OPERATION MIDLAND
Train services & Carriage Workings 1955

Jubilee 4-6-0 45626 'Seychelles' of Derby starts an evening express out of No.4 platform at St Pancras during the summer of 1957 shortly before St Pancras and St Pancras Junction signalboxes were replaced by a new box which was located to the right of the photographer. A curiosity of St Pancras was the naming of running lines with the up and down main lines being referred to as the East Departure and the West Arrival respectively whilst the up and down slow lines were called the West Departure and East Arrival lines. The normal names - up and down fast/slow - did not start until Cambridge Street which was situated at the far end of the gasometers. The proximity of the two boxes at St Pancras was because one dealt with the station only whilst the other, St Pancras Junction, signalled the throat of the terminus and the access to Somers Town goods station, Church Street sidings and St Pancras coal depot. (V.R. Webster/Kidderminster Railway Museum).

The Midland route was as interesting to contemplate as it was difficult to provide services for. Consisting of a number of loops, each of which served the most important cities on the system, it was impossible to design a series of trains that could be despatched from St Pancras to serve all major points in succession – as was the case, for example, with the Great Northern – and therefore each city served had to be considered in isolation from the rest.

The main line ran in a straight line from London to Leeds via Leicester and Chesterfield and whilst this was the shortest route, it ignored both Derby and Nottingham. The first of the Midland loops diverged at Glendon, just north of Kettering, to serve Nottingham; rejoining the main line at Trowell, a short distance north of Toton marshalling yard whilst the second diverged at Trent Junction, about ten miles north of Loughborough, to serve Derby; the main line being rejoined at Clay Cross a short distance south of Chesterfield.

Thus it was next to impossible to devise service that, for example, could run from London to Leeds calling at both Nottingham and Derby. A qualification is used since there were occasional instances of Manchester trains serving both; the overall time however was such that the trains concerned were of limited use for through passengers.

Sheffield was also situated on a loop that ran from Chesterfield to Rotherham although in this case the direct line had almost no passenger potential and was almost exclusively used in order to keep goods traffic away from the congestion of Sheffield.

The Midland also had two important branches, both of which were of sufficient magnitude to be regarded as main lines in their own right. The first of these was the Manchester route which diverged from the Derby 'loop' at Ambergate whilst the second was the West of England main line which ran from Derby to Bristol via Burton, Birmingham and Gloucester.

Although the Midland included Birmingham in its list of cities, the fact it could only be accessed via Derby put it out of consideration so far as through services from London were concerned: under no circumstances was it possible to run from St Pancras to New Street in anything like the two-hour yardstick established by Euston or Paddington. Goods trains, however, continued to operate between St Pancras and Birmingham until the 1960's.

The best-known of the Midland's services were the Anglo-Scottish trains between London and Edinburgh and Glasgow; much of the respect accorded them being due to the fact they were something of an underdog in relation to the faster services of the East and West coast routes. These services also attracted considerable affection thanks to the magnificence of the

country traversed north of Leeds; a feature that contrasted strongly with the rather mediocre views seen from the compartments of its competitors.

In its pre-1914 heyday the Midland had put up a lively fight for a share of the day Anglo-Scottish trade with departures from London at 06.00, 09.30, 11.30 and 13.30. Its position had been temporarily strengthened by the 1914-18 travel regulations which decreed that the Midland was the 'official' route between London and Glasgow – Euston being for Perth, Inverness and Aberdeen – but change came with the grouping of 1923 when Euston and St Pancras became part of the same family. Surprisingly the new management – much of which had a Midland background – did not bring the axe down on the Midland services and in fact the only change of note was that the 13.30 St Pancras to Glasgow was retimed to leave London an hour and a half earlier. Much of the reason for the maintenance of the service was that they were regarded less as Anglo-Scottish workings so much as London – Leeds and Leeds – Glasgow services and it was operationally convenient to run them as through services.

Happily this philosophy was continued by British Railways from 1948 onwards and although the midday service disappeared as a casualty of the war, an Edinburgh (09.05) and Glasgow (10.00) service remained in operation until the Beeching cuts of the 1960's. The night trains – less prone to competition and important for mail and parcels – also continued until this time.

*Thanks for assistance
with illustrations and text is due to:
Brian Wainwright, Michael Bentley, H. Townley,
Glynn Waite, D. Lord, Andrew Newman,
Audie Baker, Richard Hall, L.M. Hobdey,
W.L.Good, W. Stubbs. V.R. Webster.*

MIDLAND RAILWAY EXPRESS SERVICES : DOWN 1909/10

Station	1	2	3	4	5	6	7	8	9	10	11	12	13	14	15	16	17	18
Train							05.00		09.25		08.00	09.30				11.17		
From							St P		L'pool		St P	St P				Cambs		
ST PANCRAS	00.00	00.05	00.15			02.45	05.00				08.00	09.30		10.00	10.05		10.25	
St Albans		00.34					05.28											
Harpenden		00.43																
Luton		00.54					05.35				08.35				10.44			
BEDFORD		01d21	01c31				06D05				09b02				11c09			
Wellingborough			01.53								09b23							
Kettering			02.05								09c36				11c40	11c52	12.44	
M. Harborough																		
LEICESTER	01.53	02.25	02.40		04.32		07.05	(07.05)				11.22		11.45	12.15		13.17	
LEICESTER	01.58	02.28	02.45		04.43		07.10	07.25				11.25		11.48	12.20			
Loughborough																		
Trent	02d27						07I46											
NOTTINGHAM											10.40	(10.40)				12.52		
NOTTINGHAM									09.10	10.45	10.50					12.55		
BRISTOL		23.33			01.03							08.00	08.55			09.45		10.45
BATH																		
Mangotsfield		23.50										08.18	09.09					
GLOUCESTER		00.35			01.55							09.00	09.52			10.30		11.30
GLOUCESTER		00.50			02.12							09.02	09.55			10.32		11.35
Cheltenham					02e29							09b15	10b09			10c45		11c49
WORCESTER																		
WORCESTER																		
Kings Norton																		
BIRMINGHAM		02.00			03.40						10.20	11.17			11.42			12.45
BIRMINGHAM		02.12			03.55						10.25	11.23			11.47			12.50
Tamworth					04.20						10.59	11z46						
Burton		02.52			04b41						11b09	12c07						
DERBY		03.08	03.10	03.30	05.00	05.17		08.05		09.56	11.08	11.25	12.25		12.57	12.38		13.43
DERBY			03.28	03.38		05.24		08.08		10.02	11.12	11.30			13.02	12.43		13.47
Matlock								08.37										
Millers Dale								09b04										
Chinley								09.25			12c13				14d10			
MANCHESTER				05.25		06.42		09.52			12.42			13.40	14.38			
Alfreton																		
Chesterfield			04e05				08d29			12z00	11c35	12c08	12c29	12.33		13d17		
SHEFFIELD			04.25				08.50				12.00	12.33		12.53		13.40	13.52	
SHEFFIELD			04.38				08.57	09.42			12.03			12.58		13.45	13.57	14.03
Rotherham											11.08	12.13				13.56	14.07	14.13
Cudworth			05.04								11d30	12c34				14b26	14.32	
Normanton			05e32													14c42		
LEEDS	04.03		05.47				09.52				12.00	13.10	13.28			15.00		15.15
LEEDS	04.08						10.10				12.05		13.33			15.06		
Shipley											12.23					15.24		
BRADFORD							10.30				12.32					15.44		
Keighley																		
Skipton																		
Hellifield										11.04			14.24					
Appleby										12.06								
CARLISLE	06.25									12.40			15.50					
Destination	G'gow								Hull	G'gow			G'gow	BDX			N'cle	Hull

> a: arrived one minute earlier,
> b: arrived two minutes earlier,
> etc.
> z: slip coach.

MIDLAND RAILWAY EXPRESS SERVICES : UP 1909/10

Station	1	2	3	4	5	6	7	8	9	10	11	12	13	14	15
Train				02.25	21.30	02.25	23.00	23.00	23.00			08.30		06.15	07.45
From				Leeds	Glasgow	Leeds	Glasgow	Glasgow	Glasgow			Notts		Heysham	L'pool
CARLISLE					00.27		01.35	01.45							
Appleby															
Hellifield														07.10	
Skipton															
Keighley								03.25						07.30	
BRADFORD	21.05														07.40
Shipley	21.15														07.50
LEEDS	21.43			02.50		03.56								08.03	08.18
LEEDS	22.00		02.25	02.55		04.00								08.08	08.22
Normanton	22q32		02.42	03.20											08d57
Cudworth				03c37											
Rotherham	23.09			03.56		04.50	04.55								09z14
SHEFFIELD	23.19			04.05	03.53	(04.05)	05.05							08.56	09.22
SHEFFIELD	23.29			(04.27)	04.02	04.27			07.20	08.00				09.02	09.27
Chesterfield	23d52					04d50			07.38	08c26					09c50
Alfreton															
MANCHESTER		00.00							07.30					08.30	
Chinley		00f39													09e11
Millers Dale										08c16					
Matlock															
DERBY	00.25	02.00				05.35				08.50	08.57				
DERBY	00.55	02.22	02.25					06.15	08.00	08.05	08.55		09.05		
Burton								06b31	08.21			09.13	09d27		
Tamworth								06.50	08.43			(To	09.47		
BIRMINGHAM			03.20					07.25	09.15			B'tol)	10.13		
BIRMINGHAM			03.28					07.38	09.30				10.40		
Kings Norton								07.50							
WORCESTER															
WORCESTER															
Cheltenham			04f36					08c49	10.29				11b40		
GLOUCESTER			04.48					09.00	10.40				11.52		
GLOUCESTER			05.00					09.05	10.45				11.55		
Mangotsfield			05.40					09.47	11.36						
BATH															
BRISTOL			06.00					10.05	11.52				12.45		
NOTTINGHAM									08.22					10.28	10.33
NOTTINGHAM								06.35	08.25	08.38				(10.40)	10.40
Trent	01.13			05f03		05c45									
Loughborough	01.25							06.59			08.32	09z18			
LEICESTER	01.42	03.00				06.10		07.15			08.48	09.32		10.15	
LEICESTER	01.52	03.08				06.15		07.20			08.50	09.37		10.20	
M. Harborough	02.16	03.32										09.13			
Kettering	02b34					06c03		07c55			09e34	09c50	10b10		11c48
Wellingborough	02.46		04d02									10b02			
BEDFORD	03d11		04e25			07b10						10b36			
Luton	03.40		04.59			06.52						10.45			12z35
Harpenden															
St Albans	03.55		05.13												
ST PANCRAS	04.20		05.40			07.30	08.05		09.20	10.40	10.55	11.23	11.32	12.05	13.15
Destination									L'pool						

MIDLAND RAILWAY EXPRESS SERVICES : DOWN 1909/10

Train		14.20		12.00		13.30				14.17	15.30			
From		L'pool		St P		St P				Bristol	St P			
ST PANCRAS	11.30		12.00		12.15	13.30		14.05	14.50		15.30	15.45	16.30	16.55
St Albans					12.43									
Harpenden														
Luton	12.09				12.59							16.24		
BEDFORD					13c24				15c08			16c49		
Wellingborough					13d49							17b12		
Kettering					14b00				15c37		16c49	17b24		18c19
M. Harborough												17.52		
LEICESTER	13.25		13.55	(13.55)	14.40	15.15			16.15			18.10	18.25	
LEICESTER	13.28		14.00	14.05	14.45	15.18			16.20			18.15	18.30	
Loughborough														
Trent												18b41		
NOTTINGHAM			14.38						16.35	17.45				19.17
NOTTINGHAM			14.43						16.38	17.50				19.20
BRISTOL				12.20		12.55			14.10 14.17			15.25		
BATH														
Mangotsfield									14.30			15.40		
GLOUCESTER						13.42			15.05 15.07			16.18		
GLOUCESTER						13.45			15.08 15.10			16.22		
Cheltenham				13c18		13c59			15d24			16d37		
WORCESTER														
WORCESTER														
Kings Norton														
BIRMINGHAM				14.20		15.00			16.05 16.25			17.38		
BIRMINGHAM				14.28		15.05			16.15 16.28			17.45		
Tamworth									16.40			18.12		
Burton				15b05		15b46			16b59 17b11			18c32		
DERBY				15.23	15.30	16.05			16.55	17.26	(17.26)	18.50	19.05	
DERBY				15.28	15.37	16.08			16.57	17.30	17.38	18.57	19.10	
Matlock					16.02						18.05			
Millers Dale					16c28						18d37			
Chinley					16c48					17.56		20c12		
MANCHESTER			15.50		17.20					18.25	19.17	20.40		
Alfreton														
Chesterfield			15c30			16d44		17c26		18d09	18z30	19c30 19d42	20.00	
SHEFFIELD		16.20	15.50			16.35			17.47	18.30	18.45	19.50 20.05	20.20	
SHEFFIELD			15.55			16.40 16.44		17.10	17.52	18.33	18.50 18.54 18.58	20.24	20.28	
Rotherham			16.04				17.05		18.03		19.10		20.37	
Cudworth			16b24						18.23		19.27		20.54	
Normanton			16c41							19d15				
LEEDS	15.25		17.00			17.32			18.55	19.30	19.40		21.15	
LEEDS	15.32		17.10			17.37			19.00	19.35	19.55		21.26	
Shipley			17.27						19.20	19.52	20.19		21.45	
BRADFORD			17.35						19.30	20.00	20.28		21.55	
Keighley														
Skipton														
Hellifield	16.24	16.32				18.27								
Appleby		17.33												
CARLISLE	17.50	18.06				19.53								
Destination	G'gow	E'bro				G'gow	BDX York Hull		Notts		BDX Hull			Hull

MIDLAND RAILWAY EXPRESS SERVICES : UP 1909/10

Train	07.40		07.40		09.15		09.38 09.40			10.25	11.25		12.02	10.04	12.17	12.17	12.55
From	BFS		BFS		L'pool		Hull Hull			BFS	L'pool		BDX	N'cle	BFS	BFS	L'pool
CARLISLE																	
Appleby																	
Hellifield																	
Skipton																	
Keighley																	
BRADFORD					08.15		09.40			10.25		10.45			12.17		
Shipley					08.24		09.48			10.35		10.54			12.23		
LEEDS					08.45		10.05			10.50		11.17			12.50		
LEEDS					08.57		10.15			10.55		11.20			13.00		
Normanton					09b16					11.12		11.37					
Cudworth					09c33			11.11				11.50					
Rotherham							11.11 11.31			11.44				13z20	13.45		
SHEFFIELD					10.00		11.05 11.23 11.45					12.17		13.18	13.28 13.55		
SHEFFIELD	09.32				10.20		11.08					12.20		(13.32)	13.32 14.00		
Chesterfield	09c57				10c42							12d42					
Alfreton																	
MANCHESTER		09.20			10.15		10.20 10.55			12.00		12.20			13.50		
Chinley					10c48		10c58 11d36					13b11			14e26		
Millers Dale							11c18					13c32					
Matlock							11.29										
DERBY	10.38	10.50	(10.38)		11.22		11.57 12.30 12.35					14.15		14.22	(14.22)		15.18
DERBY	(10.53)	10.53	10.55	11.00			12.03 (12.40) 12.40					13.45 14.20		14.28	14.47		15.22
Burton			11.09	11c18			12b58								15b03		
Tamworth															15.21		
BIRMINGHAM			11.48	11.57			13.40							15.20	15.45		
BIRMINGHAM			11.54	12.03			13.45							15.27	15.50		
Kings Norton																	
WORCESTER																	
WORCESTER																	
Cheltenham			13d03				14b49							16c51			
GLOUCESTER			12.58	13.14			15.00						16.30	17.02	(17.02)		
GLOUCESTER			13.03	13.18			15.03 15.10						16.35	17.05	17.12		
Mangotsfield							15.42										
BATH				14.08			16.00								18.01		
BRISTOL			13.52				15.58						17.25	17.58			
NOTTINGHAM										13.25	14.50			14.55			
NOTTINGHAM										13.30	14.58						
Trent																	
Loughborough																	
LEICESTER		11.28				12.22	12.45			13.58	14.23						15.00
LEICESTER		11.30				12.25	12.50			14.02	14.28						16.00
M. Harborough											14.49						
Kettering		12c12					13c26			14b34	15b05			16b02			16c37
Wellingborough							13b38				15b16						
BEDFORD							14c00				15d39						17c04
Luton							14.28				16.06						17.30
Harpenden																	
St Albans							14.43										
ST PANCRAS		13.25				13.57 14.10	15.10			15.47 16.00 16.43				17.20			18.05
Destination			B'mth						B'tol	B'mth						B'mth	

3

MIDLAND RAILWAY EXPRESS SERVICES : DOWN 1909/10

Station	17.35 StP (1)	(2)	17.40 StP (3)	18.00 StP (4)	(5)	18.30 StP (6)	(7)	20.15 (8)	20.40 (9)	21.30 (10)	00.45 L'pool (11)	(12)	(13)	19.00 Bristol (14)
ST PANCRAS	17.35		17.40	18.00		18.30		20.15	20.40	21.30				
St Albans									21.09					
Harpenden									21.19					
Luton			18.17						21.30					
BEDFORD			18c43			19c29			21d58	22c31				
Wellingborough									22b22					
Kettering			19.10			19c13			22b34					
M. Harborough									22.53					
LEICESTER	19.27					20.27		22.00	23.15					
LEICESTER	19.30	19.35				20.30	20.37	22.05	23.23		23.50			
Loughborough		19.52					20.58		23.43					
Trent		20b04		20.10			21.14							
NOTTINGHAM					20.20		21.27	22.37	23.53					
NOTTINGHAM					20.28			22.40	23.55			00.05		
BRISTOL				16.52			19.00	19.55						
BATH														
Mangotsfield				17.05			19.15	20.08						
GLOUCESTER				17.55			20.00	20.53						
GLOUCESTER				17.57			20.15	20.57						
Cheltenham				18d12			20d30	21d14						
WORCESTER							21.06							
WORCESTER							21.10							
Kings Norton														
BIRMINGHAM				19.15			21.55	22.15						(21.55)
BIRMINGHAM				19.18			(23.25)	22.23						23.25
Tamworth				19z43										23.58
Burton				20c01				23c06						00e22
DERBY		20.22		20.20		21.05			23.25	00.10	00.27	00.35	00.38	
DERBY		20.30		20.38		21.08			23.30			(00.54)	00.54	01.00
Matlock		20.56												
Millers Dale		21b24				21.56								
Chinley		21e46												
MANCHESTER	21.22	22.12				22.35								05.05
Alfreton														
Chesterfield				21c13	21d45			23.20		00c05		01b28		
SHEFFIELD				21.10	21.40	22.12		23.40	00.25			01.50		
SHEFFIELD				21.14				23.44				01.58		
Rotherham														
Cudworth														
Normanton												02h54		
LEEDS				22.03				00.35	01.45			03.10		
LEEDS				22.06				00.38	01.50					
Shipley														
BRADFORD												04.05		
Keighley														
Skipton														
Hellifield				22.54					02.42	02.52				
Appleby														
CARLISLE								02.50	04.15	04.30				
Destination		Burton		Heysham				Stranraer	G'gow	G'gow				

MIDLAND RAILWAY EXPRESS SERVICES : UP 1909/10

Station	14.05 York (1)	09.20 G'gow (2)	14.25 BFS (3)	15.30 L'pool (4)	15.00 York (5)	15.20 BDX (6)	10.30 E'bro (7)	11.00 G'gow (8)	15.30 L'pool (9)	16.20 Mtr (10)	15.20 Hull (11)	15.00 Hull (12)	17.00 L'pool (13)	17.00 Hull (14)	13.30 G'gow (15)	14.15 E'bro (16)	17.30 G'gow (17)
No.																	
CARLISLE		12.05					13.10	13.30							15.58	16.42	20.28
Appleby																17.23	21.20
Hellifield						14.50		15.10							17.35	18.23	22.19
Skipton																	
Keighley																	
BRADFORD	13.30		14.25				15.27										
Shipley	13.36						15.33										
LEEDS	13.56		14.25	14.45			15.52	15.58							18.23	19.13	23.30
LEEDS	14.00		14.30	14.50			(16.02)	16.02							18.27	19.18	
Normanton																	
Cudworth	14c33									16.36		18.22					
Rotherham			15.38		15.43	16.20	16.28			17.09						20.04	
SHEFFIELD	15.08	15.12		15.53		16.30	16.38	16.56		17.19	17.03		18.55	19.17			
SHEFFIELD	(15.18)	15.18				16.40	(16.58)	16.58							19.22		
Chesterfield		15c44	16z00			17e06		17.24									
Alfreton																	
MANCHESTER					16.15				16.20				17.50				
Chinley									16f59								
Millers Dale																	
Matlock																	
DERBY		16.20	16.30			17.40			17.57	(17.57)			19.15				
DERBY	16.20	(16.35)	16.35			17.45			18.03	18.15			19.18		19.45		
Burton			16c53							18b35					20b05		
Tamworth			17.08							18.53					20.26		
BIRMINGHAM			17.35			18.45				19.20					20.52		
BIRMINGHAM			17.40							19.25					21.00		
Kings Norton																	
WORCESTER															22.00		
WORCESTER															22.05		
Cheltenham			18c50							20b28					22d44		
GLOUCESTER			19.02							20.42					22.58		
GLOUCESTER			19.05							20.45					23.05		
Mangotsfield			19.44							21.29					23.44		
BATH																	
BRISTOL			20.00							21.45					00.00		
NOTTINGHAM	16.50				(16.50)												
NOTTINGHAM	(17.00)				17.00												
Trent		16c08						17b56							20c15	20c59	
Loughborough									18.30				19z40				
LEICESTER		16.32			18.05			18.20	18.47				19.53			21.23	
LEICESTER		16.35			18.10			18.24	18.50				19.55			21.27	
M. Harborough													20.16				
Kettering		17.08			18c10				17c27							21.58	
Wellingborough					18b22				17b39								
BEDFORD									20c01				20.58				
Luton					19.05				20.29				21.23	21.48			
Harpenden									20.40								
St Albans																	
ST PANCRAS		18.39			19.42	19.55			20.15	21.10			22.00			22.25	23.15
Destination							L'pool										

4

Being a Railwayman and an enthusiast sometimes had its perils. On the 9th June 1952 one of the authors was engaged in trials between Glasgow and Dumfries with Austerity 2-10-0 90772 of Motherwell when it had to be put inside at Auldgirth with a hot crosshead, seven miles short of Dumfries. Seeing the signals off for the down Thames-Clyde, he grabbed his camera and sauntered across the line to find a good position from which to take a snap of a Holbeck Scot working hard. Hardly had his foot touched the four-foot of the down main when 45586 'Mysore' burst into view with sufficient suddenness to prompt a reasonably senior Motive Power officer to execute an athletic parabola before being devoured by the 5XP which was sparing no effort in taking a run at Thornhill bank. The resulting photograph was fortuitous rather than planned! "The driver must have recognised me," commented the photographer afterwards. "He didn't bother to blow the whistle." The appearance of an Edge Hill Jubilee on the 10.00 St Pancras - Glasgow was something of a mystery and 45586 probably took over at Carlisle from an ailing Scot.

The problem of routing was of particular significance to the Scottish trains since to run them via both the Derby and Nottingham loops would have entailed a considerable cost in overall running time. The eventual solution was to run the Edinburgh service via Nottingham and the Glasgow train via Trent and Chesterfield. The question of overall timings had been so sensitive in Midland days that at least one train ran direct from Chesterfield to Rotherham, its Sheffield portion being detached at Chesterfield and run separately to Sheffield. Such extremes died during the great war and were not revived.

Although the jewel in the Yorkshire crown was Leeds – where the Midland fought a losing battle with the Great Northern – Bradford was too important to be ignored and the Midland used it as a terminus for almost all its Leeds services; Forster Square being more convenient for the marshalling and maintenance of stock. However the reversal at Leeds put the Midland at a disadvantage with the Great Northern and to counter this and at the same time give some of the stations in the Huddersfield and Halifax areas a direct service with London, many Forster Square services carried a subsidiary portion which was removed at Sheffield and run to Bradford Exchange via the connection between Royston Junction and Thornhill Midland Junction.

This dual Bradford service not only survived the grouping but flourished between the war and resulted in the curious sight of the midday arrival from St Pancras consisting of two Bradford sections: one starting from Forster Square at 07.30 and the other leaving Bradford Exchange

LMS Fleet Summary						
Main line			**Suburban**			
Code	**Type**	**Built**	**Code**	**Type**		**Built**
BCK	Brake Composite Corridor	304	BT	Brake Third (Non-corridor)		1341
BFK	Brake First Corridor	73	BTL	Brake Third Lavatory (Non-corridor)		273
BFO	Brake First Open	5	C	Composite (Non-corridor)		931
BTK	Brake Third Corridor	1826	CL	Composite Lavatory (Non-corridor)		200
BTO	Brake Third Open	231	F	First (Non-corridor)		132
CK	Composite Corridor	1356	FL	First Lavatory (Non-corridor)		30
CLUB	Club Car	2	T	Third (Non-corridor)		1616
CO	Composite Open	54		**TOTAL**		**4523**
FK	First Corridor	114				
FO	First Open	136				
RB	Restaurant Buffet	5				
RC	Restaurant Composite	31				
RF	Restaurant First	95				
RK	Kitchen Car	108				
RT	Restaurant Third	44				
RTO	Restaurant Third	121				
SLC	Composite Sleeping Car	25				
SLF	First Sleeping Cat	103				
SLT	Third Sleeping Car	125				
TK	Third Corridor	1044				
TO	Third Open	2130				
-	Articulated & Misc	160				
TOTAL		**8092**				

1955 · LONDON to MANCHESTER		
Train	**Arrive**	**Time**
00.40 Euston	04.35 London Road	3.55
04.18 St Pancras	09.49 Central	5.31
07.55 Euston	11.24 London Road	3.29
08.15 St Pancras	13.05 Central	4.50
08.30 Euston	12.33 London Road	4.03
09.45 Euston	13.10 London Road	3.25
10.00 Marylebone	15.08 London Road	5.08
10.15 St Pancras	14.30 Central	4.15
11.45 Euston	15.30 London Road	3.45
12.15 Marylebone	17.39 London Road	5.24
14.15 St Pancras	18.35 Central	4.20
14.45 Euston	18.46 London Road	4.01
15.20 Marylebone	20.27 London Road	5.07
15.45 Euston	19.56 London Road	4.11
16.15 St Pancras	20.50 Central	4.35
16.30 Euston	20.14 London Road	3.44
16.50 Marylebone	22.08 London Road	5.18
18.00 Euston	21.30 London Road	3.30
18.18 Marylebone	23.24 London Road	5.06
18.40 St Pancras	23.08 Central	4.28
22.00 Marylebone	04.02 London Road	6.02

To the passenger, Birmingham New Street was a depressingly dirty place; to the railway enthusiast it was about as close to heaven as one could get without 8P Pacifics. New Street consisted of two stations side by side and although it appeared to be a single location, neither the Midland or North Western halves had much to do with each other and the only movement of note between them was the Pines Express which transferred from the Midland to the North Western (and vice-versa) at New Street.
A peculiarity of New Street (Midland) was that it hosted very few starting services; the reason being that apart from one short bay, all four platforms served through lines and the shunting and running-round that accompanied empty stock movements would have prejudiced the smooth running of the line. Thus, Westbound services tended to start as empty stock from Saltley whilst trains in the other direction ran in (either as ECS or as a local train) from Kings Norton.
From the enthusiasts point of view, the main drawback to New Street was the lack of large engines. The two through LNW services to Glasgow saw rebuilt Royal Scot 4-6-0's but all other expresses on both sides of the stations normally saw anything larger than a 5XP Jubilee 4-6-0. Above, Jubilee 45674 of 'Duncan' blows off as it waits for the right-away with an express for Bristol.

ten minutes earlier. Later in the afternoon the 09.05 from Bradford Central ran into St Pancras at 13.21 and was followed fifteen minutes later by the 09.20 ex Forster Square.

Such things were all very colourful but were of little benefit to through traffic since the advantages lay so heavily with the Great Northern who could with ease in 1939 better the Midland's best Leeds – London time of 3 hours 49 minutes by three quarters of an hour in Pullman splendour or by sixty-five minutes with the streamlined West Riding Limited. The idea of the Midland being able to compete by knocking a full hour off the schedule of the 07.30 Bradford – St Pancras was laughable.

Although the Midland's West Riding expresses relied heavily on intermediate traffic, there was a reluctance to slow them down by diverting them to either Derby or Nottingham and of the seven principal day trains between Leeds and St Pancras, five ran direct from Chesterfield to Leicester. The remaining two ran via Nottingham and lost around twenty minutes each as a result.

The greatest casualty of the grouping was Manchester and Merseyside and while the LMS was seemingly content to do battle with the Great Northern, it was not prepared to countenance out and out competition between Euston and St Pancras and thus one of the first cuts to be made by the new order was the excising of the through Liverpool portions that had run on the rear of most St Pancras to Manchester expresses. The Board was less keen to concentrate its Manchester services on Euston and even though the level LNW route permitted start to stop speeds of very nearly a mile a minute – by 1939 the 18.00 from Euston was running to Manchester in three and a quarter hours – many of the Midland's slower Manchester trains were lopped from the timetable, leaving the principal expresses much as they had been. Of these, the fastest (by

1939) was the 10.30 from St Pancras which with stops at Leicester and Derby ran to Manchester in three hours and thirty-five minutes.

Unfortunately British Railways took a less charitable view of parallel London Midland services and although the St Pancras – Manchester service was allowed to continue in being, users received the impression that no-one had told Derby that the war had ended since about forty minutes had been added to the prewar timings whilst the mid-day service which had disappeared during the war, was not reinstated until the last few years of operation when the temporary suspension of most LNW services obliged the Midland to operate an

1955 : LONDON to LEEDS			
Train	Arrive		Time
03.50 Kings Cross	09.04	Central	5.14
07.50 Kings Cross	11.23	Central	3.33
08.50 Kings Cross	12.26	Central	3.36
09.00 St Pancras	13.42	City	4.42
10.00 St Pancras	14.31	City	4.31
10.18 Kings Cross	14.42	Central	4.24
11.45 St Pancras	16.32	City	4.47
12.05 Kings Cross	15.19	Central	3.14
13.18 Kings Cross	17.19	Central	4.01
14.00 St Pancras	18.47	City	4.47
14.18 Kings Cross	18.26	Central	4.08
15.15 St Pancras	20.12	City	4.57
15.45 Kings Cross	20.12	Central	4.27
16.50 St Pancras	21.50	City	5.00
17.30 Kings Cross	21.02	Central	3.32
18.10 Kings Cross	22.24	Central	4.14
21.05 St Pancras	02.13	City	5.08
21.15 St Pancras	02.39	City	5.24
22.45 Kings Cross	3.28	Central	4.43
23.50 St Pancras	06.20	City	6.30

1955 : LONDON to SHEFFIELD			
Train	Arrive		Time
09.00 St Pancras	12.33	Midland	3.33
10.00 St Pancras	13.10	Midland	3.10
10.00 Marylebone	13.57	Victoria	3.57
11.45 St Pancras	15.20	Midland	3.35
12.15 Marylebone	16.20	Victoria	4.05
14.00 St Pancras	17.30	Midland	3.30
15.15 St Pancras	18.56	Midland	3.41
15.20 Marylebone	19.18	Victoria	3.58
16.50 St Pancras	20.27	Midland	3.37
16.50 Marylebone	20.40	Victoria	3.50
18.18 Marylebone	21.55	Victoria	3.37
18.33 St Pancras	21.53	Midland	3.20
21.05 St Pancras	01.01	Midland	3.56
21.15 St Pancras	01.21	Midland	3.06
22.00 Marylebone	02.47	Victoria	4.47
23.50 St Pancras	04.36	Midland	4.46

Black Five 45277 and Jubilee 45598 (both of Kentish Town) approach Luton at speed with the down Waverley, the 09.00 St Pancras to Edinburgh, in 1959. Both engines have eased off in order not to breach the 75 mph limit between Harpenden and Luton and the Jubilee is clearly being fired in readiness for the rather sharp bank to Leagrave. Following the 1957 Midland accelerations the Waverley was upgraded from Special Limit to XL limit timings which meant that a Jubilee 4-6-0 had to be assisted on any load greater than nine vehicles. For some time 2P 4-4-0's had been used as pilots to overloaded 5XP 4-6-0's but by 1959 there numbers had dwindled to such an extent that class 5 4-6-0's had to be regularly substituted. The problems imposed by XL load were a decisive factor in the introduction of class 7 engines to the Midland.

enhanced service of Manchester trains .

Forty minutes seemed a great deal to add to a three and a half hour schedule but in fact the post-war service was not as bad as it appeared. Much of the additional time was due less to management inertia than to the increased weight of trains and, more especially, to the number of additional stops that had been inserted into the schedules. In 1910 the 10.00 St Pancras - Manchester had done the journey in two hundred and twenty minutes - 52 mph - with only one stop, Leicester. By 1939 the train also called at Derby yet, thanks to the new 5XP 4-6-0's, the running time had been reduced by five minutes. In 1955 the same service took two hundred and fifty-five minutes *but made no less than seven intermediate stops*. Since stopping a train cost anything from five to eight minutes, it is not difficult to see that had the 10.15 St Pancras to Manchester of 1955 had five of its stops cancelled then the overall running time would have been very close to what it had been in 1938. Given that trains tended to be a coach or two heavier in 1955, it can be appreciated that the post-war standard of work demanded was in no way inferior to that of 1939.

If the Midland had to play second fiddle in Leeds and Manchester, there was no doubting its

Arr	Station	Dep	Day
	Nottingham	07.35	1
08.09	Derby	08.15	
12.00	Bristol	01.10	2
09.55	Bradford	07.30	3
13.42	Bristol	16.45	
23.02	York	12.20	4
18.26	Bristol	14.15	5
20.00	York	09.43	6
11.50	Sheffield	10.10	7
12.09	Birmingham	08.05	8
13.03	Newcastle	15.57	
21.05	Birmingham	06.40	9
11.04	Bradford	17.25	
19.23	Sheffield	09.09	10
13.21	St Pancras	17.30	
20.47	Nottingham	(07.35)	

...robably a record for a cyclic diagram; the above six-...oach set took a nominal eleven-days to get back to its ...arting point although with the intervention of week-...nds, the cycle actually took a fortnight to complete. ...he workings included the interesting instance of the ...t leaving London on one day, appearing in Bristol ...e next and being seen in York a couple of days ...ter.

PASSENGER TRAIN TIMINGS			
London to Leicester (Start to top)			
	Ordinary Express	Limited Load	Special Limit	XL Limit
---	---	---	---	---
4P	11:340	9:300	8:270	7:220
5MT	12:390	11:345	10:310	8:255
5XP	14:440	12:390	11:350	9:300
7P	16:510	14:450	13:405	10: 350
St Pancras	**0.00**	**0.00**	**0.00**	**0.00**
Kentish Town	4.00	4.00	4.00	4.00
Hendon	13.00	11.00	11.00	10.30
St Albans	31.00	28.00	28.00	23.00
Luton	44.00	40.00	38.00	32.00
Bedford	**63.00**	**59.00**	**55.00**	**47.00**
Oakley	66.00	62.00	58.00	50.00
Sharnbrook Summit	75.00	70.00	65.00	56.00
Wellingborough	81.00	76.00	70.00	60.50
Kettering	**87.00**	**84.00**	**77.00**	**68.00**
Desborough	90.00	93.00	84.00	74.30
Market Harborough	95.00	98.00	89.00	79.00
LEICESTER	**120.00**	**118.00**	**110.00**	**95.30**

There were four categories of passenger train timings on the London Midland, ranging from the basic 'ordinary' timings (often referred to as Full Load Timings') to the fastest band, XL (Express Limit) timings. The difference between the slowest and fastest was quite marked - nearly twenty-five minutes between London and Leicester, for example - and depended on the class of engine and the load being hauled. A 5XP 4-6-0 could haul 14 coaches (440 tons) on ordinary timings but only 11 (350 tons) on Special Limit trains. · The XL timings did not appear on the Midland until the introduction of class 7P 4-6-0's in 1957. If the booked type of engine was not available and, for example, a 5MT 4-6-0 engine, had to be turned out for an eleven coach Special Limit train, then a pilot engine would have to be provided.

LMS TIMETABLE (1938/9)

Train																			
From												07.45 St P				09.05 St P			
ST PANCRAS	02.25			04.25					07.45			08.25				09.05		09.25	10.00
St Albans				04.55					08.15									09.51	
Harpenden									08.26									10.01	
Luton				05.14					08.37			09.01						10.10	
BEDFORD				05.47					09.04									10.34	
Wellingborough	03h41			06e14					09.27			09b37						11b54	
Kettering	03c54			06c28					09.39			09b49	09.51					11.05	11b13
Manton																			
Melton Mowbray																			
M. Harborough				06.47								10.05							
LEICESTER	04.26			07.13								10.24							11.44
LEICESTER	04.39			07.23			08.25					10.28							11.48
Loughborough				07.40			08.40					10.43							
Trent																			
NOTTINGHAM													11.00			11.08			
NOTTINGHAM					07.45					09.05						11.12			
BRISTOL		01.10												07.42					
BATH																			
Mangotsfield														07.58					
GLOUCESTER		02.02												08.38					
GLOUCESTER		02.20												08.42					
Cheltenham		02f38												08c57					
WORCESTER																			
WORCESTER											07.57								
Kings Norton																			
BIRMINGHAM		04.01									08.57			10.04					
BIRMINGHAM		04.15	06.50					08.43			09.01			10.10					
Tamworth		04.45	07.14								09.32			10.33					
Burton		05.10	07.33								09.50			10.52					
DERBY	05.17	05.30	07.50	08.01	08.15		09.00	09.24		09.36	10.06		11.03	11.07					
DERBY	05.24			08.06	08.20		09.04	09.30		09.40	10.15		11.11	11.16					
Belper										09.49									
Ambergate				08.22						10.01									
Matlock				08.36						10.17		11.34							
Bakewell										10.30									
Millers Dale				09c02						10b45		11b57							
Chinley										11.06		12b18							
Stockport																			
Cheadle Heath										11.23									
Didsbury																			
MANCHESTER	06.47			09.45			10.24			11.37		12.40							
Alfreton																			
Chesterfield								09.59			10.43		12.02		11.52				12.45
SHEFFIELD					09.06			10.19			11.04		12.21		12.12		(12.12)		
SHEFFIELD			07.55		09.11	09.18		10.24			11.16		12.31		12.17		12.35		
Rotherham			08.06		09.21			10.34			11.36				12.45				
Swinton															12.55				
Cudworth					09.37	09.46									13.07				
Normanton			08.35																
LEEDS			08.50		10.06			11.15								13.05			13.48
LEEDS			08.57		10.22	10.20		11.20								13.10			13.53
Newlay																			
Shipley					10.40			11.38											
BRADFORD			09.19		10.47			11.45											
Keighley																			
Skipton						10.55										13.43			
Hellifield						11f17													14d42
Appleby																			15.34
CARLISLE						12.40										15.14			16.09
Destination					H'fax	G'gow					York			York		E'bro	BDX		G'gow

> *a: Arrived one minute earlier,*
> *b: arrived two minutes earlier,*
> *etc.*
> *z: slip coach.*

1955 : LONDON to NOTTINGHAM

Train	Arrive		Time
01.45 Marylebone	04.50	Victoria	3.05
09.00 St Pancras	11.25	Midland	2.25
10.00 Marylebone	12.52	Victoria	2.52
12.15 Marylebone	15.14	Victoria	2.59
14.00 St Pancras	16.17	Midland	2.17
15.15 St Pancras	17.37	Midland	2.22
15.20 Marylebone	18.16	Victoria	2.56
16.50 St Pancras	19.17	Midland	2.27
16.50 Marylebone	19.36	Victoria	2.46
17.30 St Pancras	20.47	Midland	3.17
18.18 Marylebone	20.56	Victoria	2.38
19.10 St Pancras	21.40	Midland	2.30
19.55 St Pancras	23.17	Midland	3.22
21.05 St Pancras	23.41	Midland	2.36
22.00 Marylebone	01.28	Victoria	3.28

position in Sheffield which, with a population of half a million, was only slightly smaller than Leeds. It did not enjoy a monopoly but the service via Retford to Kings Cross was indirect whilst the post-war Great Central had a reputation for being slow and infrequent. This last was entirely deserved since the up Master Cutler, 07.50 Victoria to Maylebone, ran to London in three hours and thirty-three minutes which was only ten minutes slower than the fastest Midland time. The remainder of the Great Central service took around the four-hour mark to reach London which was about half an hour longer than the normal Midland express time. The Great Northern timings were similar to those of the Great Central although it did find a chink in the Midland's armour; the weakness being a lack of a good evening business train from Sheffiel[d] to London. The last Midland express of th[e] day was the up Waverley which left Sheffiel[d] at the rather early time of 16.46 and the onl[y] Midland train afterwards was the indirect 18.3[?] which meant changing at Derby and connectin[g] with the 17.55 Manchester – St Pancras. Th[e] Great Central contribution was the 17.05 fro[m] Victoria (16.00 ex Manchester, London Road[)] which took four and a quarter hours to reac[h] Marylebone and was fifteen minutes slowe[r] than the 17.39 to Kings Cross with a change a[t] Retford. It was however the Great Norther[n] which put the others to shame by stopping th[e] 17.03 Newcastle to Kings Cross at Retford i[n] order to connect with the 17.00 Manchest[er] to Cleethorpes which left Sheffield Victor[ia] at 18.24. By using this combination of trai[ns]

LMS TIMETABLE (1938/9)

Train	21.15	21.55	02.55		07.45		07.20	05.35			08.05	07.45	09.20	09.05
From	G'gow	E'bro	Leeds		Nott		BDX	Hey			L'pool	B'ford	M'ter	BDX
CARLISLE	00.05	00.37												
Appleby														
Hellifield														
Skipton		02.25						06.55						
Keighley	02.10							07.15						
BRADFORD									07.30			07.45		09.20
Shipley									07.38			07.53		09.27
Newlay												08.07		
LEEDS	02.33	03.00							07.41	07.54		08.13		09.42
LEEDS	02.41	02.55	03.10						(08.00)	08.00		08.20		09.47
Normanton		03.11	03.35									08.37		
Cudworth			03.49					08.13				08.53		
Swinton														
Rotherham			04.09					08.29				09.11		
SHEFFIELD	03.31	04.03	04.19					08.39	08.50			09.21	10.09	10.36
SHEFFIELD	03.41	04.17	04.42	07.15			08.05	(09.00)	09.00	09.05		09.26	10.13	10.40
Chesterfield			05.13	07.36			08.33	09.28	09.30			09.47	10.34	
Alfreton														
MANCHESTER						07.20					08.55			
Didsbury														
Cheadle Heath / Stockport														
Chinley											09.36			
Millers Dale						08b11					10e00			
Bakewell														
Matlock						08.27					10.18			
Ambergate														
Belper														
DERBY			05.55			08.50	09.03				10.19	10.40	(10.19)	
DERBY			06.12	08.00	08.22	08.55	09.08				10.24	10.46	10.52	
Burton			06.28			08.38	08.55	09.27				10.40	11.07	
Tamworth			06.50			08.55		09.48					11.27	*(Ex*
BIRMINGHAM			07.17			09.16		10.16				11.18	11.51	*LNW)*
BIRMINGHAM			07.30			09.23		10.30				11.25	(12.10)	12.10
Kings Norton			07.45			09.35		10.47						
WORCESTER								11.23						
WORCESTER								11.28						
Cheltenham			08d50			10d23		12d02			12b20		13d14	
GLOUCESTER			09.00			10.31		12.12			12.28		13.22	
GLOUCESTER			09.05			10.36					12.33		13.27	
Mangotsfield			09.45			11.23								
BATH													14.15	
BRISTOL			10.00			11.36					13.25			
NOTTINGHAM		05.16		07.00	08.19						10.10		11.14	
NOTTINGHAM		05.28			08.23						10.14		11.18	
Trent	04e39			07.16										
Loughborough				07.28	08.26	09.17								
LEICESTER	05.04			07.45		08.46	09.33	10.17			11.17			11.54
LEICESTER	05.10			07.50		08.52	09.37	10.21			11.21			11.57
M. Harborough				08.11		09.13								
Melton Mowbray					08.45			10.40						
Manton					09.05			11.00						
Kettering		06e33		08b29	09c31			11b27						
Wellingborough				08b40										
BEDFORD				09b01				11c55						
Luton		07.22			10.20	10.50		12.22					12.55	
Harpenden														
St Albans														
ST PANCRAS	07.07	08.00		09.55	10.35	10.50	11.20	12.00	12.54	13.00		13.21		13.36
Destination													B'mth	

journey time of no more than three hours and forty minutes was achieved which was an astonishing achievement for a routing that involved a change of trains.

With a population of almost three hundred and twenty thousand people and an assured demand for travel to London, Nottingham was large enough to have warranted an express service of its own, especially as its position on a loop line placed in it the shadow of Leicester population: two hundred and eighty thousand which had a far better service. A 5XP and an eight coach dining set performing two 130-minute round trips per day might have been a profitable consideration but the Midland always more conscious of the needs of coal rather than people – preferred to divert an occasional main line express rather than give the city a service of its own. The few sets that were based at Nottingham were used for the semi-fasts trains that either called at the seven or eight major intermediate stops or ran via Leicester and, taking more than three hours for the journey, were of little relevance to through traffic.

Nottingham businessmen who wished to be in London for a meeting at ten in the morning and wanted to do the journey in something better than two and a half hours were in for a disappointment since the only service that came close to fitting the bill was the up Edinburgh sleeper which left Nottingham at 06.00 – far too early for most business tastes in the 1950's – but had to eke out 32 minutes of extra time that had been inserted into the running times in order to prevent the train from reaching London in the middle of the rush hour. There was also a London train at 06.40 but this ran via Trent and made innumerable stops before reaching St Pancras at 09.55. Its one redeeming feature was a restaurant car in which some of the ennui of the extended journey could be passed. The service designed for business travel was the 07.00 Sheffield – London which left Nottingham at 08.15 and ran to London in two and a quarter hours; a timing not noticeably inferior to the best the line had been capable of in earlier times. There was always a danger that the train would arrive at Nottingham with every seat taken by passengers who had boarded at Sheffield, Chesterfield and Alfreton and while third class travellers had to fight for seats, first class passengers joining at Nottingham were cosseted by the attachment of a three-coach dining section; the majority of seats being first class.

There was very little competition from other quarters at Nottingham. The Great Central could only offer – assuming one ignored the 06.20 ex Victoria which took almost five hours

Train	09.25			09.25				11.20			09.15		10.35						
From	St P			St P				St P			Paignton		B'mth						
ST PANCRAS			10.30			10.55	11.20	12.00	12.30			13.00		14.10	14.30	14.40	15.25	16.30	16.35
St Albans							11.45					13.26				15.06			
Harpenden							11.55									15.16			
Luton						11.34	12.04					13.41				15.25			17.12
BEDFORD						11.57	12.29					14.05				15.51		17.22	17.36
Wellingborough						12c19	12b49					14b25				16b17			
Kettering	11.18					12b32	12.59	13b13	13.18			14b38				16b29	16b44		18.02
Manton																			
Melton Mowbray						13.20						15.22							
M. Harborough	11.36								13.35										
LEICESTER	11.56		12.09	(11.56)				13.44	14.04	14.09					16.09	17.08		18.15	
LEICESTER	(12.20)		12.13	12.20				13.48		14.13					16.13			18.19	
Loughborough				12.37															
Trent																			
NOTTINGHAM						13.44						15.45		16.13			17.38		
NOTTINGHAM						13.48						15.50		16.17			17.43		
BRISTOL		09.05			10.35						12.35					14.20			
BATH												12.44							
Mangotsfield		09.20			10.50											14.38			
GLOUCESTER		10.00			11.23						13.18	13.32				15.11			
GLOUCESTER		10.06			11.27						13.23	13.37				15.16			
Cheltenham		10b19			11d41						13d37	13d51				15c29			
WORCESTER																			
WORCESTER																			
Kings Norton																			
BIRMINGHAM		11.18			12.35						14.31	14.45				16.24			
BIRMINGHAM		11.28			12.42						14.37	15.04				16.30			
Tamworth		11.52														16.55			
Burton		12.12			13.18						15.11	15.42				17.14			
DERBY		12.26	12.43	12.58	13.33						14.43	15.25	15.58		16.43	17.29		18.52	
DERBY		12.31	12.48	13.04	13.40						14.48	15.33	16.05		16.48	17.35		18.57	
Belper																			
Ambergate																			
Matlock				13.27														19.21	
Bakewell				13.40															
Millers Dale				13b55											17c31				
Chinley				14c16														19c59	
Stockport																			
Cheadle Heath											15.55							20.13	
Didsbury																			
MANCHESTER			14.05	14.40							16.08				18.10			20.26	
Alfreton																			
Chesterfield		13.02				14.31						16.04	16.37	16.57			18.06	18.25	
SHEFFIELD		13.23			14.29	14.51		15.02				16.25	16.47	16.58	17.17		18.27	18.45	
SHEFFIELD		13.28			14.36			15.07				16.30	16.52		17.23		18.34	18.50	
Rotherham		13.38			14.46								17.02		17.33		18.44	19.00	
Swinton					14.55														
Cudworth		13.56											17.20		17.50				
Normanton		14.12													18.05				
LEEDS		14.29						15.55				17.24			18.21			19.41	
LEEDS		14.35						16.02				17.29			18.28			19.46	
Newlay															18.42				
Shipley		14.53										17.46			18.59			20.03	
BRADFORD		15.01										17.54			19.06			20.10	
Keighley																			
Skipton																			
Hellifield								16f54											
Appleby																			
CARLISLE								18.12											
Destination						N'ctle		G'gow				BDX				N'cle			

to reach London – the up Master Cutler which left at 08.46 but did not reach Marylebone until 11.23. The Great Northern had virtually given up the fight for Nottingham passenger traffic but for the adventurous one through service for Kings Cross left Victoria at 07.33, reaching London at 10.50. The main reason for the train was to serve the intermediate stations on the Nottingham – Grantham branch but, of course, it was available for through Nottingham traffic. Formed of a five-coach set of BR Mark1 vehicles with three LNER carriages being added at Grantham, the train had no return working and therefore posed something of a mystery to amateur railway operators who wondered how the stock made its way back to Nottingham. In fact the eight vehicles formed the 17.00 Kings Cross to Peterborough 'Parli', the 19.52 Peterborough – Grantham and the 22.00 Grantham – Nottingham.

In addition to the demand for London services, bookings to the North West were relatively high; a fact that had always caused problems since Nottingham was rather off the beaten track so far as London – Manchester services were concerned. In most cases a change of trains was necessary at Derby but some alleviation was granted by the introduction after the grouping of a through train from Nottingham to Liverpool via Manchester; the service leaving at around nine in the morning and returning from Liverpool in the late afternoon. Taking half an hour longer than its pre-1914 equivalent – a great many intermediate stops had been added – it was nonetheless quite a good service by the reckoning of the 1950's since it was not only direct but included catering facilities. In British Railways days it was the last link between the Midland and Merseyside. There was no corresponding service based at Liverpool but for passengers in the opposite direction the 09.00 Manchester to St Pancras was routed via Nottingham and Melton, an arrangement that involved some interesting contortions at Trent Junction and added about half an hour to the usual Manchester – London running time.

Another interesting feature of Nottingham operation was the through morning service to Bristol; the only West of England service not to originate at either Bradford or York/Newcastle There was no return working and in order

LMS TIMETABLE (1938/9)

Station	09.40			08.15				10.50	14.35					09.30		10.03
From	H'fax			N'cle				H'fax	Leic					G'gow		E'bro
CARLISLE														11.55		12.42
Appleby																13.21
Hellifield																14b19
Skipton																14.36
Keighley																
BRADFORD					10.25			10.38				12.20	12.32		14.18	
Shipley					10.31			10.44				12.26	12.38		14.24	
Newlay																
LEEDS					10.47			11.02				12.44	12.55	14.20	14.39	15.08
LEEDS					10.52			11.07				12.50	13.00	14.26	14.44	15.13
Normanton								11.23								
Cudworth								11.39								
Swinton																
Rotherham				11.21				11.55				13.22	13.47		15.28	
SHEFFIELD	10.54			11.42		12.05	12.10	13.42	13.58					15.15	15.38	16.02
SHEFFIELD	11.00			11.47		(12.18)	12.18	13.47	13.55	14.03				15.20	15.43	16.07
Chesterfield				11.48			12.39	14.07	14.16	14.24					16.05	16.27
Alfreton																
MANCHESTER	10.00								12.25				14.00			16.25
Didsbury																
Cheadle Heath	10.14															
Stockport																
Chinley													14.29			
Millers Dale													14c52			
Bakewell																
Matlock													15.09			
Ambergate																
Belper																
DERBY	11.26			12.18		12.40	(12.40)	13.47				14.52	15.31		16.36	17.43
DERBY	11.33		12.05	(12.46)		12.46	12.55	13.54				14.57	15.36		16.43	17.48
Burton							13.12					15.12				
Tamworth																
BIRMINGHAM					13.33	13.50						15.48			17.34	
BIRMINGHAM					13.39	14.00						15.54			17.40	
Kings Norton																
WORCESTER							14.45									
WORCESTER							14.48									
Cheltenham					14b34	15c19						16c50			18c36	
GLOUCESTER					14.42	15.29	(15.29)					16.58			18.44	
GLOUCESTER					14.48	15.35	15.40					17.02			18.50	
Mangotsfield							16.30					17.49			19.25	
BATH						16.21										
BRISTOL					15.32		16.43					18.05			19.40	
NOTTINGHAM								13.19			14.55				17.07	
NOTTINGHAM								13.25			14.59				17.11	
Trent																
Loughborough			12.27													18.09
LEICESTER	12.04	12.14	12.43					14.26		15.05			16.07	16.41		18.25
LEICESTER	12.09	12.18	12.48					14.30	14.35	15.08			16.11	16.46		18.29
M. Harborough			13.12						14.59							
Melton Mowbray												15.24			17.34	
Manton																
Kettering			13d32					14b22		15.16		16b10			18.10	
Wellingborough		12b58	13d46							15b27		16b20				
BEDFORD			14c12							15.48	16.05	16b41				
Luton		13.36	14.41								16.38					19.42
Harpenden											16.47					
St Albans											16.58					
ST PANCRAS	13.48	14.07	15.22					15.32	16.10	16.47	17.20	17.35	17.50	18.25	19.20	20.12
Destination					Paignton	B'mth										

rovide the stock for the service a complex ten-day carriage diagram had to be devised which llowed the 17.30 St Pancras to Nottingham to rovide the coaches for the Bristol service.

Of all the locations served by the Midland, here is no doubt that Leicester was the most avoured. With a population of two hundred and eighty thousand it deserved a fast and egular service to London although it has to be aid that most of its good fortune derived from is position on the main line rather than especial ttentions of the railway although it was unusual or an express to be booked to pass the station ithout stopping and in fact the only booked ervice in 1955 not to stop was the 18.33 St ancras – Sheffield. Older staff recalled pre-014 days when a number of expresses were ooked to be divided at Leicester, one such being the 12.00 ex St Pancras the leading section of which went forward non-stop to Manchester; the rear section leaving five minutes later for Bradford. In addition to the division, the train was notable in that the Bradford section was routed via Nottingham.

One of the busier Midland stations, much of Leicester's passenger activities involved the interaction between local and main line trains while it was also the crossroad of the main line and the cross-country route between Birmingham and the Eastern Counties. Apart from a handful of semi-fast trains to London which came under the aegis of London district local services, there were no main line originating services from Leicester – the largest passenger engines allocated locally were a mere nine class 5 4-6-0's - and, like Nottingham, where a service specifically designed for London traffic might have been expected, there was none, reliance being placed on services from the North. The most obvious gap, similar to that of Nottingham, affected business travel in that there was no express service which gave an arrival in London before ten in the morning. The nearest was 06.40 from Nottingham which ran via Trent to leave Leicester at 07.35 and although it arrived in London at 09.55 and had a restaurant car, it was something of a semi-fast service and a far cry from the non-stop expresses that operated later in the day and were booked at all but a mile a minute start to stop. The dearth of business expresses was repeated from London in the evening when there was a gap of two and a half hours between the 16.25 and 18.40 departures from St Pancras. The intervening 17.30 was too

LMS TIMETABLE (1938/9)

Train			16.55				18.20		18.30							00.05
From			St P				St P		St P							St P
ST PANCRAS	16.55	17.00		17.32		18.20		18.30		18.35	20.15	21.15	21.30	23.50	00.05	
St Albans											20.42					
Harpenden																
Luton										19.14	21.00			00.33		
BEDFORD				18b37						19.45	21.28			01.02	01.19	
Wellingborough		18.11								20h22	21e54		22b47	01g49		
Kettering		18b23	18.29	19b04				19b47		20d37	22e10	22c41	23b00	02c03		
Manton			18.55													
Melton Mowbray			19.19													
M. Harborough				19.20						21.02					02.21	
LEICESTER	18.41			19.39				20.19		21.23	22.49		23.35	02.00	02.43	
LEICESTER	18.45			19.42				20.24			22.58		23.42	02.14	02.50	
Loughborough				19.56											03.09	
Trent				20.07									00c15			
NOTTINGHAM		19.21	19.41	20.18		20.23					23.41					
NOTTINGHAM		19.26				20.28					23.50					
BRISTOL					17.00					19.20	20.00			23.45		
BATH																
Mangotsfield										19.40	20.23					
GLOUCESTER					17.43					20.21	21.03			00.45		
GLOUCESTER					17.48					20.25	21.10			00.58		
Cheltenham					18c01					20d42	21f28			01e15		
WORCESTER											22.05					
WORCESTER											22.10					
Kings Norton																
BIRMINGHAM					18.57					21.55	22.58			02.20		
BIRMINGHAM					19.05					22.05						
Tamworth					19.28					22.30						
Burton					19.48					22.50						
DERBY					20.04			20.57	(20.57)	23.06	23.38			02.52	03.21	(03.21)
DERBY					20.10			21.02	21.10	23.14				03.10	03.49	03.55
Belper									21.26							
Ambergate									21.32							
Matlock									21.52							04g26
Bakewell									22.10							
Millers Dale								21.43	22.23							
Chinley								22b01								
Stockport																05.25
Cheadle Heath																
Didsbury								22.16								
MANCHESTER								22.27								05.25
Alfreton																
Chesterfield		20.06			20.41	21.08				23.47			01.14	04.02		
SHEFFIELD	20.00	20.26			21.02	21.28	(21.28)			00.10				04.23		
SHEFFIELD	20.06	20.31				21.33	21.40			00.15				04.37		
Rotherham						21.43						00.56		04.47		
Swinton																
Cudworth														05.06		
Normanton														05.23		
LEEDS		21.21				22.24					01.10	01.41	01.59	05.58		
LEEDS		21.35				22.30					01.25	01.50	02.12			
Newlay																
Shipley		21.53				22.53										
BRADFORD		22.02				23.00										
Keighley	BDX												02.37			
Skipton												02.25				
Hellifield												02e47	03d09			
Appleby																
CARLISLE										03.50		04.15	04.38			
Destination							BDX		Buxton	G'gow		E'bro	G'gow			Mtr (V)

slow to be taken seriously by regular travellers.

By the 1950s the most picturesque elements of the West of England route had evaporated and niceties such as through coaches from Bristol to Manchester and Scotland had give way to a more austere series of expresses to either Bradford, York or Newcastle. With a norm of four and a half hours for the 166 miles between Bristol and Sheffield – 37 mph – they were scarcely in the first flight of expresses although much of the time taken was due to the number of stops that had to be made: Gloucester, Cheltenham, Birmingham and Burton were too important to be ignored whilst several lesser points were usually added for good measure.

A peculiar point concerning Midland timing practices was the way in which Temple Meads was regarded as the boundary of the civilised world. With the disappearance of the Railway Companies, it might have been expected that Midland services would have been routinely extended to start at Paignton or Plymouth yet it took twenty-five years for the penny to drop and in the meantime Bristol remained the starting point for almost all workings. The exception was the Devonian which ran to and from Paignton and Plymouth but this was not a post-1948 innovation; the working dating back to a long standing arrangement between the LMS and GWR. A more recent innovation was the running of through coaches between Cardiff and Newcastle, an interesting if complicated arrangement whereby the Bristol section had to run into the Great Western station at Gloucester to be attached to the Cardiff section.

A further sign of the sanctity of compan[y] boundaries was evident at Worcester were [it] was perfectly possible for Midland trains t[o] call yet few did so, partly because of the ext[ra] time involved but mainly because the tab[oo] of crossing into what prior to 1948 had bee[n] foreign territory remained. The only expres[s] to make the detour into Shrub Hill was the nig[ht] mail from Bristol to Sheffield although a throug[h] train was run each morning from Worcester t[o] York.

By the mid-1950s most of the stock to b[e] found in Midland expresses was of LMS desig[n] as well it might be since the interwar years ha[d] seen a programme of carriage building on a[n] extraordinary scale. A summary of main li[ne]

LMS TIMETABLE (1938/9)

Train	15.35	12.15	16.09					18.40		19.10				17.30
From	York	G'gow	BDX					York		N'cle				G'gow
CARLISLE		14.45												20.40
Appleby		15.25												21.30
Hellifield		16d28												22d43
Skipton														23.02
Keighley														23.18
BRADFORD				16.40							21.00	21.20		
Shipley				16.48							21.10	21.32		
Newlay											21.26	21.49		
LEEDS		17.11		17.01							21.40	22.05		23.41
LEEDS		17.16		17.23							22.00	22.15		00.05
Normanton											22.18	22.35		
Cudworth		17.33												
Swinton								19.31						
Rotherham	16.30			18.05				19.40			22.53	23.08		
SHEFFIELD	16.40			18.16				19.50		22.45	23.03	23.22		01.02
SHEFFIELD	16.50	17.35		18.21				20.00		(23.18)	23.18	23.45		01.18
Chesterfield	17.17	17.56		18.42				20.21			23.46	00.10		01.45
Alfreton														
MANCHESTER			16.34	17.50	18.20				19.25				00.00	
Didsbury														
Cheadle Heath				17.48					19.39					
Stockport			16.50										00.25	
Chinley			17.20		18.27				20.03				00.32	
Millers Dale			17b44		18.46				20c29					
Bakewell			17.54						20.38					
Matlock			18.05		19.02				20.50					
Ambergate			18.18											
Belper									21.14					
DERBY	17.49			19.10	19.24	19.38		21.58	21.25		00.18	00.48	02.00	02.22
DERBY	18.06			19.15	19.45	19.49	20.00	21.02	21.35		00.35	01.10	02.20	02.35
Burton	18.25			19.31			20.21				00.53			02.55
Tamworth	18.47						20.42				01t34			
BIRMINGHAM	19.15			20.06			21.05	22.10			02.00			03.40
BIRMINGHAM	19.20			20.16			21.18				02.50			03.52
Kings Norton														
WORCESTER	20.13						22.18				03.33			
WORCESTER							22.26				03.45			
Cheltenham				21c12			23f06				04h19			05e00
GLOUCESTER				21.20			23.16				04.29			05.17
GLOUCESTER				21.25			23.30				04.40			05.28
Mangotsfield				21.59							05.21			06.14
BATH														
BRISTOL				22.11			00.15				05.37			06.35
NOTTINGHAM		18.36	19.11						22.04					
NOTTINGHAM	17.25	18.40												
Trent		18c53												
Loughborough							20.12							
LEICESTER		19.17				18.16	20.28				01.50		03.00	
LEICESTER		19.22				18.20	20.33				02.00	02.05	03.10	
M. Harborough												02.35	03.46	
Melton Mowbray	17.50													
Manton	18.13													
Kettering	18b40	19b37	19.55					21.10				03k03		
Wellingborough	18c52							21.19				03g20	04f14	
BEDFORD	19o27	20b03						21d43			03e09	03l54	04g43	
Luton	19.54							22.12			03.47	04.26	05.18	
Harpenden														
St Albans											04.06	04.45	05.35	
ST PANCRAS	20.25	20.55	21.10				21.59	22.49			04.30	05.15	06.00	
Destination														

and suburban vehicles, showing the year and type, are given in the tables which may be useful in allowing the reader to identify the types of vehicles – the number of seats are the key - used in each service. Although prepared with every care, the list should be regarded as a guide rather than a gospel since it does not take into account the various reclassification, etc, that some types of coaches underwent. This book is concerned more with the use made of coaches rather than the coaches themselves and for greater detail of the design and classification of vehicles, the reader is urged to turn to one of the several authoritative works that deal with the topic.

From the seating details given in the train tables in the main body of the book, it should be possible for the reader to establish within reasonable bounds the exact type of vehicle used in each service. However, operators tended to be somewhat vague about carriage classifications and unless a specific instruction was given to provide a particular vehicle, train marshalling staff were guided solely by the type and seating accommodation; a procedure that sometimes led to some curious inclusions in main line workings. If, for example, the 42-seat Third Corridor diagrammed for the 20.55 Bradford – Bristol happened to be crippled a few hours before departure and the only 42-seat replacement was some venerable pre-grouping vehicle then no-one – apart, perhaps, from the knowledgeable line side observer - would regard its use as being in any way remarkable. As it happened there were usually sufficient spare LMS vehicles available to allow trains to retain a reasonably modern look although now and again museum pieces did make an appearance.

The energies expended by the LMS in keeping its carriage fleet up to date cannot be understated and although coach production was almost a side-show compared to the running of trains and building of engines, the construction of nearly thirteen thousand passenger vehicles over twenty-five years – construction was suspended during the war years - meant two new carriages taking to the rails every week day which was an amazing industrial performance. During the sixteen years from 1924 annual production

After easing off for the curves north of St Albans, Millhouses (Sheffield) Jubilee 4-6-0 45654 'Hood' opens up and appears to prepare for a fast run into St Pancras on Saturday 4th April 1953. Although engines of only moderate power and at their best with loads of twelve coaches or less, the Jubilee's were very speedy engines and (as anyone who stood on Bedford Midland Road will testify) took every advantage of the falling gradients. Speeds in excess of 90 mph were by no means uncommon.

MAIN LINE ARRIVALS & DEPARTURES : DERBY MIDLAND

Train	From	Arr	C/W	Formation	Dep	Destination
			954	1: BG	00.09	Normanton
21.55	Leeds	23.07	949	1: BG	00.38	Worcester
20.10	St Pancras	23.40	908	1: BG	01.25	Newcastle
20.10	St Pancras	23.40	909	1: BG	01.25	York
23.50	St Pancras	03.20	920	1: BG	03.57	Nottingham
19.10	St Pancras	22.15	49	6: BTK, TK, 2CK, TK, BTK	06.18	Nottingham
18.15	Llandudno	22.02	441	6: BTK, TK, 2CK, TK, BTK	07.20	Llandudno
20.10	St Pancras	23.40	32	8: BTK, TK, CK, FK, TK, BTK, 2TK	08.05	St Pancras
14.15	St Pancras	16.52	32A	1: BTK	08.05	St Pancras
16.15	St Pancras	19.01	24B	1: FK	09.00	St Pancras
16.45	Bristol	20.22	153	2: TK, RC	10.24	Bristol
16.45	Bristol	20.22	24A	1: TK	10.48	St Pancras
16.45	Bradford	19.29	43A	1: RB	11.10	Bradford
18.40	St Pancras	21.17	119	7: 2TK, CK, RF, 2 TO, BTK	12.05	St Pancras
08.15	St Pancras	11.19	28A	2: RC. TO	15.35	St Pancras
20.10	St Pancras	23.40		1: TK	15.35	St Pancras
10.15	St Pancras	12.50	29A	1: CK	15.35	St Pancras
01.10	Bristol	05.36	43B	1: TPO	19.52	Bristol
18..33	St Pancras	20.53	907	1: BZ	21.27	Manchester
			952	1: BG	22.10	Sheffield
			953	1: BG	22.10	Sheffield
23.50	St Pancras	03.20	919	1: BG		
21.20	Blackpool	06.00	985	1: BG		

MAIN LINE ARRIVALS & DEPARTURES : MANCHESTER CENTRAL

Train	From	Arr	C/W	Formation	Dep	Destination
			932	BG	00.05	Derby
			933	BG	00.05	Leicester
22.10	Liverpool		934	BG	00.05	St Pancras
16.15	Derby	19.08	27A	1: CK	00.05	St Pancras
16.15	St Pancras	20.50	27C	1: TK	00.05	St Pancras
18.40	St Pancras	23.08	907	BZ	00.05	St Pancras
			935	2: BG	00.05	St Pancras
			936	BG	00.05	Derby
22.10	Liverpool		937	BG	00.05	Derby
16.15	St Pancras	20.50	23	8: BTK, CK, FK, RF, TO, 2 TK, BTK	07.20	St Pancras
18.40	St Pancras	23.08	30	4: BTK, 2 CK, BTK	07.24	Derby
14.15	St Pancras	20.50	24	8: BTK, CK, FK, RF, TO, 2 TK, BTK	09.00	St Pancras
16.15	St Pancras	20.50	24C	1: CK	09.00	St Pancras
04.18	Leicester	09.49	26A	2: TK	11.35	Nottingham
09.06	Nottingham	11.29	48	8: BTK, TK, CK, RB, CK, TK, BTK, BG	11.40	Liverpool
04.18	St Pancras	09.49	26	6: BTK, FK, CK, 2 TK, BTK	13.50	St Pancras
08.15	St Pancras	13.05	28C	1: TK	16.00	St Pancras
10.15	St Pancras	14.30	31	4: BTK, 2 CK, BTK	16.00	St Pancras
10.15	St Pancras	14.30	123	2: KB, TO	16.00	St Pancras
10.15	St Pancras	14.30	29	3: CK, TK, BTK	16.00	St Pancras
15.30	Liverpool	16.15	48	8: BG, BTK, TK, CK, RB, CK, TK, BTK	16.32	Nottingham
08.15	St Pancras	13.05	25	8: BTK, CK, FK, TO, 2 TK, BTK, BG	17.55	St Pancras
04.18	St Pancras	09.49	901	1: BG	17.55	St Pancras

MAIN LINE ARRIVALS & DEPARTURES : LEEDS CITY (MIDLAND)

Train	From	Arr	C/W	Formation	Dep	Destination
19.23	Nottingham	21.50	906	1: BG	01.15	Carnforth
23.50	St Pancras	06.24	21B	2: SLF, SLT	02.45	St Pancras
18.20	Hull	20.17	913	1: VANFIT	02.50	Carlisle
07.55	Sheffield	08.50	931A	1: BG	02.55	Kings Norton
			943	1: BG	02.55	Derby
			96	3: BTK, CK, BTK	02.55	Kings Norton
07.00	Barnsley	08.15	975	1: BG	02.55	Barnsley
			914	1: BG	02.59	Glasgow
02.10	Sheffield	03.37	442	3: BTK, CK, BTK	06.30	Sheffield
23.50	St Pancras	06.24	915	1: BG	06.55	Bradford
23.50	St Pancras	06.24	916	1: BG	06.55	Bradford
23.50	St Pancras	06.24	917	1: BG	06.55	Bradford
23.50	St Pancras	06.24	22	4: 2TK, CK, BTK	06.55	Bradford
03.16	Normanton	03.37	954	1: BG	07.20	Bradford
02.10	Sheffield	03.37	948	1: BG	07.20	Bradford
02.10	Sheffield	03.37	951	1: BG	07.20	Bradford
02.10	Sheffield	03.37	950	1: BG	07.20	Bradford
02.10	Sheffield	03.37	953	1: BG	07.20	Bradford
16.00	Glasgow	21.41	11	9: BTK, 2TK, 2CK, 2TK, BTK, BG	10.35	Glasgow
16.40	Kilmarnock	21.41	11A	2: CO RC	10.35	Kilmarnock
			960	1: BG	21.55	Birmingham
			961	1: BG	21.55	Birmingham
			962	1: BG	21.55	Bristol
23.50	St Pancras	06.24	924	1: BG	22.12	St Pancras
02.10	Sheffield	03.37	952	1: BG		

MAIN LINE ARRIVALS & DEPARTURES : BRISTOL

Train	From	Arr	C/W	Formation	Dep	Destination
07.43	Nottingham	12.00	42	6: BTK, TK, 2 CK, TK, BTK	01.10	Sheffield
07.43	Nottingham	12.00	42A	1: TK	01.10	Sheffield
	Plymouth		930	1: BG	01.10	Sheffield
21.55	Leeds	04.35	931	1: BG	01.10	Sheffield
19.52	Derby	23.56	43B	1: TPO	01.10	Derby
19.52	Derby	23.56	974	1: BG	01.10	Gloucester/Sheffield
20.55	Bradford	04.35	85	3: TK, CK, BTK	07.35	Bradford
16.45	Bradford	23.56	43	6: BG, TK, 2 CK, TK, BTK	07.35	Bradford
08.15	Newcastle	15.52	57	5: BTK, RT, CK, TK, BTK	08.45	Newcastle
12.37	Newcastle	20.27	64	10: BTK, 5 TK, TO, RC, FK, BTK	10.20	Newcastle
12.00	York	18.26	44	6: BTK, TK, 2 CK, TK, BTK	14.15	York
12.00	York	18.26	150	2: 2TK	14.15	York
			152	3: 3TK	14.15	Sheffield
07.30	Bradford	13.42	40	6: BTK, TK, 2 CK, TK, BTK	16.45	York
10.24	Derby	13.42	153	2: TK, RC	16.45	Derby
07.30	Bradford	13.42	40A	2: TK	16.45	York
07.43	Nottingham	12.00	153A	1: TK	16.45	Derby
02.15	Derby	07.25	932	1: BG	16.45	York
19.05	Newcastle	05.20	66	9: BG, BTK, 2 TK, CK, BG, 3 TPO	19.20	Newcastle
23.30	Sheffield	05.20	947	1: BG	19.20	Sheffield/Bradford
19.52	Derby	23.56	969	1: BG		
16.45	Bradford	23.56	967	1: BG		
16.45	Bradford	23.56	968	1: BG		
21.55	Leeds	04.35	962	1: BG		
20.55	Bradford	04.35	964	2: 2BG		
20.55	Bradford	04.35	966	1: BG		
20.10	Newcastle	21.00	980	1: BG		
21.00	Durham	21.00	981	1: BG		
20.33	W. Hartlepool	21.00	983	1: BG		

The tables above (and on following pages) show the stock needed for the main line services from several major Midland centres together with the carriage working reference and the inward service. Although suburban and local trains added considerably to the number of trains, they generally remained in set formations and did not need the marshalling operations that main line services often required.

The start from Sheffield for up trains was a bad one with a four mile climb to Dore and Totley at around 1 in 100 for which eleven minutes was allowed. It was a four-track section over which Chinley and Manchester trains used the slow lines, the fast lines being used by services to Derby, Nottingham and London. 5XP 4-6-0 45651 'Shovell' of Bristol passes Dore with a West of England train in December 1960; the engine in rather poor shape with every sign of a perspiring fireman and little evidence of steam.

MAIN LINE ARRIVALS & DEPARTURES : NOTTINGHAM MIDLAND

Train	From	Arr	C/W	Formation	Dep	Destination
12.50	St Pancras	16.22	27	10 : BTK, SFO, RT, TO, 2CK, BTK, 2TK	06.40	St Pancras
17.30	St Pancras	20.47	24A	1 : TK	06.40	St Pancras
17.30	St Pancras	20.47	42A	1 : TK	07.35	Bristol
17.30	St Pancras	20.47	46	6 : BTK, TK, 2CK, TK, BTK	07.35	Bristol
17.30	St Pancras	20.47	153A	1 : TK	07.35	Bristol
17.30	St Pancras	20.47	86	1 : CK	07.50	Derby
14.00	St Pancras	16.17	117	3 : FK, FO, RT	08.15	St Pancras
16.25	St Pancras	19.48	47	10 : BTK, 5TK, 2CK, TK, BTK	08.28	St Pancras
15.30	Liverpool	19.31	48	8 : BTK, TK, CK, RB, CK, TK, BTK, BG	09.06	Liverpool
08.37	Leicester	09.32	902	1 : BG	12.50	Newark
06.18	Nottingham	07.06	49	6 : BTK, TK, 2CK, TK, BTK	13.25	St Pancras
19.10	St Pancras	21.40	49A	4 : BTK, TK, TO, CAFÉ	13.25	St Pancras
09.00	St Pancras	11.25	5A	1 : CK	17.50	Sheffield
			906		19.23	Carnforth
18.45	St Pancras	23.10	910	1 : BG	23.52	Edinburgh
19.40	Luton	23.10	911	1 : BG	23.52	Carlisle
			973	1 : BG	23.55	Derby
03.57	Derby	04.37	920	1 : BG		
03.57	Derby	04.37	937	1 : BG		
03.57	Derby	04.37	938	1 : BG		

MAIN LINE ARRIVALS & DEPARTURES : BIRMINGHAM NEW STREET (MIDLAND)

Train	From	Arr	C/W	Formation	Dep	Destination
21.55	Leeds	01.35	960	1 : BG	02.15	Bailey Gate
06.09	Kings Norton	06.21	38	6 : BTK, TK, 2CK, TK, BTK	06.40	Bradford
07.40	Kings Norton	07.52	39	6 : BTK, TK, 2CK, TK, BTK	08.05	Newcastle
02.55	Leeds	07.56	96	3 : BTK, CK, BTK	08.05	Kings Norton
06.57	Cleethorpes	11.13	87	5 : BTK, TK, CK, TK, BTK	12.15	Gloucester
10.10	Sheffield	12.09	50	6 : BTK, TK, 2CK, TK, BTK	12.30	Kings Norton
10.25	Manchester LR	12.29	74	7 : BCK, CK, TK, TO, RT, CO, BTK	12.42	Bournemouth W
10.10	Sheffield	12.09	68	2 : BTK, CK	12.42	Bournemouth W
10.15	Liverpool LS	12.29	72	2 : BTK, CK	12.42	Bournemouth W
12.40	Kings Norton	12.55	90	3 : 2TK, BCK	13.45	Yarmouth Beach
12.40	Kings Norton	12.55	91	2 : TK: BCK	13.45	Norwich City
12.40	Kings Norton	12.55	89	2 : TK, BCK	13.45	Cromer
09.45	Bournemouth W	14.23	73A	2 : BTK, CK	14.33	Liverpool LS
09.45	Bournemouth W	14.23	73	6 : BCK, CK, TK, TO, RT, CO, BTK	14.33	Manchester (Mayfield)
09.45	Bournemouth W	14.23	69	2 : BTK, CK	14.38	Sheffield
14.03	Kings Norton	14.15	69A	1 : TK	14.38	Sheffield
09.42	Cromer	15.38	92	2 : TK: BCK	15.46	Kings Norton
09.00	Yarmouth Beach	15.38	93	3 : 2TK, BCK	15.46	Kings Norton
09.31	Bnorwich City	15.38	94	2 : TK: BCK	15.46	Kings Norton
08.15	Derby	09.15	980	1 : BG	16.10	Bristol
02.08	York	09.15	982	1 : BG	16.10	Bristol
02.08	York	09.15	983	1 : BG	16.10	Bristol
02.08	York	09.15	982	1 : BG	16.10	Bristol
13.51	Gloucester	15.59	88	5 : BTK, TK, CK, TK, BTK	16.50	Cleethorpes
08.06	Sheffield	15.59	132	3 : BTK, CK, BTK	17.15	Derby
16.40	Kings Norton	16.55	96	3 : BTK, CK, BTK	17.15	Derby
15.57	Newcastle	21.05	39	6 : BTK, TK, 2CK, TK, BTK	21.25	Kings Norton
19.05	Sheffield	21.05	69A	1 : TK	21.25	Kings Norton
			939	1 : BG	23.35	Leicester
			940	1 : BG	23.35	Leicester
20.55	Bradford	01.35	963	1 : BG		
02.55	Leeds	07.56	944	1 : BG		

MAIN LINE ARRIVALS & DEPARTURES : SHEFFIELD MIDLAND

Train	From	Arr	C/W	Formation	Dep	Destination
06.30	Sheffield	08.25	442	3 : BTK, CK, BTK	02.10	Leeds (03.41)
			950	1 : BG	02.10	Leeds (03.41)
18.33	St Pancras	21.53	14	7 : BTK, 3 TK, 2 CK, BTK	07.00	St Pancras
01.10	Bristol	06.59	42	6 : BTK, TK, 2CK, TK, BTK	07.50	Bradford
01.10	Bristol	06.59	42A	1 : TK	07.50	Bradford
01.10	Bristol	06.59	930	1 : BG	07.50	Leeds
01.10	Bristol	06.59	931	1 : BG	07.50	Bradford
19.42	Derby	21.18	132	3 : BTK, CK, BTK	08.06	Gloucester
22.10	Derby	23.28	133	4 : 3 TK, BCK	08.06	Gloucester
15.15	St Pancras	18.56	14	3 : RF, TO, TK	08.58	St Pancras
			38A	1 : TK	09.07	Bradford
17.25	Bristol	19,23	38	6 : BTK, TK, 2CK, BTK	09.09	St Pancras
09.43	Bristol	10.46	50	6 : BTK, TK, 2CK, BTK	10.10	Birmingham
09.45	Bournemouth	16.33	69	2 : BTK, CK	10.10	Bournemouth
18.33	St Pancras	21.53	126	2 : RF, TO	12.11	St Pancras
17.50	Nottingham	20.00	126A	1 : CK	12.11	St Pancras
09.15	Hull	11.03	129	6 : BTK, CK, 2 TK, BTK,T. (LNER)	15.10	Hull
16.15	York	18.06	52	8 : BTK, TK, 2 CK, 3 TK, BTK	17.15	Gloucester
14.38	Birmingham	16.33	69A	1 : TK	19.05	Birmingham
			971	1 : BG	19.18	Derby
			946	1 : BG	21.37	Edinburgh
19.20	Bristol	00.48	947	1 : BG	23.30	Bristol
			925	1 : BG	23.50	St Pancras
14.15	Bristol	18.42	152	3 : 3 TK		
02.35	Gloucester	07.35	974	1 : BG		

MAIN LINE ARRIVALS & DEPARTURES : BRADFORD

Train	From	Arr	C/W	Formation	Dep	Destination
16.24	Leeds	17.04	128	5 : BTK, TK, CK, TK, BTK (LNER)	06.42	York
15.15	St Pancras	20.50	124	7 : BFK, 2 CK, 3 TK, BTK	07.15	St Pancras
07.50	Sheffield	09.55	40	6 : BTK, TK, 2 CK, TK, BTK	07.30	Bristol
			40A	2 : 2TK	07.30	Bristol
16.22	Scarborough	19.00		10 : BTK, TK, 2 CK, 5 TK, BTK	08.46	Scarborough
16.50	St Pancras	22.42		10 : BTK, TK, TO, RK, FO, FK, BFK, CK, BTK	09.12	St Pancras
08.15	Plymouth	19.09	35	6 : BTK, TK, CK, RC, TO, BTK	09.25	Newton Abbot
09.15	Paignton	19.09	33	5 : BTK, CK, 2 TK, BTK	09.25	Paignton
14.00	St Pancras	19.26	15	7 : BTK, 2 CK, 3 TK, BTK	10.30	St Pancras
07.50	Sheffield	09.55	15A	1 : TK	10.30	St Pancras
11.45	St Pancras	17.15		11 : TK, BTK, 3 TK, TO, RK, FO, FK, CK, BTK	11.50	St Pancras
10.42	Hull	12.57	LNER	7 : BTK, 2TK, FK, CK, BTK	14.57	Hull
10.15	York	11.44	LNER	6 : BTK, TK, CK, TK, BTK	15.50	Leeds/Newcastle
07.35	Bristol	14.03	A	6 : BG, TK, 2CK, TK, BTK	16.45	Bristol
				2 : 2 BG	16.45	Bristol
11.10	Derby	14.03		1 : RB	16.45	Bristol
06.40	Birmingham	11.04	38	6 : BTK, TK, 2CK, TK, BTK	17.25	Sheffield
			972	1 : BG	18.05	Derby
			949	1 : BG	20.55	Derby
07.35	Bristol	14.03	85	3 : BTK, CK, TK	20.55	Bristol
			963	1 : BG	20.55	Birmingham
			964	2 : BG	20.55	Bristol
			949	1 : BG	20.55	Bristol
			970	1 : BG	21.20	Leicester
06.55	Leeds	07.40	21	6 : 2 TK, CK, BTK, 2BG	21.20	St Pancras
06.55	Leeds	07.40	915A	1 : BG	21.20	St Pancras
06.55	Leeds	07.40	916A	1 : BG	21.20	St Pancras
09.08	Sheffield	11.04	38A	1 : TK		

Type	Seats	Dia	1924	1925	1926	1927	1928	1929	1930	1931	1932	1933	1934	1935	1936	1937	1938	1939	1940-4	1945	1946	1947	1948	1949	1950	1951	1952	1953	TOTALS
BCK	12/32	1754	29																										29
BCK	12/32	1755			30	25																							55
BCK	12/32	1704						50																					50
RTO	42	1706				25																							25
BCK	12/24	1720							50																				50
BCK	9/21	1850									20																		20
BCK	6/21	1939											2																2
BCK	9/21	1911												2															2
BCK	12/21	1932													51														51
BCK	12/21	2010																20											20
BFK	27	1654				25																							25
BFK	16	1717						5				1																	6
BFK	27	1845								15																			15
BFK	27	1910												1			8												9
BFK	18	1961														3													3
BFK	30	2168																						15					15
BFO - LOUNGE	10	1741					5																						5
BT	72	1771		74																									74
BT	72	1703			30	117	100																						247
BT	84	1733								3																			3
BT	72	1735								73	45	65	142				1												326
BT (Push & Pull)	72	1790								7																			7
BT	84	1841									6																		6
BT (Push & Pull)	72	1856										17		2		1													20
BT (LTSR)	84	1914											4																4
BT	72	1907										61	30																91
BT	72	1964														64	49	94						60		170			437
BT (Push & Pull)	72	2122																						30	15				45
BT (LTSR)	84	1770	8	20																									28
BT (LTSR/CATHCART)	84	1772			23	4	4	4																					35
BT (NLR)	72	1723								3						3													6
BT (NLR)	72	1797									2	2				4													8
BT (NLR)	84	1783									2	2																	4
BTK	40	1712	8																										8
BTK	32	1758		14																									14
BTK	40	1696			100			25				1																	126
BTK	40	1730							50	50																			100
BTK	24	1851											54																54
BTK	24	1852											16																16
BTK	24	1905												127	125	163													415
BTK	24	1963													24														24
BTK	24	1971															1												1
BTK	24	1968														64	90	130		125	100								509
BTK	24	2123																					120						120
BTK	24	2161																						125	314				439
BTL	56	1685			50	50	148																						248
BTL	56	1737							25																				25
BTO	40	1746			35																								35
BTO	40	1693				35	20																						55
BTO	40	1913											20																20
BTO	48	1946														64	6												70
BTO	44	2008															5	46											51
C	24/72	1701		49	131	88																							268
C	24/72	1767		30																									30
C	24/72	1734							43	100																			143
C	24/72	1849									20	89																	109
C	24/72	1921										25	20	32	27		36	40						70	10				260
C	32/50	2189																									45	35	80
C (Cathcart)	40/48	1766			19																								19
C (Cathcart)	40/48	1766A																										6	6
C (LTSR)	40/36	1764	2																										2
C (NLR)	48/24	1732							3																				3
C (NLR)	48/24	1731							3																				3
C (NLR)	48/24	1786									2	2																	4
C (NLR)	48/24	1785									2	2																	4
CK	18/32	1694	41	75	35	50																							201
CK	24/24	1751		5																									5
CK	18/32	1752		25																									25
CK	18/32	1716							50																				50
CK	18/24	1791								48																			48
CK	18/24	1859										35																	35
CK	18/24	1898											70																70
CK	18/24	1925												90	90														180
CK	18/24	1969													70	33	114												217
CK	18/24	2117																			125	160							285
CK	18/24	2159																						150	90				240
CL	21/54	1736							25																				25
CL	21/54	1686			20			125																					145
CL (LTSR)	22/44	1763	4																										4
CL (LTSR)	31/46	1765			4	4	4	4																					16
CL (LTSR)	31/46	1788							6					4															10
CLUB	40	1922											1																1
CLUB	17	2020															1												1
CO	12/35	1744	5	10																									15
CO	18/18	1862									9																		9
CO	18/18	1984											1																1
CO	18/18	1903											10	10			4	5											29
			97	272	507	398	281	238	341	266	121	389	317	344	432	194	298	336		125	225	160	120	450	429	170	45	41	6596

averaged almost 640 coaches – slightly over 2 vehicles per working day – whilst output ranged from 345 in 1932 as a result of the great depression to almost one thousand in 1936. Many of the vehicles were run of the mill Third and Brake Third Corridors (2870 coaches) and the like whilst a third of the output was stock for local and suburban services.

In some cases one wonders what sort of return was realised since of the respectable fleet of Kitchen-only cars built, only sixteen saw daily use with an additional seven being employed on services to Llandudno and Windermere on summer week-ends. This meant that something approaching eighty vehicles had no visible purpose and although special trains run for parties provided some employment, much of the fleet must have been greatly underemployed. It is all the more curious since the LMS was sensitive about the weight to passenger ratio of its trains – a typical Midland express minus locomotive weighed slightly less that 0.9ton per passenger – and the inclusion of Kitchen Car[s] which carried no payload did nothing to improv[e] train-load statistics. On the other side of th[e] coin, the Kitchen Cars did allow large number[s] of passengers to be fed, a good example bein[g] the pre-war Thames-Clyde express which wi[th] its Kitchen flanked by a Composite Open an[d] two Third Opens, could serve one hundred an[d] twenty diners at one sitting. This compared wit[h] the more conventional arrangement whereb[y] seventy-two passengers could be catered f[or]

Type	Seats	Dia	1924	1925	1926	1927	1928	1929	1930	1931	1932	1933	1934	1935	1936	1937	1938	1939	1940-4	1945	1946	1948	1949	1950	1951	1952	1953	TOTALS
F	64	1858										4	1															5
F	64	1997															4							15				19
F	64	1702	4		25	20	30																					79
F (Cathcart)	80	1760			10																							10
F (LTSR)	64	1759	6																									6
F (LTSR)	64	1762			2	2	2	2																				8
F (LTSR)	64	1787									3			2														5
FK	39	1698	3																									3
FK	39	1747		10																								10
FK	33	1748			10																							10
FK	33	1920											1															1
FK	22	1909											12															12
FK	33	1930													11	7	12											30
FK	22	1960														3												3
FK	36	2121																					30					30
FK	36	2162																						15				15
FL	52	1761				30																						30
FO	36	1742		35	30																							65
FO	42	1917												10	14	27												51
FO	42	2160																							20			20
RB	24	1848									1																	1
RB	24	1948												4														4
RC	12/30	1743		6																								6
RC	12/18	1811									12																	12
RC	12/18	1938												10	3													13
RF	24	1810							6		6																	12
RF	24	1857										4																4
RF	24	1900										4		4	4	4												16
RF	24	2120																										0
RF	24	1718							12																			12
RFO - SEMI	30	1707				5																						5
RFO - SEMI	30	1719							10		1																	11
RFO - SEMI	42	1902											25			10												35
RK	0	1697	8	30	20		15																					73
RK	0	1855										2																2
RK	0	1912											1		20	5	7											33
RT	24	1901										10																10
RT	24	1923												10	4	10												24
RT	24	1861										10																10
RTO	42	1699		35																								35
RTO	42	1721						50																				50
RTO	42	1722						25																				25
RTO	42	1981														9												9
RTO	42	2153																2										2
SLC	6/16	1781							6		6																	12
SLC	6/14	1947												13														13
SLF	12	1739	10																									10
SLF	12	1705		10		12	10	9	1																			42
SLF	12	1926												20	6													26
SLF	12	2166																							25			25
SLT	28	1709				50	25		10																			85
SLT	28	1863										15																15
SLT	22	2169																							10	15		25
T	108	1700		100	50	50	218	50	56																			524
T	108	1784							128	4	104																	236
T	108	1906										54	25	25	110	170	137	70										591
T	108	2124																					30	15	40			85
T (LTSR)	108	1768	102																									102
T (LTSR)	108	1769			12	12	12	12																				48
T (LTSR)	108	1789							18				12															30
TK	64	1756	50																									50
TK	56	1710	5																									5
TK	64	1695	35	45	80		75																					235
TK	56	1782							10																			10
TK	42	1860									30																	30
TK	42	1899									35	289	65	75	40	89	18											611
TK	42	36															3											3
TK	42	2170																					100					100
TO	56	1353	61																									61
TO	56	1692		50		180	200	125																				555
TO	56	1745		100	100																							200
TO	56	1738							25																			25
TO	42	1795							50	1																		51
TO	56	1897								200																		200
TO	56	1807									99																	99
TO	56	1904										25	100															125
TO	60	1915												120	256													376
TO	60	1915A														4												4
TO	56	1999														49	34				150	200						433
TO	56	2021															1											1
TRIPLET COMPOSITE	32/204	1995										33																33
TWIN THIRD	100	1965										44																44
TWIN THIRD	112	1966										44																44
TWIN COMPOSITE	18/87	1967										22																22
TWIN (FIRST)	40	2014															6											6
TWIN (FIRST)	71	2015															2											2
TWIN (FIRST)	72	2138															4											4
TWIN (KITCHEN THII	44	2016															2											2
TWIN THIRD	70	2017															6											6
TWIN THIRD	60	2018															6											6
			284	411	339	316	617	223	379	241	224	193	456	266	527	425	299	163		150	230	35	145	15	75	15		6028

LMS PASSENGER CARRIAGE STOCK 1923 - 1953

sing a two-coach dining set which typically onsisted of a restaurant car and an open coach.

Problems arose with the Manchester route here train weights had to be kept to a minimum f fast timings were to be achieved and it was ver the Peak District that the economics of the itchen Cars was demonstrated to be somewhat awry. To meet the high demand for lunch on the 12.20 ex Manchester and for Dinner on the 18.25 from St Pancras, the working was equipped with a three-car dining section consisting of a First Open, a Kitchen Car and a Third Open that allowed a sitting for eighty-four passengers but which was not very much more than could be catered for in an ordinary two-coach arrangement. Both, however, were soundly eclipsed by the fact that no less than one hundred and twenty-two diners could be accommodated in the 07.20 Manchester – St Pancras/14.25 St Pancras – Manchester, the catering portion of which consisted of a

Served also by the Great Central and the LDEC, Chesterfield was an important Midland Railway crossroads; the lines from Derby and Nottingham merging at Clay Cross, a few miles to the south of Chesterfield whilst a short distance to the North, Tapton Junction was the point of divergence for the Sheffield and Barrow Hill lines. Black 5 4-6-0 44817 of Kentish Town passes mid-way between Tapton Junction and Chesterfield with a Sheffield - St ancras express and overhauls 4F 0-6-0 3991 of Burton on the up goods line with a mineral service from Rotherham.

Restaurant First sandwiched between a pair of Third Open coaches. With no deadweight to be hauled yet with large sittings being accommodated, the 07.20 from Manchester demonstrated that the arguments supporting Kitchen-Only cars were not especially sound and many of the vehicles found themselves obsolete before they had entered service.

The Midland did not abandon the use of Kitchen Cars altogether but their post-war employment was limited to the 10.00 St Pancras – Glasgow, 11.45 St Pancras – Bradford (the former mid-day Scottish service) and the 16.50 St Pancras – Bradford. All had been replaced by conventional restaurant cars by the mid-1960's although it should be noted that the problems associated with the type did not prevent British Railways from building a further forty examples.

Although St Pancras did not see anything like the overnight traffic dealt with at Kings Cross or Euston, the Midland ran three sleeping cars each night from St Pancras: the 21.05 to Edinburgh Waverley, the 21.15 to Glasgow St Enoch and the 23.50 to Leeds City. With their return workings, the there trains accounted for fourteen sleeping cars plus four LNER vehicles which alternated with the LMS vehicles in the Edinburgh working. Strictly speaking, the Edinburgh service was not available for sleeping car passengers travelling to or from London although the author never heard of this restriction being applied and indeed used the up train very frequently since it reached London

at a far more civilised hour than the East Coast services.

Since nearly two thousand five hundred LMS coaches were built between 1945 and 1953 it is not surprising that they dominated services from both St Pancras and Euston until the early 1960's whilst many remained in main line service, particularly from Euston, until 1965 after which they disappeared quite rapidly. Because multiple-units had taken over many branch and secondary services from 1960, the scope for relegating LMS coaches was very limited and those that remained in service after about 1963 could often be seen in front line service. The author can still remember an especially lively trip in an LMS coach on the Mancunian in 1965 when the AC electric locomotive which took over the train at Nuneaton set about knocking an hour off the steam schedule that still prevailed. The remaining Manchester – Marylebone service consisted very largely of LMS stock right up to the end of the Great Central whilst many other examples could be found on the North & West route between Crewe and Pontypool Road and on stopping trains between Manchester Central and Derby.

The BR Standard coaches which appeared in the early 1950's seemed to take an eternity to become established and it was not until the early 1960's that they posed a serious threat to the LMS status quo. The extent to which BR stock had gained a toehold by 1955 is shown in the individual train tables where of the 235 passenger vehicles that left St Pancras daily,

only 84 were of post-nationalisation design: a proportion that was larger than it appeared at the time and appreciably greater than could be found at any other London terminus at the time. Why this should be is a matter for conjecture but the Midland was going through a lengthy period of subservience to the West Coast and one suspects that the relatively high – one third – proportion of BR standard coaches working out of St Pancras was connected with the rather poor opinion the public had of them. Most people employed on the Midland felt the system to be something of a Cinderella in London Midland circles and there was no reason why coaching stock should have been excluded from this opprobrium.

The main sections of most regular service were diagrammed in the usual way with some sets working the same pair of services day in, day out whilst others took several days to get back to the starting point of their working. Few train though worked a service with some adjustment being made: the 08.15 St Pancras to Manchester for example, consisting of a basic eight coach formation to which three other vehicles were added; two running no further than Derby and the third running through to Manchester but returning to London in a different train from that worked by the main portion of the 08.15. Both the main sections and the subsidiary coaches were for the most part clearly diagramme and once the components were placed in working, they remained there indefinitely. No all coaches were so carefully programmed an

MIDLAND MAIN LINE : 1955

Train	21.05		21.53	02.55	02.55				07.35	09.15				
From	G'gow		E'bro	Leeds	Leeds				Notts	Wolves				
No.	10	219	16	219	219	32	40	44	229		48	50	233	56
CARLISLE	23.55		00.36											
Appleby														
Hellifield														
Skipton			02e31											
Keighley	02e02													
BRADFORD						06.42								07.15
Shipley						06.52								07b23
Newlay						07.08								
LEEDS	02.33		03.06			07.24								07.38
LEEDS	02.45	02.55	03.16											07.45
Normanton		03.20		03.45										
Cudworth				04d09										
Swinton														
Rotherham				04i39										08b43
SHEFFIELD	03.51		04.22	04.48										08.52
SHEFFIELD	04.02		04.35	05.03			07.00						08.06	08.58
Chesterfield				05e30			07b24						08b35	09b22
Alfreton							07.43							
MANCHESTER												07.20		
Didsbury												07.32		
Cheadle Heath														
Stockport														
Chinley														
Millers Dale												08.13		
Bakewell														
Matlock												08b31		
Ambergate														
Belper														
DERBY	04.54			06.00	(06.03)							08.53		09.04
DERBY	05.01		(06.40)	06.18	06.40		08.05		08.15			09.00		09.09
Burton					06c58				08c33				09b29	
Tamworth					07B17				08.52				09c52	
BIRMINGHAM					07.56				09.15				10.24	
BIRMINGHAM					08.05				09.21				10.32	
Kings Norton					08.23				09.34				10.45	
Bromsgrove													11.08	
WORCESTER									10.06				11.29	
WORCESTER									10.11				11.35	
Ashchurch										(Ex			12.08	
Cheltenham									10e43	GW)			12b22	
Churchdown														
GLOUCESTER									10.54	11.26			12.34	
GLOUCESTER									10.59	11.30				
Mangotsfield									11b46					
BATH														
BRISTOL									12.00	12.25				
NOTTINGHAM			05.48		07.06		08.10							
NOTTINGHAM			06.00			06.40	08.15				08.28			
Trent						06b57								
Loughborough						07b11		08b36				09b23		
LEICESTER	05.40					07.30		08.51				09.38		10.26
LEICESTER	05.47					07.35		08.55				09.43		10.31
M. Harborough						08b00		09b17						
Melton Mowbray			(Via								08b58			
Manton			Melton)					08.58			09.18			
Kettering	06b26		07f16			08c20		09b33			09b48			
Wellingborough						08c33					09b59			
BEDFORD						08b55					10c22			
Luton			08c29								10b51	10c59		11b46
Harpenden														
St Albans														
ST PANCRAS	08.05		09.12			09.55	10.31	10.45			11.25	11.31		12.18
Destination						York				Penz				
Arr						08.19								

MIDLAND MAIN LINE : 1955

	204	43	208	37	294	York	55	302	Hull	216	Clee	65	71	75
Train	01.10		06.40		08.02	10.15		07.54	10.42	07.35	06.57			
From	Bristol		B'ham		B'ham	York		Worcs	Hull	Bristol	Clee			
No.	204	43	208	37	294		55	302		216		65	71	75
ST PANCRAS				04.18								08.15	09.00	09.05
St Albans				04f53										09b37
Harpenden														09.47
Luton				05g14								08b58	09b41	09b58
BEDFORD				05f42										10d24
Wellingborough				06e08								09c39		10c48
Kettering				06e24								09c53	10c25	11b01
Manton													(Via	
Melton Mowbray													Manton)	
M. Harborough				06c43								10c12		11b19
LEICESTER				07.05							10.05	10.33		11.40
LEICESTER				07.13							10.10	10.39		
Loughborough				07b31							(Via	10c58		
Trent											Nun)			
NOTTINGHAM													11.25	
NOTTINGHAM							09.06						11.30	
BRISTOL	01.10									07.35				
BATH														
Mangotsfield										07d52				
GLOUCESTER	02.00									08.31				
GLOUCESTER	02.13									08.36				
Churchdown														
Cheltenham	02g35									08e55				
Ashchurch										09b10				
WORCESTER	03.06													
WORCESTER	03.14							07.54						
Bromsgrove	03f40							08b17						
Kings Norton					07.40									
BIRMINGHAM	04.05				07.52			08.52		10.05	11.13			
BIRMINGHAM	04.30		06.40		08.05			09.00		10.12				
Tamworth	04c58		07e10					09c35						
Burton	05d21		07c32		08c45			09c56						
DERBY	05.36		07.48	07.53	08.59		09.37	10.13		11.03		11.19		
DERBY	05.50		07.58	08.10	09.04		09.44	10.18		11.10		11.25		
Belper							09.56	10.32						
Ambergate				08.20										
Matlock				08c39			10b13					11c52		
Bakewell							10.26							
Millers Dale				09c05			10b41					12b17		
Chinley							11b03					12b39		
Stockport														
Cheadle Heath														
Didsbury														
MANCHESTER				09.49			11.29					13.05		
Alfreton														
Chesterfield	06c27		08b41		09b38			10b58						12b14
SHEFFIELD	06.48		09.02		09.59			11.19		12.02				12.33
SHEFFIELD		07.50	09.08		10.05			11.27		12.08				12.39
Rotherham			09b19		10b16			11b38		12b19				
Swinton								11.48						
Cudworth			09b41							12b42				
Normanton		08b38	10b01							13b03				
LEEDS		08.58	10.25							13.24				13.42
LEEDS	06.55	09.15	10.35	10.37		10.58			12.12	13.30				13.50
Newlay	07.10	o09.26				11.15			12.28					
Shipley	07d30	09.43	10c57			11.32			12.45	13b51				
BRADFORD	07.40	09.55	11.04			11.44			12.57	13.58				
Keighley			11b01											
Skipton			11d17											14c30
Hellifield			11c36											14b48
Appleby			12c37											15b48
CARLISLE			13.11											16.29
Destination			G'gow		N'cle		L'pool	York						E'bro
Arr			15.53		13.03		12.25	12.50						19.15

b: Arrived two minutes earlier, c: Arrived three minutes earlier. etc.

MIDLAND MAIN LINE : 1955

Train From / No.	60	239	70		247	74	84	10.25 M'ter 220	12.15 B'ham	09.10 Hull 251	251	08.15 N'cle 287	09.22 B'ford 251
CARLISLE													
Appleby													
Hellifield													
Skipton													
Keighley													
BRADFORD			07.30	08.46		09.12					09.25		
Shipley			07b38	08b54		09b20					09b33		
Newlay													
LEEDS			07.53	09.10		09.35					09.49		
LEEDS		08.03				09.42					09.56		
Normanton		08b25									10b19		
Cudworth		08b46									10b41		
Swinton										10.45			
Rotherham		09b08								10.54	11b05	11c13	
SHEFFIELD		09.18								11.03	11.14	11.22	
SHEFFIELD	09.09	09.25			10.10	10.51					11.20	11.28	
Chesterfield	09b33	09b49			12b34	11b15						11d54	
Alfreton													
MANCHESTER		07.24	09.00										
Didsbury		07.41	09.12										
Cheadle Heath													
Stockport													
Chinley		08c19	09b38										
Millers Dale		08b48	10e05										
Bakewell		09.04											
Matlock		09b22	10c24										
Ambergate		09.41											
Belper		09.47											
DERBY		10.01 / 10.18	10.46		11.04						12.10	12.24	
DERBY		10.24	10.51		11.09		12.05				12.17	12.31	
Burton		10b41			11b26		(Ex					12c49	
Tamworth					11b46		LNW)						
BIRMINGHAM		11.23			12.09						13.12	13.28	
BIRMINGHAM		11.30			12.15						13.21	13.35	
Kings Norton					12.29								
Bromsgrove					12.52								
WORCESTER					13.16			(13.16)			14.11		(14.11)
WORCESTER					(13.20)			13.20			(14.16)		14.16
Ashchurch								13b54					
Cheltenham		12e33						12g49	14d10			14e38	14e48
Churchdown													
GLOUCESTER		12.44						14.00	14.21			14z49	15.02
GLOUCESTER		12.50						14.05			15z02	15.08	15.20
Mangotsfield													
BATH								15.01					16.21
BRISTOL		13.42									15.52	16.00	
NOTTINGHAM	10.18		11.18										
NOTTINGHAM	10.24		11.23										
Trent													
Loughborough	10b54						12b28						
LEICESTER						12.21	12.44						
LEICESTER						12.26	12.50						
M. Harborough							13b14						
Melton Mowbray			(Via										
Manton			Melton)										
Kettering	11b47		12b31				13c33						
Wellingborough			12b41				13c44						
BEDFORD	12d17						14c07						
Luton	12c47		13b27				14b36						
Harpenden													
St Albans													
ST PANCRAS	13.21		14.01			14.08	15.12						
Destination				Scar				B'mth			Paign		B'mth
Arr				11.14				17.32			19.25		19.23

z : GWR Station

MIDLAND MAIN LINE : 1955

Train / From / No.	81	308	87	93	310		99	236	238	109	240	117
Train								09.45		16.22	09.15	
From								B'mth		Scar	P'ton	
No.	81	308	87	93	310		99	236	238	109	240	117
ST PANCRAS	10.00		10.15	10.40			11.45			12.50		14.00
St Albans				11b14						13c23		
Harpenden				11b25								
Luton				11b36						13e42		
BEDFORD				12c02						14c08		
Wellingborough				12b26						14c32		
Kettering			11c36	12c40			13c13			14c46		
Manton												(Via
Melton Mowbray												Manton)
M. Harborough				13b05						15b04		
LEICESTER	11.48		12.08	13.33			13.48			15.25		
LEICESTER	11.52		12.13				13.52					
Loughborough			12b29									
Trent							14b19					
NOTTINGHAM												16.17
NOTTINGHAM												16.25
BRISTOL		08.45			10.20						12.30	
BATH								12.01				
Mangotsfield		09c01			10b35							
GLOUCESTER		09z48			11.11			12.53			13.30	
GLOUCESTER		10z04		10.15	11.18			12.58			13.36	
Churchdown		*z : GWR Station*										
Cheltenham		10f23		10e35	11e37			13e22			13d54	
Ashchurch				10b48								
WORCESTER				**11.20**								
WORCESTER												
Bromsgrove					12.16			13.56			14.33	
Kings Norton						12.40						
BIRMINGHAM		11.29			12.43	12.55		14.23			15.00	
BIRMINGHAM		11.39			12.52			14.33	14.38		15.10	
Tamworth		12d05						(To				
Burton		12d26			13b31			LNW)	15b17		15b49	
DERBY		12.40	12.50		13.45				15.31		16.03	
DERBY		12.45	12.55		13.52				15.37		16.09	
Belper												
Ambergate												
Matlock			13c21									
Bakewell												
Millers Dale			13b44									
Chinley			14b05									
Stockport												
Cheadle Heath												
Didsbury												
MANCHESTER			14.30									
Alfreton												
Chesterfield	12b51	13b20			14b26				16c12		16b43	17b11
SHEFFIELD	13.10	13.41			14.47		15.20		16.33		17.04	17.30
SHEFFIELD	13.20	13.47		14.53	15.10		15.26				17.10	17.37
Rotherham		13b58		15c05	15b21						17c22	
Swinton												
Cudworth											17b45	18b10
Normanton											18b06	
LEEDS	14.31						16.32				18.30	18.47
LEEDS	14.37					16.24	16.40			18.33	18.43	18.56
Newlay						16.37						
Shipley						16.54	17b00			18b53	19b02	19b15
BRADFORD						17.04	17.08			19.00	19.09	19.22
Keighley												
Skipton												
Hellifield												
Appleby												
CARLISLE	16.55											
Destination	G'gow	N'cle			N'cle	Hull		M'ter				
Arr	19.41	16.57			18.30	17.10		16.35				

MIDLAND MAIN LINE : 1955

	90	94	102	293	112	116	122	301	132	140	265	136
Train				12.20			09.20	12.40	10.05			
From				York			G'gow	N'cle	E'bro			
CARLISLE							12.05		12.58			
Appleby									13.39			
Hellifield									14c39			
Skipton									14c55			
Keighley												
BRADFORD	10.30		11.50					14.57			15.50	
Shipley	10b38		11b58					15b05			15b58	
Newlay											16.14	
LEEDS	10.54		12.14			14.21		15.25	15.27		16.28	
LEEDS	11.02		12.20			14.27			15.33			
Normanton												
Cudworth												
Swinton												
Rotherham				13b39				15c33	16b31			
SHEFFIELD	12.05		13.26	13.48			15.36	15.45	16.40			
SHEFFIELD	12.11		13.32	13.54			15.44	15.55	16.46		17.15	
Chesterfield	12b32		13b56	14b18				16b19	17b07		17b39	
Alfreton												
MANCHESTER					13.50					16.00		
Didsbury												
Cheadle Heath												
Stockport												
Chinley					14b25							
Millers Dale					14b49					16b55		
Bakewell												
Matlock					15b07					17c14		
Ambergate												
Belper												
DERBY					14.48	15.29		16.48		17.38	18.08	
DERBY					14.57	15.35		16.57		17.45	18.13	
Burton					15c14			17c16			18d38	
Tamworth											19f07	
BIRMINGHAM					15.53			18.00			19.33	
BIRMINGHAM		13.45			15.59		16.50	18.08			19.42	
Kings Norton		(Via					(Via					
Bromsgrove		Nun)					Nun)				20.17	
WORCESTER											20.41	
WORCESTER											20.46	
Ashchurch					16.48						21c20	
Cheltenham					17f06			19f12			21f38	
Churchdown												
GLOUCESTER					17.17			19.23			21.49	
GLOUCESTER					17.24			19.28				
Mangotsfield					18d10			20e13				
BATH												
BRISTOL					18.26			20.27				
NOTTINGHAM	13.15		14.48						17.53			
NOTTINGHAM	13.21	13.35	14.55						18.00			18.15
Trent		13b51				16c46						
Loughborough		14b09			15b58				18b08			
LEICESTER		14.35	14.58			16.14			18.24			
LEICESTER		14.40	(To			16.25	17.17	(18.06)	18.30			
M. Harborough		15b10	Yar)			16b49						
Melton Mowbray	(Via		15c26						(Via			18d53
Manton	Melton)								Melton)			19b20
Kettering	14c26	15c29	16b20			17b07	17d57		19b10			19c55
Wellingborough		15c40	16b30			17d19						20e10
BEDFORD		16b02	16c53			17c47						20d36
Luton		16b31				18b16			20e04			21c11
Harpenden						18.26						21.21
St Albans						18b37						21b32
ST PANCRAS	15.39	17.05	17.52	18.14		19.00	19.19		20.38	20.15		21.56
Destination							Clee	Hull				
Arr							21.28	17.17				

23

Train	123	256	320	131	137	141	147	141	324	153	165	169
From				11.40 B'mth	16.50 B'ham			10.35 Penz	16.25 St P			
No.	123	256	320	131	137	141	147	141	324	153	165	169
ST PANCRAS	14.15			15.15	16.15	16.25	16.50			17.30	18.33	18.40
St Albans												
Harpenden												
Luton						17e11				18b12		
BEDFORD						17b35				18f41		
Wellingborough							18c04			19c05		
Kettering				16c37	17b44	18.06	18c17		18.27	19b18		20b00
Manton				(Via			(Via		18b58			
Melton Mowbray				Manton)			Manton)		19b24			
M. Harborough										19b36		
LEICESTER	16.13				18.00	18.19				19.57		20.30
LEICESTER		15.35	16.17		18.06	18.23				20.02		20.38
Loughborough		15b54			18b24					20b20		20b56
Trent		16b11			18b37					20b33		
NOTTINGHAM		16.22		17.37	18.51		19.17		19.48	20.47		
NOTTINGHAM				17.43	18.58		19.23					
BRISTOL			14.15					16.09	16.45			
BATH		13.58										
Mangotsfield									17b00			
GLOUCESTER		14.50	15.06					17.05	17.42			
GLOUCESTER	13.51		15.11					17.09	17.47			
Churchdown												
Cheltenham	14c09		15e32					(To	18e05			
Ashchurch	14c23							GW)				
WORCESTER	14.52											
WORCESTER	14.57											
Bromsgrove	15b25		16.11						18.45			
Kings Norton	15d48											
BIRMINGHAM	15.59		16.38						19.12			
BIRMINGHAM			16.45						19.22			
Tamworth			17b09						19c47			
Burton			17b28						20d08			
DERBY	16.52		17.42		19.01				20.22		20.53	21.17
DERBY	16.57		17.47		19.06				20.30		21.03	21.27
Belper												
Ambergate												
Matlock					19c33							21b53
Bakewell												
Millers Dale	17d43				19c59							22.17
Chinley	18b05				20b21							22b39
Stockport												
Cheadle Heath	18b21											
Didsbury					20.38							22.56
MANCHESTER	18.35				20.50							23.08
Alfreton												
Chesterfield			18b21	18e35			20c08		21b04		21b34	
SHEFFIELD			18.42	18.56			20.27		21.25		21.53	
SHEFFIELD			18.48	19.04			20.36		21.37			
Rotherham			18b59	19b15			20c48		21b48			
Swinton									21.58			
Cudworth												
Normanton							21c27					
LEEDS			20.12				21.50					
LEEDS			20.18				22.05					
Newlay												
Shipley			20b37				22b29					
BRADFORD			20.44				22.37					
Keighley												
Skipton												
Hellifield												
Appleby												
CARLISLE												
Destination			York		Clee			Wolves	York			
Arr			20.00		21.28			19.23	23.02			

MIDLAND MAIN LINE : 1955

Station	15.30	16.15			16.45	15.57		16.45	20.00	19.05	16.00		19.05		
From	L'pool	York			B'ford	N'cle		B'ford	Linc	N'tle	G'gow		N'tle		
No.			269	166	269	311		269	273	317	174	277	317	182	190
CARLISLE											18.50				
Appleby											19d36				
Hellifield											20b40				
Skipton											21e00				
Keighley											21b14				
BRADFORD				16.45				17.25					20.55	21.20		
Shipley				16d55				17b33					21d07	21d30		
Newlay													21.21	21.47		
LEEDS				17.10				17.48				21.41	21.35	22.01		
LEEDS				17.20				17.55					21.55	22.15		
Normanton								18b18					22d19	22f42		
Cudworth								18b44						23b05		
Swinton		17.39						19.04								
Rotherham		17b54		18c19		18b46		19b14						23d30		
SHEFFIELD		18.06		18.28		18.55		19.23		22.45	(22.47)	23.03		23.39		
SHEFFIELD				18.35		19.05	(23.30)					23.20	23.30	23.50		
Chesterfield				19c00									23c57	00c15		
Alfreton															
MANCHESTER	16.32		17.55												00.05
Didsbury															
Cheadle Heath															00.20
Stockport	16b50														
Chinley	17b25		18c31												
Millers Dale	17b53		18b55												
Bakewell	18.03														
Matlock	18.14		19e16												
Ambergate															
Belper	18.29														
DERBY	18.40		19.29	19.38	(19.29)	19.58						00.11	00.27	00.45	02.00
DERBY	18.48		(19.52)	19.48	19.52	20.05			21.43			00.21	00.38	01.00	02.30
Burton					20e12	20b22			22c05			00d41	00d58		
Tamworth					20d34				22.24				01n31		
BIRMINGHAM					21.59	21.05	(20.59)					01.35	01.57		
BIRMINGHAM					(21.20)		21.20					01.51	02.30		
Kings Norton															
Bromsgrove															
WORCESTER													03.12		
WORCESTER													03.25		
Ashchurch							22b27								
Cheltenham							22f46					03h01	04g01		
Churchdown															
GLOUCESTER							22.58					03.13	04.13		
GLOUCESTER							23.08					03.29	04.22		
Mangotsfield												04i21	05e10		
BATH															
BRISTOL							23.56					04.35	05.20		
NOTTINGHAM	19.29														
NOTTINGHAM															
Trent															
Loughborough				20c12										01c27	
LEICESTER				20.28										01.44	03.09
LEICESTER				20.36										02.05	03.35
M. Harborough														02i37	04j08
Melton Mowbray															
Manton															
Kettering				21c15										03j04	04j34
Wellingborough				21c26										03h21	05i52
BEDFORD				21d50										03i54	05n30
Luton				22d21										04j33	06k10
Harpenden															
St Albans														04e52	06f30
ST PANCRAS				22.55										05.16	06.54
Destination															

MIDLAND MAIN LINE : 1955

	173	175	177	185	326	185	191	29	199
Train						21.05			
From						St P			
ST PANCRAS	19.10	19.55	20.10	21.05		21.15			23.50
St Albans		20c30	20c42						
Harpenden			20.52						
Luton		20d49	21d05						00c42
BEDFORD		21d19	21d31						01f10
Wellingborough			21d56				22d41		01e37
Kettering	20b38	21c55	22e12	22d39			22d56		01e53
Manton	*(Via*								
Melton Mowbray	*Manton)*								
M. Harborough			22b30						02c13
LEICESTER		22.30	22.51				23.31		02.34
LEICESTER		22.38	23.00				23.41		02.42
Loughborough		22b56	23c19						
Trent				(Via					
				Manton)					
NOTTINGHAM	21.40	23.17		23.41					
NOTTINGHAM	21.46			23.52					
BRISTOL					19.20				
BATH									
Mangotsfield					19i42				
GLOUCESTER					20.18				
GLOUCESTER					20.25				
Churchdown									
Cheltenham					20f45				
Ashchurch									
WORCESTER									
WORCESTER									
Bromsgrove					21.24				
Kings Norton									
BIRMINGHAM					21.48				
BIRMINGHAM					22.40				
Tamworth					23g09				
Burton					23c29				
DERBY	22.15		23.40		23.45		00.16		03.20
DERBY					23.56		00.24		03.33
Belper									
Ambergate									
Matlock									
Bakewell									
Millers Dale									
Chinley									
Stockport									
Cheadle Heath									
Didsbury									
MANCHESTER									
Alfreton									
Chesterfield							01d00		04g15
SHEFFIELD				01.01	00.48	(01.01)	01.21		04.36
SHEFFIELD				(01.11)	01.00	01.11	01.31	02.10	04.51
Rotherham							01d44		05d04
Swinton									
Cudworth									05c28
Normanton								03q16	05l59
LEEDS						02.13	02.39	03.37	06.20
LEEDS						02.23	02.50		
Newlay									
Shipley									
BRADFORD									
Keighley							03g21		
Skipton						03g05			
Hellifield						03c24			
Appleby						04b24			
CARLISLE						05.02	05.17		
Destination					N'cle	E'bro	G'gow		
Arr					04.21	07.54	08.30		

there was considerable daily use of loose vehicles which had no inward or return working. While this may suggest that one end of the system was continuously being denuded whilst a glut amassed at the other, in fact the number of additional trains and unscheduled strengthening vehicles run each week tended to keep matters more or less balanced whilst the daily reporting of stock by stations to the Rolling Stock HQ enabled any significant imbalances to be corrected at an early stage. The usual procedure for making up trains was for the night shift to take the core sections of trains – which were normally kept to their cyclic workings - and to add whatever subsidiary coaches were called for, often without much attention being paid to what the latter had worked in with. The main thing was to marshal trains of the correct stock for the following morning and in pursuit of this aim, niceties of diagramming sometimes had to take second place.

The problems of dealing with undiagrammed passenger rolling stock were as nothing compared to the business of putting parcels trains together and although it is a topic on the periphery of the subject covered by this book, it can be seen that in many cases full brakes and the like worked in to various destinations and had no obvious return working. Part of the reason for this apparent imbalance was because the BG's shown in the tables were those included in passenger train formations and many either returned to their points of origin in parcels trains or had no specific balancing working. A glut of vehicles because of the lack of return workings was not the problem it might appear to be since parcels traffic often fluctuated quite dramatically at short notice and a reserve of vehicles had to be maintained in order to meet sudden peaks of demand. As with passenger rolling stock, each station liaised every morning with the district rolling stock office where decisions were taken on the movement of empty vehicles.

So far as the authors are aware, little if anything has been written before about the detail of passenger operations on the Midland and it is hoped that this contribution will go some small way to filling the vacuum. The book – which, like others in the series, is a medium of information and not a work of art! - does not cover the whole picture since neither time nor space would allow us to deal with local services or summer Saturday workings and we have therefore had to content ourselves with the main line workings, although we hope that there is enough meat on this particular bone to satisfy most appetites.

While the workings are those of the Summer 1955 timetable, the detail shown is generally representative of the post-nationalisation steam period since the changes that were made tended on the whole to be of a minor nature.

The order of trains follows that of the 195 timetable which will act as an index in addition to its more obvious use. Up and down trains are shown on alternate pages. The individual train tables show the formation of each service from the engine backwards although where a reversal is made en route - trains to Scotland and Bradford reverse in Leeds City - the order shown is that South of Leeds.

We hope that the following pages will n merely help to satisfy the thirst for detail that is the hallmark of any self-respecting railway historian b will fit into place another part or two to the jigsaw of railway operating history.

By the early 1950's the passenger standardisation goals set by the LMS had been all but fulfilled on the Southern section of the Midland where 5XP 'Jubilee' 4-6-0's were diagrammed to the faster expresses with Black Five 4-6-0's working the semi-fast and most of relief services.   The last major centre of non-standard LMS steam was Bedford whose 4-4-0 Compounds were replaced by BR Standard 4MT 4-6-0's in 1955 which, with 2-6-4 and 2-6-2 tanks for the inner-suburban workings, handled most of the local duties.   The principal source of variety came from BR Standard designs, especially the 5MT 4-6-0, from 1951 onwards.   On 4th April 1954 Black Five 4-6-0 44963 (Derby) brings a semi-fast service past St Albans North and prepares to stop in the station whilst, below, 45560 'Prince Edward Island' of Nottingham crows a warning as it approaches St Albans at speed with an up express.

The 10.20 Bristol - Newcastle calls at Gloucester Eastgate on Wednesday 13th May 1959 behind 5XP 4-6-0 45660 'Rooke' of Bristol.   Evidently there has been some reason to anticipate traffic that is heavier than normal since an additional open coach has been inserted between the second vehicle and the restaurant car.   This service was a joint working with the North Eastern and consisted of an LMS and LNER set of coaches with alternated daily; the return working being the 12.37 Newcastle - Bristol.   It is interesting to note that the train is in reverse formation.

Although not the flagbearer it had once been, the St Pancras to Manchester service continued to be an important element of the Midland timetable although the 5XP 4-6-0's were sometimes hard pressed north of Derby where a coach or two often had to be removed in order to lighten trains sufficiently for a reasonable standard of running to be maintained over Peak Forest.   45652 'Hawke' of Trafford Park runs into Millers Dale with an express from St Pancras in 1958 shortly before class 7 Royal Scot 4-6-0's and Britannia Pacifics arrived on the route.   Shortly after the picture was taken 45652 and several other Jubilee 4-6-0's were transferred to Kentish Town following the arrival of six Britannia Pacifics at Trafford Park.

06.55 LEEDS to BRADFORD (07.40)

C/W	Previous working	Vehicle	Type	From	To	Next working
1	22 23.50 St Pancras - Leeds (06.20)	THIRD CORRIDOR (42)	LMS	LEEDS	BRADFORD	21.20 Bradford - St Pancras (05.16)
2	22 23.50 St Pancras - Leeds (06.20)	THIRD CORRIDOR (42)	LMS	LEEDS	BRADFORD	21.20 Bradford - St Pancras (05.16)
3	22 23.50 St Pancras - Leeds (06.20)	COMPOSITE CORRIDOR (24/18)	BR	LEEDS	BRADFORD	21.20 Bradford - St Pancras (05.16)
4	22 23.50 St Pancras - Leeds (06.20)	BRAKE THIRD CORRIDOR (24)	LMS	LEEDS	BRADFORD	21.20 Bradford - St Pancras (05.16)
5	915 23.50 St Pancras - Leeds (06.20)	FULL BRAKE	LMS	LEEDS	BRADFORD	21.20 Bradford - St Pancras (05.16)
6	916 23.50 St Pancras - Leeds (06.20)	FULL BRAKE	LMS	LEEDS	BRADFORD	21.20 Bradford - St Pancras (05.16)

Although shown in the timetables as a local service between Leeds and Bradford, the 06.55 was in fact the concluding leg of the 23.50 St Pancras to Leeds, the train's sleeping cars having been detached and left in Leeds. For those who could get a seat in London and had little trouble sleeping, the train was about the most civilised way of getting from London to Bradford and with luck a fairly good night's rest was possible. The service was measurably better than the night train from Kings Cross, the passengers of which were turned onto the streets of Bradford at four in the morning. It was less convenient for local passengers who often had difficulty finding a seat because of the sprawl of sleeping Londoners in every compartment.

The seven vehicles on the service returned to London at 21.20 but excluded the sleeping cars which remained in Leeds until the early hours of the following morning to be attached to the Glasgow - St Pancras overnight express.

One aspect of the service, of use to the Leeds-based enthusiast but not obvious from a casual look in the timetable, was the fact that it led to an interesting way of getting to the Lancashire coast. By changing at Shipley one could pick up the 07.23 Bradford to Liverpool which ran via Skipton, Colne and the LYR. It was not the sort of journey that many would want to repeat but it made a change from the usual route via Manchester.

01.10 BRISTOL to SHEFFIELD (06.59)

C/W	Previous working	Vehicle	Type	From	To	Next working
1	43B 19.50 Derby - Bristol (00.03)	T.P.O.	LMS	BRISTOL	DERBY	19.50 Derby - Bristol (00.03)
2	930 17.05 Plymouth - Bristol	FULL BRAKE	LMS	BRISTOL	SHEFFIELD	07.50 Sheffield to Bradford
3	931	FULL BRAKE	LMS	BRISTOL	SHEFFIELD	07.50 Sheffield to Leeds
4	42A 07.43 Nottingham - Bristol (12.09)	THIRD CORRIDOR (42)	LMS	BRISTOL	SHEFFIELD	07.50 Sheffield to Bradford
5	42 07.43 Nottingham - Bristol (12.09)	BRAKE THIRD CORRIDOR (24)	LMS	BRISTOL	SHEFFIELD	07.50 Sheffield to Bradford
6	42 07.43 Nottingham - Bristol (12.09)	THIRD CORRIDOR (42)	LMS	BRISTOL	SHEFFIELD	07.50 Sheffield to Bradford
7	42 07.43 Nottingham - Bristol (12.09)	COMPOSITE CORRIDOR (18/24)	LMS	BRISTOL	SHEFFIELD	07.50 Sheffield to Bradford
8	42 07.43 Nottingham - Bristol (12.09)	COMPOSITE CORRIDOR (18/24)	LMS	BRISTOL	SHEFFIELD	07.50 Sheffield to Bradford
9	42 07.43 Nottingham - Bristol (12.09)	THIRD CORRIDOR (42)	LMS	BRISTOL	SHEFFIELD	07.50 Sheffield to Bradford
10	42 07.43 Nottingham - Bristol (12.09)	BRAKE THIRD CORRIDOR (24)	LMS	BRISTOL	SHEFFIELD	07.50 Sheffield to Bradford
11	97A	FULL BRAKE	LMS	BRISTOL	GLOUCESTER	02.35 Gloucester - Sheffield (07.35)

In contrast to the corresponding Bradford - Bristol night train which contained a miserly three passenger coaches, the northbound train was quite well equipped; using the six vehicles that had arrived with the 07.43 Nottingham - Bristol plus a loose Third Corridor. In addition it conveyed a TPO for Derby - a quick turn-round vehicle that only spent just over an hour in Bristol, having arrived in Temple Meads with the 16.45 ex Bradford - and three parcels vans, one of which came off at Gloucester to continue on to Sheffield in the 02.35 Gloucester - Sheffield parcels train. One of the full brakes was involved in a very long run, having left Penzance in the 11.30 departure that morning. Although advertised as terminating in Sheffield, in fact most of the train continued forward to Leeds and Bradford as the 07.50 express.

07.50 SHEFFIELD to BRADFORD (09.55)

C/W	Previous working	Vehicle	Type	From	To	Next working
1	931 01.10 Bristol - Sheffield (06.59)	FULL BRAKE	LMS	SHEFFIELD	LEEDS	
2	930 01.10 Bristol - Sheffield (06.59)	FULL BRAKE	LMS	SHEFFIELD	BRADFORD	
3	42 01.10 Bristol - Sheffield (06.59)	THIRD CORRIDOR (42)	LMS	SHEFFIELD	BRADFORD	07.30 Bradford - Bristol (13.37)
4	42 01.10 Bristol - Sheffield (06.59)	BRAKE THIRD CORRIDOR (24)	LMS	SHEFFIELD	BRADFORD	07.30 Bradford - Bristol (13.37)
5	42 01.10 Bristol - Sheffield (06.59)	THIRD CORRIDOR (42)	LMS	SHEFFIELD	BRADFORD	07.30 Bradford - Bristol (13.37)
6	42 01.10 Bristol - Sheffield (06.59)	COMPOSITE CORRIDOR (18/24)	LMS	SHEFFIELD	BRADFORD	07.30 Bradford - Bristol (13.37)
7	42 01.10 Bristol - Sheffield (06.59)	COMPOSITE CORRIDOR (18/24)	LMS	SHEFFIELD	BRADFORD	07.30 Bradford - Bristol (13.37)
8	42 01.10 Bristol - Sheffield (06.59)	THIRD CORRIDOR (42)	LMS	SHEFFIELD	BRADFORD	07.30 Bradford - Bristol (13.37)
9	42 01.10 Bristol - Sheffield (06.59)	BRAKE THIRD CORRIDOR (24)	LMS	SHEFFIELD	BRADFORD	07.30 Bradford - Bristol (13.37)

Although shown in the timetable as a train in its own right, the 07.50 was actually a continuation of the overnight service from Bristol but spent an hour at Sheffield unloading parcels traffic before going forward to Leeds and Bradford. During that time a slow train for Leeds left at 07.10 and since it was regarded as the obvious connection for stations to the north, the 07.50 was advertised as being independent of the Bristol service. (Since the slow connection reached Leeds only six minutes ahead of the faster 07.50, the wisdom of this advice is questionable - especially as passengers for Bradford who changed and caught the 07.10, found themselves back on the Bristol train at Leeds!).

Calling only at Rotherham and Normanton, the 07.50 was a fast train to Leeds and in fact ran to timings that were faster than some of the London - Bradford expresses. After a leisurely reversal at Leeds, for which seventeen minutes was allowed, the tone of the service changed considerably as it continued forward as a stopping train, calling at all stations except Holbeck. On reaching Bradford the stock was berthed until the next morning when the majority of the vehicles formed the 07.30 to Bristol. This was a useful piece of diagramming since it gave Forster Square the opportunity to make good any immediate shortfall in coaching stock.

00.05 MANCHESTER CENTRAL to ST PANCRAS (06.54)

	C/W	Previous working	Vehicle	Type	From	To	Next working
1	932		FULL BRAKE	LMS	MANCHESTER	DERBY	02.10 Derby - Bristol
2	933		FULL BRAKE	LMS	MANCHESTER	LEICESTER	
3	934	22.10 Liverpool - Manchester (23.37)	FULL BRAKE	LMS	MANCHESTER	ST PANCRAS	
4	27A	16.15 Derby - Manchester (19.08)	COMPOSITE CORRIDOR (18/24)	LMS	MANCHESTER	ST PANCRAS	
5	27C	16.15 St Pancras - Manchester (20.50)	THIRD CORRIDOR (42)	LMS	MANCHESTER	ST PANCRAS	16.15 St Pancras - Manchester (20.50)
6	907	18.40 St Pancras - Manchester (23.08)	BRAKE VAN	BZ	MANCHESTER	ST PANCRAS	18.40 St Pancras - Manchester (23.08)
7	935		FULL BRAKE	LMS	MANCHESTER	ST PANCRAS	
8	936		FULL BRAKE	LMS	MANCHESTER	ST PANCRAS	
9	937		FULL BRAKE	LMS	MANCHESTER	DERBY	03.57 Derby - Nottingham
10	938	22.10 Liverpool - Manchester (23.37)	FULL BRAKE	LMS	MANCHESTER	DERBY	03.57 Derby - Nottingham
11	939	23.35 Birmingham - Leicester	FULL BRAKE	LMS	LEICESTER	ST PANCRAS	
12	940	23.35 Birmingham - Leicester	FULL BRAKE	LMS	LEICESTER	ST PANCRAS	
13	941	20.37 Bolton - Leicester	FULL BRAKE	LMS	LEICESTER	ST PANCRAS	
14	942	20.37 Bolton - Leicester	FULL BRAKE	LMS	LEICESTER	ST PANCRAS	
15	-	20.37 Bolton - Leicester	VANFIT	Fish	LEICESTER	ST ALBANS	
16	-	20.37 Bolton - Leicester	VANFIT	Fish	LEICESTER	LUTON	

Overnight trains ran from St Pancras to Edinburgh, Glasgow and Leeds yet Manchester was omitted; the long standing midnight express from London having been expunged from the timetable during the war, never to be reinstated. Parcels traffic from Lancashire was far too heavy to allow the overnight equivalent from Manchester to be threatened and for good measure a pair of passenger coaches were added which, provided one could get a seat, gave one six or seven hours sleep and reached London at a civilised time of day unlike the services to Marylebone and Euston both of which arrived at their respective termini at 05.05.

With the weight of parcels traffic handled two passenger vehicles was all that could be handled especially since parcels traffic could fluctuate considerably and an allowance had to be made in order for peaks of output to be handled. Three vehicles were detached at Derby and another at Leicester where the service was amalgamated with the overnight parcels train from Bolton with a pair of Birmingham - London brakes being added, taking the load up to twelve vehicles between Leicester and Luton.

21.05 GLASGOW ST ENOCH to ST PANCRAS (08.05)

	C/W	Previous working	Vehicle	Type	From	To	Next working
1	21B	23.50 St Pancras - Leeds (06.24)	SLEEPING CAR THIRD	LMS	LEEDS	ST PANCRAS	23.50 St Pancras - Leeds (06.24)
2	21B	23.50 St Pancras - Leeds (06.24)	SLEEPING CAR FIRST	LMS	LEEDS	ST PANCRAS	23.50 St Pancras - Leeds (06.24)
3		17.10 Ayr - Kilmarnock (21.45)	TPO	LMS	KILMARNOCK	CARLISLE	03.11 Carlisle - Ayr (06.12)
4	95		THIRD CORRIDOR (42)	LMS	GLASGOW	CARLISLE	
5	8	21.15 St Pancras - Glasgow	FULL BRAKE	LMS	GLASGOW	ST PANCRAS	21.15 St Pancras - Glasgow
6	8	21.15 St Pancras - Glasgow	COMPOSITE CORRIDOR (18/24)	LMS	GLASGOW	ST PANCRAS	21.15 St Pancras - Glasgow
7	8	21.15 St Pancras - Glasgow	SLEEPING CAR FIRST	LMS	GLASGOW	ST PANCRAS	21.15 St Pancras - Glasgow
8	8	21.15 St Pancras - Glasgow	SLEEPING CAR FIRST	LMS	GLASGOW	ST PANCRAS	21.15 St Pancras - Glasgow
9	8	21.15 St Pancras - Glasgow	SLEEPING CAR THIRD	LMS	GLASGOW	ST PANCRAS	21.15 St Pancras - Glasgow
10			THIRD CORRIDOR (42)	LMS	CARLISLE	ST PANCRAS	
11	8	21.15 St Pancras - Glasgow	THIRD CORRIDOR (42)	LMS	GLASGOW	ST PANCRAS	21.15 St Pancras - Glasgow
12	8	21.15 St Pancras - Glasgow	THIRD CORRIDOR (42)	LMS	GLASGOW	ST PANCRAS	21.15 St Pancras - Glasgow
13	8	21.15 St Pancras - Glasgow	THIRD CORRIDOR (42)	LMS	GLASGOW	ST PANCRAS	21.15 St Pancras - Glasgow
14	8	21.15 St Pancras - Glasgow	BRAKE THIRD CORRIDOR (24)	LMS	GLASGOW	ST PANCRAS	21.15 St Pancras - Glasgow

Like its opposite number from Edinburgh, the Midland's Glasgow - St Pancras sleeper got its passengers into London at a civilised time which was a much preferable arrival to staggering half asleep around Euston or Kings Cross at an uncomfortably hour of morning. Unlike the Edinburgh service which arrived after the busiest part of the rush hour, the Glasgow train passed the threshold at Bedford at the worst possible time and usually stopped at every signal south of Leagrave as it queued behind the 06.25 Bedford - St Pancras stopping train. The Kettering - London section which could be reeled off in an hour was booked to take 91 minutes and even though the sleeper might be halted innumerable times by signals, a punctual arrival was usually recorded in St Pancras.

The load conveyed extended well beyond through Glasgow to London traffic; one item of especial interest, although it came no further south than Carlisle, being a TPO letter-sorting vehicle from Ayr which returned northwards after connecting with the down West Coast Postal from Euston. Two sleeping cars were attached at Leeds whilst the train reversed and its 7P 'Rebuilt Scot' 4-6-0 gave way to a 5XP 4-6-0. These vehicles were the return working of the sleeping section of the 23.50 St Pancras - Leeds, the remainder of the 23.50 coming south in the 21.28 ex Bradford which was considered too early a departure for sleeping car passengers. The formation, above, is in the order after leaving Leeds.

02.55 LEEDS to KINGS NORTON (08.23)

	C/W	Previous working	Vehicle	Type	From	To	Next working
1	102	18.20 Birmingham - Derby (19.49)	NON-CORRIDOR THIRD (108)	LMS	DERBY	BIRMINGHAM	18.20 Birmingham - Derby (19.49)
2	984	21.20 Blackpool - Leeds (01.11)	FULL BRAKE	LMS	LEEDS	SHEFFIELD	
3	980	Newcastle - Normanton	FULL BRAKE	LMS	NORMANTON	DERBY	08.15 Derby - Bristol
4	983	West Hartlepool - Normanton	FULL BRAKE	LMS	NORMANTON	DERBY	08.15 Derby - Bristol
5	981	Durham - Normanton	FULL BRAKE	LMS	NORMANTON	DERBY	08.15 Derby - Bristol
6	982	York - Normanton	FULL BRAKE	LMS	NORMANTON	DERBY	08.15 Derby - Birmingham
7	985	21.20 Blackpool - Leeds (01.11)	FULL BRAKE	LMS	LEEDS	DERBY	
8	931A	07.50 Sheffield - Leeds (09.55)	FULL BRAKE	LMS	LEEDS	DERBY	
9	96	22.05 Sheffield - Leeds (23.38)	BRAKE THIRD CORRIDOR (32)	LMS	LEEDS	KINGS NORTON	16.40 Kings Norton - Birmingham (16.55)
10	96	22.05 Sheffield - Leeds (23.38)	COMPOSITE CORRIDOR (18/32)	LMS	LEEDS	KINGS NORTON	16.40 Kings Norton - Birmingham (16.55)
11	96	22.05 Sheffield - Leeds (23.38)	BRAKE THIRD CORRIDOR (32)	LMS	LEEDS	KINGS NORTON	16.40 Kings Norton - Birmingham (16.55)
12	944	07.50 Sheffield - Leeds (09.55)	FULL BRAKE	LMS	LEEDS	BIRMINGHAM	
13	975	07.00 Barnsley - Leeds (08.15)	FULL BRAKE	LMS	LEEDS	CUDWORTH	04.25 Cudworth - Barnsley

Although it was primarily a parcels service, the 02.55 pulled out of Leeds in the wake of the overnight Glasgow - London express and provided a useful connection for passengers travelling to stations between Leeds and Sheffield. For much of its journey it was a heavy train by Midland standards, consisting of eight vehicles as far as Normanton where it was swollen to twelve by the addition of four vehicles from the North Eastern. The formation of the train made an interesting study and although the three-coach passenger section ran only between Leeds and Birmingham (Kings Norton), the other vehicles joined from points as far afield as Blackpool, Newcastle and West Hartlepool. In contrast to these widely travelled components, the rear of the train was brought up by a local parcels vehicle for Barnsley via Cudworth. Rather surprisingly since it left Leeds only ten minutes after the departure of the 21.05 ex St Enoch, no Scottish vehicles were included in the formation; a feature that led to some frenetic manual activity at Leeds as several barrow loads of parcels from Scotland were transferred to the various sections of the 02.55.

By the time it commenced the latter stages of its journey, the train's load had lightened considerable as vehicles were dropped at Cudworth, Sheffield and Derby; the last point seeing the North Eastern section transferred to the rear of the 07.35 Nottingham - Bristol. As though by way of exchange, the three-coach passenger section was strengthened by a non-corridor third for the rush-hour traffic between Derby and Birmingham.

Black Five 44828 of Leeds (Holbeck) runs into Chesterfield Midland with an up express on 10th June 1950. Although the slightly larger 5XP's 'Jubilee' 4-6-0's were the preferred choice for express motive power, the fact that only sixty-nine of the class were allocated to Midland sheds (Leeds: 18, London: 13, Bristol: 12, Sheffield: 10, Nottingham: 6, Manchester: 6 and Derby: 4) meant that it was inevitable that Black 5's would shoulder a high proportion of relief work as well as covering for 5XP's when called upon. The haulage difference between the two classes was forty-five tons: a 5XP being allowed 390 tons on most sections of the Midland main line as opposed to 345 tons for a 5MT.

	C/W Previous working	Vehicle	Type	From	To	Next working
1	11 16.00 Glasgow - Leeds (21.41)	**FULL BRAKE**	LMS	LEEDS	GLASGOW	16.00 Glasgow - Leeds (21.41)
2	11 16.00 Glasgow - Leeds (21.41)	**BRAKE THIRD CORRIDOR (24)**	LMS	LEEDS	GLASGOW	16.00 Glasgow - Leeds (21.41)
3	11 16.00 Glasgow - Leeds (21.41)	**THIRD CORRIDOR (42)**	LMS	LEEDS	GLASGOW	16.00 Glasgow - Leeds (21.41)
4	11 16.00 Glasgow - Leeds (21.41)	**THIRD CORRIDOR (42)**	LMS	LEEDS	GLASGOW	16.00 Glasgow - Leeds (21.41)
5	11 16.00 Glasgow - Leeds (21.41)	**COMPOSITE CORRIDOR (24/18)**	BR	LEEDS	GLASGOW	16.00 Glasgow - Leeds (21.41)
6	11 16.00 Glasgow - Leeds (21.41)	**COMPOSITE CORRIDOR (24/18)**	BR	LEEDS	GLASGOW	16.00 Glasgow - Leeds (21.41)
7	11 16.00 Glasgow - Leeds (21.41)	**THIRD CORRIDOR (42)**	LMS	LEEDS	GLASGOW	16.00 Glasgow - Leeds (21.41)
8	11 16.00 Glasgow - Leeds (21.41)	**THIRD CORRIDOR (42)**	LMS	LEEDS	GLASGOW	16.00 Glasgow - Leeds (21.41)
9	11 16.00 Glasgow - Leeds (21.41)	**BRAKE THIRD CORRIDOR (24)**	LMS	LEEDS	GLASGOW	16.00 Glasgow - Leeds (21.41)
10	11A 16.40 Kilmarnock - Leeds (21.41)	**RESTAURANT COMPOSITE (12/18)**	LMS	LEEDS	KILMARNOCK	16.40 Kilmarnock - Leeds (21.41)
11	11A 16.40 Kilmarnock - Leeds (21.41)	**COMPOSITE OPEN (18/18)**	LMS	LEEDS	KILMARNOCK	16.40 Kilmarnock - Leeds (21.41)

10.35 LEEDS to GLASGOW ST ENOCH (15.53)

Leeds was well served by Scottish expresses during the morning and perhaps the only weakness in the arrangement was that both trains left within an hour of each other rather than being spread out between, say, eight and eleven. However, most would agree that Leeds would have been fortunate to have had one train let alone two, especially as both were expresses of the first order. The first to depart was the North Briton at 09.15 which ran to Glasgow via York, Newcastle and Edinburgh, arriving in Queen Street at 14.52. The second was the unnamed Midland service which left at 10.35 and arrived in St Enoch at 15.53, ostensibly nineteen minutes faster although the respective distances covered were 278 and 228 miles. The more efficient of the two services was undoubtedly the North Briton since the entire train worked to Glasgow and back in the same day, a daily mileage of 556 miles which for many years stood as a record. The Midland service was balanced by the 16.00 Glasgow to Leeds but since the down train arrived in St Enoch only seven minutes before the up train was due to depart, two sets of stock were needed with the 10.35 remaining idle for over twenty-four hours in Glasgow although it was not unknown for the South Western to utilise it to work a local train during the morning rush hour from Paisley to St Enoch. Not all of the 10.35 went through to Glasgow since, in order to maximise the utility of the dining section, the restaurant car and its companion vehicle was removed at Kilmarnock in order to be attached to the up train when it called a couple of hours later.

5MT 4-6-0 44856 of Derby has been pressed into Manchester - London express service and appears to be filling the boiler after the long slog from Manchester to Peak Forest. By 1958, the time of the photograph, the introduction of 7P's to the route should have reduced the opportunities for Black Fives on express work but in fact they continued to play a part in class 1 work until Type 4 diesels took over in 1962.

Although popularly supposed to be 5MT engines, the two class 5 2-6-0 (parallel and taper boiler) classes were actually goods engines and barred from all passeng trains other than those running to the slowest timings. As a result their use on passenger workings tended to be confined to excursions and cross-country relief trai although they were actually cleared to haul greater passenger loads than a Black Five 4-6-0. The reason for this anomaly was that the 2-6-0 was actually a goods engi and not mixed traffic and as such was allowed to take a load 10% greater than a class 5 mixed traffic engine. 42960 of Longsight restarts an excursion from Blackpo away from Chinley.

	C/W	Previous working	Vehicle	Type	From	To	Next working
1	38	06.09 ECS Kings Norton - Birmingham (06.21)	BRAKE THIRD CORRIDOR (24)	LMS	BIRMINGHAM	BRADFORD	17.25 Bradford - Sheffield (19.23)
2	38	06.09 ECS Kings Norton - Birmingham (06.21)	THIRD CORRIDOR (42)	LMS	BIRMINGHAM	BRADFORD	17.25 Bradford - Sheffield (19.23)
3	38	06.09 ECS Kings Norton - Birmingham (06.21)	COMPOSITE CORRIDOR (18/24)	LMS	BIRMINGHAM	BRADFORD	17.25 Bradford - Sheffield (19.23)
4	38	06.09 ECS Kings Norton - Birmingham (06.21)	COMPOSITE CORRIDOR (18/24)	LMS	BIRMINGHAM	BRADFORD	17.25 Bradford - Sheffield (19.23)
5	38	06.09 ECS Kings Norton - Birmingham (06.21)	THIRD CORRIDOR (42)	LMS	BIRMINGHAM	BRADFORD	17.25 Bradford - Sheffield (19.23)
6	38	06.09 ECS Kings Norton - Birmingham (06.21)	BRAKE THIRD CORRIDOR (24)	LMS	BIRMINGHAM	BRADFORD	17.25 Bradford - Sheffield (19.23)
7	38A		THIRD CORRIDOR (42)	LMS	SHEFFIELD	BRADFORD	

For all its position as Britain's second or third city, remarkably few long distance trains started their journeys at Birmingham; heavy reliance being placed on the Bristol - Derby expresses together with the presumption that most passengers coming in from the west alighted at New Street and therefore balanced the numbers who joined the train at Birmingham. Since, however, the first arrival from Bristol did not reach New Street until 10.05, Birmingham was obliged to start two services off, one being the 06.40 to Bradford and the other, the 08.05 to Newcastle.

Although travelling to different parts of the country, the two services were not entirely unrelated since many of the West of England expresses were worked by a complex eleven-day carriage cycle which happened to cover both the Bradford and the Newcastle working and in fact the set working the 06.40 had the previous day formed the 08.05 Birmingham - Newcastle. What was even more interesting was that the cycle also included London and meant that on three consecutive days the same set of coaches worked the 15.57 Newcastle - Birmingham, the 06.40 Birmingham - Bradford and the 17.30 St Pancras - Sheffield. Since the cycle also included the 01.10 Bristol - Bradford and the 12.00 York - Bristol, it is difficult to find another set of coaches that worked to such a varied programme.

The 06.40 itself lay on the very margins of what constituted express work and called at all the important points en route plus several of those that were not. With a Black 5 4-6-0 at its head, there was little to distinguish it from the numerous semi-fast trains on the system except that it played a small part in the Anglo-Scottish trade by connecting at Derby with the 04.18 St Pancras to Manchester and at Leeds with the 10.35 to Glasgow. It is doubtful if there were many through passengers from London by this route although it was the only service that allowed one to reach Glasgow before four in the afternoon.

	C/W	Previous working	Vehicle	Type	From	To	Next working
1	26	13.50 Manchester - St Pancras (18.11)	BRAKE THIRD CORRIDOR (24)	LMS	ST PANCRAS	MANCHESTER	13.50 Manchester - St Pancras (18.11)
2	26	13.50 Manchester - St Pancras (18.11)	THIRD CORRIDOR (42)	LMS	ST PANCRAS	MANCHESTER	13.50 Manchester - St Pancras (18.11)
3	26	13.50 Manchester - St Pancras (18.11)	THIRD CORRIDOR (48)	BR	ST PANCRAS	MANCHESTER	13.50 Manchester - St Pancras (18.11)
4	26	13.50 Manchester - St Pancras (18.11)	COMPOSITE CORRIDOR (24/18)	BR	ST PANCRAS	MANCHESTER	13.50 Manchester - St Pancras (18.11)
5	26	13.50 Manchester - St Pancras (18.11)	FIRST CORRIDOR (42)	BR	ST PANCRAS	MANCHESTER	13.50 Manchester - St Pancras (18.11)
6	26	13.50 Manchester - St Pancras (18.11)	BRAKE THIRD CORRIDOR (24)	BR	ST PANCRAS	MANCHESTER	13.50 Manchester - St Pancras (18.11)
7	901	17.55 Manchester - St Pancras (22.55)	FULL BRAKE	LMS	ST PANCRAS	MANCHESTER	
8	902	20.36 Leicester - St Pancras (22.55)	FULL BRAKE	LMS	ST PANCRAS	WELLINGBOROUGH	07.02 Wellingborough - Nottingham (09.32)
9	903	20.36 Leicester - St Pancras (22.55)	FULL BRAKE	LMS	ST PANCRAS	WELLINGBOROUGH	07.02 Wellingborough - Leicester (08.09)
10	904		FULL BRAKE	LMS	ST PANCRAS	BEDFORD	
11	904		FULL BRAKE	LMS	ST PANCRAS	BEDFORD	
12	905		FULL BRAKE	LMS	ST PANCRAS	LUTON	
13	26A	15.42 Nottingham - Leicester (16.50)	THIRD CORRIDOR (42)	LMS	LEICESTER	MANCHESTER	11.35 Manchester - Nottingham (14.41)
14	26A	15.42 Nottingham - Leicester (16.50)	THIRD CORRIDOR (42)	LMS	LEICESTER	MANCHESTER	11.35 Manchester - Nottingham (14.41)

Newspaper traffic was big business for the railway generally and around four in the morning a number of trains left London for the provinces with heavy loads of newsprint. These included the 04.00 from Kings Cross to Leeds, the 04.30 Liverpool Street to Norwich and the 04.37 from Euston to Birmingham and Wolverhampton. The Midland's contribution to this activity was the 04.18 St Pancras to Manchester which left London with as many newspaper vehicles as it had passenger coaches, although the former tended to reduce as the journey proceeded. Newsprint traffic for the home counties was especially heavy with a van being devoted to St Albans and Luton traffic alone, whilst Bedford and Wellingborough required two apiece. The Wellingborough vans were of interest since they also served the intermediate stations on the main line, both vehicles being attached to the 07.02 local, one coming off at Leicester but the other continuing forward to Nottingham via Trent.

Passenger accommodation was generous given the time of day yet by the time the train left Leicester, demand was brisk enough to warrant the addition of two more coaches for the Leicester - Manchester section. Trade between the two cities was not something to be sniffed at and at 07.13 when the 04.18 pulled out of London Road, the Great Central had already despatched one - 06.45 - from Leicester Central and was preparing to run another.

Since newspaper traffic ran in one direction only, the 04.18 had no corresponding southbound working and the passenger stock returned as the 13.50 express from Manchester Central to London. The six vehicles ran as an independent set as far as Derby where they were strengthened by a four-coach dining section (off the 08.15 St Pancras to Manchester) for the rest of the journey to London.

	C/W	Previous working	Vehicle	Type	From	To	Next working
1	39	07.40 Kings Norton - Birmingham (07.52)	BRAKE THIRD CORRIDOR (24)	LMS	BIRMINGHAM	NEWCASTLE	15.57 Newcastle - Birmingham (21.05)
2	39	07.40 Kings Norton - Birmingham (07.52)	THIRD CORRIDOR (42)	LMS	BIRMINGHAM	NEWCASTLE	15.57 Newcastle - Birmingham (21.05)
3	39	07.40 Kings Norton - Birmingham (07.52)	COMPOSITE CORRIDOR (18/24)	LMS	BIRMINGHAM	NEWCASTLE	15.57 Newcastle - Birmingham (21.05)
4	39	07.40 Kings Norton - Birmingham (07.52)	COMPOSITE CORRIDOR (18/24)	LMS	BIRMINGHAM	NEWCASTLE	15.57 Newcastle - Birmingham (21.05)
5	39	07.40 Kings Norton - Birmingham (07.52)	THIRD CORRIDOR (42)	LMS	BIRMINGHAM	NEWCASTLE	15.57 Newcastle - Birmingham (21.05)
6	39	07.40 Kings Norton - Birmingham (07.52)	BRAKE THIRD CORRIDOR (24)	LMS	BIRMINGHAM	NEWCASTLE	15.57 Newcastle - Birmingham (21.05)

In terms of frequency the service between Birmingham and the North Eastern was not inadequate and in fact eight of the twelve expresses that started from New Street or the West of England terminated at either York or Newcastle. Of the remainder three ran to Bradford and one terminated in Sheffield. Unfortunately it is difficult to write as glowingly about the speed of the service since it was a rare train that did not stop at Tamworth, Burton, Chesterfield and Rotherham in addition to Derby and Sheffield. The 08.05 Birmingham - Newcastle was not much of an exception to the rule - it omitted the Tamworth stop - and formed of a Black 5 4-6-0 and half a dozen LMS coaches, resembled more a run-of-the-mill semi-fast service rather than an important cross-country express. The hapless passenger was not even granted the benefit of food until the train reached York where the North Eastern added a dining portion for the final ninety minutes of the journey. The stock of the train, which the previous day had worked the 10.10 Sheffield to Birmingham - was maintained at Kings Norton and worked the 07.40 Kings Norton to New Street before departing for Newcastle.

06.18 DERBY to NOTTINGHAM (07.06)

	C/W	Previous working	Vehicle	Type	From	To	Next working
1	49	19.10 St Pancras - Derby (22.15)	BRAKE THIRD CORRIDOR (24)	LMS	DERBY	NOTTINGHAM	13.25 Nottingham - St Pancras (17.33)
2	49	19.10 St Pancras - Derby (22.15)	THIRD CORRIDOR (42)	LMS	DERBY	NOTTINGHAM	13.25 Nottingham - St Pancras (17.33)
3	49	19.10 St Pancras - Derby (22.15)	COMPOSITE CORRIDOR (18/24)	LMS	DERBY	NOTTINGHAM	13.25 Nottingham - St Pancras (17.33)
4	49	19.10 St Pancras - Derby (22.15)	COMPOSITE CORRIDOR (18/24)	LMS	DERBY	NOTTINGHAM	13.25 Nottingham - St Pancras (17.33)
5	49	19.10 St Pancras - Derby (22.15)	THIRD CORRIDOR (42)	LMS	DERBY	NOTTINGHAM	13.25 Nottingham - St Pancras (17.33)
6	49	19.10 St Pancras - Derby (22.15)	BRAKE THIRD CORRIDOR (24)	LMS	DERBY	NOTTINGHAM	13.25 Nottingham - St Pancras (17.33)

Only sixteen miles apart, Derby and Nottingham were connected by an interestingly varied collection of local trains; a service that operated at roughly ninety-minute intervals - although there was no discernable pattern to the service - and ranged from LMS non-corridor sets worked by 2-6-4T's to mainline corridor vehicles being used in marginal time and worked by anything from a 2P 4-4-0 to a Jubilee 4-6-0. In addition there were the through trains between Derby and Lincoln which were worked at various times by D11 Director 4-4-0's and ex-GER D16 4-4-0's.

The 06.18 was formed by the set of main line stock that had arrived from London the previous night in the 19.10 St Pancras - Derby; its use as a local train being partly to supplement the ordinary local workings but also to provide a connection - with suitable accommodation - at Trent into the 06.40 Nottingham to St Pancras which reached London at 09.55, nearly an hour earlier than the first direct train: the 08.05 Derby to St Pancras.

On reaching Nottingham, the six-coach set was taken to the carriage sidings and attached to a four coach cafe-car set to form the 13.25 Nottingham - London express.

21.53 EDINBURGH (WAVERLEY) to ST PANCRAS (09.12)

	C/W	Previous working	Vehicle	Type	From	To	Next working
1	10	21.05 St Pancras - Edinburgh (07.54)	FULL BRAKE	LMS	EDINBURGH	ST PANCRAS	21.05 St Pancras - Edinburgh (07.54)
2	10	21.05 St Pancras - Edinburgh (07.54)	THIRD CORRIDOR (42)	LMS	EDINBURGH	ST PANCRAS	21.05 St Pancras - Edinburgh (07.54)
3	10	21.05 St Pancras - Edinburgh (07.54)	THIRD CORRIDOR (42)	LMS	EDINBURGH	ST PANCRAS	21.05 St Pancras - Edinburgh (07.54)
4	10	21.05 St Pancras - Edinburgh (07.54)	THIRD CORRIDOR (42)	LMS	EDINBURGH	ST PANCRAS	21.05 St Pancras - Edinburgh (07.54)
5	10	21.05 St Pancras - Edinburgh (07.54)	COMPOSITE CORRIDOR (18/24)	LMS	EDINBURGH	ST PANCRAS	21.05 St Pancras - Edinburgh (07.54)
6	10	21.05 St Pancras - Edinburgh (07.54)	COMPOSITE CORRIDOR (18/24)	LMS	EDINBURGH	ST PANCRAS	21.05 St Pancras - Edinburgh (07.54)
7	10	21.05 St Pancras - Edinburgh (07.54)	SLEEPING CAR FIRST	LMS/LNER	EDINBURGH	ST PANCRAS	21.05 St Pancras - Edinburgh (07.54)
8	10	21.05 St Pancras - Edinburgh (07.54)	SLEEPING CAR THIRD	LMS/LNER	EDINBURGH	ST PANCRAS	21.05 St Pancras - Edinburgh (07.54)
9	10	21.05 St Pancras - Edinburgh (07.54)	SLEEPING CAR COMPOSITE	LMS/LNER	EDINBURGH	ST PANCRAS	21.05 St Pancras - Edinburgh (07.54)
10	10	21.05 St Pancras - Edinburgh (07.54)	SLEEPING CAR COMPOSITE	LMS/LNER	EDINBURGH	ST PANCRAS	21.05 St Pancras - Edinburgh (07.54)
11	10	21.05 St Pancras - Edinburgh (07.54)	FULL BRAKE	LMS	EDINBURGH	ST PANCRAS	21.05 St Pancras - Edinburgh (07.54)
12		12.40 Aberdeen - Edinburgh (17.15)	FISH VAN	6-wheeled	EDINBURGH	NOTTINGHAM	

Shown in order of leaving Leeds

In the author's view this was without question the best overnight train in the British Isles and far superior to the East Coast trains where you were woken at a highly uncivilised hour in order to be dressed, washed and shaved in time to be pitched onto the platforms of Kings Cross before the rush hour started. The Midland had a far nicer sense of priorities and brought its Edinburgh sleeper into London *after* the worst of the rush hour; a policy that ensured a leisurely awakening after a long night's sleep. To lie in bed and watch the London suburban stations pass by the window was about as close to Paradise as this world would allow one to approach. An added charm of the train was the anticipation of whether one would have an LMS or LNE berth; the sleeping cars alternating nightly in continued celebration of a pregrouping joint working with the North British Railway.

The train served other purposes beside that of an Anglo-Scottish night express and left Nottingham and Kettering late enough to be considered the first of the day expresses. Its running time of 192 minutes for the 123 miles between Nottingham and London was deceptively slow and in anticipation of delays at Carlisle, Leeds or Sheffield, no less than 32 minutes was added to the normal running time of 160 minutes. (This was on top of 12 minutes at Nottingham to remove a van of fish from Aberdeen and short of a disaster, it was almost impossible for the train to reach London behind time). The formation of the train did not alter, other than the fishvan, and the vehicles in each of the two sets remained together for long periods.

06.40 NOTTINGHAM to ST PANCRAS (09.55)

	C/W	Previous working	Vehicle	Type	From	To	Next working
1	27B	17.30 St Pancras - Nottingham (20.47)	THIRD CORRIDOR (42)	LMS	NOTTINGHAM	ST PANCRAS	20.10 St Pancras - Derby (23.40)
2	27	15.35 Leicester - Nottingham (16.22)	BRAKE THIRD CORRIDOR (24)	LMS	NOTTINGHAM	ST PANCRAS	12.50 St Pancras - Leicester (15.25)
3	27	15.35 Leicester - Nottingham (16.22)	FIRST OPEN (42)	LMS	NOTTINGHAM	ST PANCRAS	12.50 St Pancras - Leicester (15.25)
4	27	15.35 Leicester - Nottingham (16.22)	FIRST OPEN (42)	LMS	NOTTINGHAM	ST PANCRAS	12.50 St Pancras - Leicester (15.25)
5	27	15.35 Leicester - Nottingham (16.22)	RESTAURANT THIRD (30)	LMS	NOTTINGHAM	ST PANCRAS	12.50 St Pancras - Leicester (15.25)
6	27	15.35 Leicester - Nottingham (16.22)	THIRD OPEN (56)	LMS	NOTTINGHAM	ST PANCRAS	12.50 St Pancras - Leicester (15.25)
7	27	15.35 Leicester - Nottingham (16.22)	COMPOSITE CORRIDOR (24/18)	BR	NOTTINGHAM	ST PANCRAS	12.50 St Pancras - Leicester (15.25)
8	27	15.35 Leicester - Nottingham (16.22)	COMPOSITE CORRIDOR (24/18)	BR	NOTTINGHAM	ST PANCRAS	12.50 St Pancras - Leicester (15.25)
9	27	15.35 Leicester - Nottingham (16.22)	BRAKE THIRD CORRIDOR (24)	BR	NOTTINGHAM	ST PANCRAS	12.50 St Pancras - Leicester (15.25)
10	27	15.35 Leicester - Nottingham (16.22)	THIRD CORRIDOR (42)	BR	NOTTINGHAM	ST PANCRAS	12.50 St Pancras - Leicester (15.25)
11	27	15.35 Leicester - Nottingham (16.22)	THIRD CORRIDOR (42)	BR	NOTTINGHAM	ST PANCRAS	12.50 St Pancras - Leicester (15.25)

Being the largest city, by far, between Sheffield and London, it might have been expected that Nottingham's business community would have been given at least one 135-minute express which would have got them to London by ten in the morning. In pregrouping days the 06.40 - a long-standing service which had the unusual Trent routing - had reached St Pancras at 09.20 but years and wars had seen so many additional stops added to its schedule that by 1955 it was little more than a semi-fast train - fortunately the restaurant car managed to survive the changes - although the non stop run from Bedford to London did something to recall past memories. Most of the passengers using the train booked from Leicester and Kettering since the 07.00 Sheffield to St Pancras left Nottingham an hour and a half after the 06.40 yet reached London only thirty-six minutes later. It has to be said that the 06.40 was always a very busy train south of Leicester and passengers joining at Bedford did not always find it easy to get a seat.

The main body of the train was a ten-coach set of coaches - the eleventh was a loose vehicle which returned in a night train to Derby - which enjoyed the curious distinction of never running over the direct route from Nottingham to London. The 06.40 ran from Nottingham via Trent and Loughborough whilst the return journey was made over the same route. The normal route from Nottingham was through Melton Mowbray to join the main line at Glendon South Junction, a short distance north of Kettering.

10.15 YORK to BRADFORD (11.44)

	C/W	Previous working	Vehicle	Type	From	To	Next working
1	128	06.42 Bradford - York	BRAKE THIRD CORRIDOR (32)	LNER	YORK	BRADFORD	15.50 Bradford - Leeds (16.28)
2	128	06.42 Bradford - York	THIRD CORRIDOR (64)	LNER	YORK	BRADFORD	15.50 Bradford - Leeds (16.28)
3	128	06.42 Bradford - York	COMPOSITE CORRIDOR (21/32)	LNER	YORK	BRADFORD	15.50 Bradford - Leeds (16.28)
4	128	06.42 Bradford - York	THIRD CORRIDOR (64)	LNER	YORK	BRADFORD	15.50 Bradford - Leeds (16.28)
5	128	06.42 Bradford - York	BRAKE THIRD CORRIDOR (32)	LNER	YORK	BRADFORD	15.50 Bradford - Leeds (16.28)
6			COMPOSITE CORRIDOR (21/32)	LNER	YORK	BRADFORD	15.50 Bradford - Leeds (16.28)
7			THIRD CORRIDOR (48)	LNER	YORK	BRADFORD	15.50 Bradford - Leeds (16.28)

This service was one of the few instances of a through service between the Midland and North Eastern - even though they shared the same station in Leeds - and was the return service (plus the addition of a pair of coaches) of the 06.42 Bradford - York. Its main purpose was to connect with the 08.12 Newcastle - Bristol at York and thereby give Tyneside a fast service to the West Riding.

09.06 NOTTINGHAM to LIVERPOOL CENTRAL (12.25)

	C/W	Previous working	Vehicle	Type	From	To	Next working
1	48	15.30 Liverpool - Nottingham (19.31)	BRAKE THIRD CORRIDOR (24)	LMS	NOTTINGHAM	LIVERPOOL	15.30 Liverpool - Nottingham (19.31)
2	48	15.30 Liverpool - Nottingham (19.31)	THIRD CORRIDOR (48)	BR	NOTTINGHAM	LIVERPOOL	15.30 Liverpool - Nottingham (19.31)
3	48	15.30 Liverpool - Nottingham (19.31)	COMPOSITE CORRIDOR (24/18)	BR	NOTTINGHAM	LIVERPOOL	15.30 Liverpool - Nottingham (19.31)
4	48	15.30 Liverpool - Nottingham (19.31)	RESTAURANT BUFFET	LMS	NOTTINGHAM	LIVERPOOL	15.30 Liverpool - Nottingham (19.31)
5	48	15.30 Liverpool - Nottingham (19.31)	COMPOSITE CORRIDOR (24/18)	BR	NOTTINGHAM	LIVERPOOL	15.30 Liverpool - Nottingham (19.31)
6	48	15.30 Liverpool - Nottingham (19.31)	THIRD CORRIDOR (48)	BR	NOTTINGHAM	LIVERPOOL	15.30 Liverpool - Nottingham (19.31)
7	48	15.30 Liverpool - Nottingham (19.31)	BRAKE THIRD CORRIDOR (24)	LMS	NOTTINGHAM	LIVERPOOL	15.30 Liverpool - Nottingham (19.31)
8	48	15.30 Liverpool - Nottingham (19.31)	FULL BRAKE	LMS	NOTTINGHAM	LIVERPOOL	15.30 Liverpool - Nottingham (19.31)

It is astonishing to recall that in pre-1914 days and in spite of the disadvantage of distance, the Midland railway had run no less than nine daily expresses between St Pancras and Liverpool Central; the fastest taking only four and a half hours. Since this was rather longer that the route from Euston, it is doubtful if the Midland ever secured a significant proportion of the through traffic and the chief advantage of the service was that it enable certain main line and CLC services to be covered by the same set of coaches - an economy that was lost on later generations of operators. The service also provided a valuable connection between the East Midlands and Merseyside; a connection that British Railways maintained in the form of the only service to run though to Liverpool from the Midland main line. Unfortunately the service left Nottingham some time before the arrival of the first train from London and it was not therefore possible to relive the experience of former times while in any case the speed of the train was rather disappointing since it called at most points to Derby and quite a number beyond. The eight vehicle set remained in the working on a daily basis and returned south in the 15.30 Liverpool - Nottingham.

07.54 WORCESTER to YORK (12.50)

	C/W	Previous working	Vehicle	Type	From	To	Next working
1	54	10.15 Gloucester - Worcester (11.20)	BRAKE THIRD CORRIDOR (24)	LMS	WORCESTER	YORK	16.15 York - Sheffield (18.06)
2	54	10.15 Gloucester - Worcester (11.20)	THIRD CORRIDOR (42)	LMS	WORCESTER	YORK	16.15 York - Sheffield (18.06)
3	54	10.15 Gloucester - Worcester (11.20)	COMPOSITE CORRIDOR (18/24)	LMS	WORCESTER	YORK	16.15 York - Sheffield (18.06)
4	54	10.15 Gloucester - Worcester (11.20)	COMPOSITE CORRIDOR (18/24)	LMS	WORCESTER	YORK	16.15 York - Sheffield (18.06)
5	54	10.15 Gloucester - Worcester (11.20)	THIRD CORRIDOR (42)	LMS	WORCESTER	YORK	16.15 York - Sheffield (18.06)
6	54	10.15 Gloucester - Worcester (11.20)	THIRD CORRIDOR (42)	LMS	WORCESTER	YORK	16.15 York - Sheffield (18.06)
7	54	10.15 Gloucester - Worcester (11.20)	THIRD CORRIDOR (42)	LMS	WORCESTER	YORK	16.15 York - Sheffield (18.06)
8	54	10.15 Gloucester - Worcester (11.20)	BRAKE THIRD CORRIDOR (24)	LMS	WORCESTER	YORK	16.15 York - Sheffield (18.06)

Worcester lay in an awkward position so far as cross-country services were concerned and northbound passengers either had to travel via Hereford or Kidderminster to connect with the Bristol - Shrewsbury/Crewe route or else take one of the Midland's stopping trains to New Street for connections to Derby and the North or the ex-LNWR. Neither was a prospect to savour and a tolerable alternative came in the form of the 09.00 Birmingham - York which started back at Worcester to give Shrub Hill its only cross-country express. The description 'express' was purely nominal and owed everything to the fact the service operated over a long distance and nothing to its running qualities which included stopping at almost every station to Derby. In actual fact the train only existed because of the difficulties in dealing with empty stock at Birmingham and it was operationally convenient to merge a Birmingham - York and a Worcester Birmingham local into one service. The stock worked into the area as the 17.16 Sheffield - Gloucester, followed by a local service from Gloucester to Worcester.

10.42 HULL to BRADFORD (12.57)

	C/W	Previous working	Vehicle	Type	From	To	Next working
1	130	14.57 Bradford - Hull (17.17)	BRAKE THIRD CORRIDOR (24)	LNER	HULL	BRADFORD	14.57 Bradford - Hull (17.17)
2	130	14.57 Bradford - Hull (17.17)	THIRD CORRIDOR (48)	BR/NER	HULL	BRADFORD	14.57 Bradford - Hull (17.17)
3	130	14.57 Bradford - Hull (17.17)	COMPOSITE CORRIDOR (24/18)	BR/NER	HULL	BRADFORD	14.57 Bradford - Hull (17.17)
4	130	14.57 Bradford - Hull (17.17)	FIRST CORRIDOR (36)	BR/NER	HULL	BRADFORD	14.57 Bradford - Hull (17.17)
5	130	14.57 Bradford - Hull (17.17)	THIRD CORRIDOR (48)	BR/NER	HULL	BRADFORD	14.57 Bradford - Hull (17.17)
6	130	14.57 Bradford - Hull (17.17)	THIRD CORRIDOR (48)	BR/NER	HULL	BRADFORD	14.57 Bradford - Hull (17.17)
7	130	14.57 Bradford - Hull (17.17)	BRAKE THIRD CORRIDOR (24)	LNER	HULL	BRADFORD	14.57 Bradford - Hull (17.17)

The principal city of the West Riding was Leeds, from which railway lines radiated like the spokes of a wheel and whilst this gave Leeds a regular, if not always speedy, series of connections with most parts of the country, it made travel between the Yorkshire provinces difficult in that a change of trains, sometime stations, was required if Leeds lay on the line of route. The fact that the railways of Leeds, even those sharing the same station, scarcely seemed to talk to each other was reflected all too clearly in the timetable and made the handful of trains that did run through rather special. Amongst this select number was the 10.42 Hull to Bradford which whilst presenting a commonplace enough sight East of Leeds, brought to the Midland the daily curious spectacle of an LNER B1 4-6-0 hauling an LNER train over foreign metals. The train was not quite as foreign in appearance as the engine since five of the seven vehicles were new BR standard coaches. The outermost coaches, however, were of LNER vintage. The engine and stock returned to Hull with the 14.57 from Bradford.

	C/W Previous working	Vehicle	Type	From	To	Next working
		06.42 BRADFORD to YORK (08.19)				
1	128 16.24 Leeds - Bradford (17.04)	**BRAKE THIRD CORRIDOR (32)**	LNER	BRADFORD	YORK	10.15 York - Bradford (11.44)
2	128 16.24 Leeds - Bradford (17.04)	**THIRD CORRIDOR (64)**	LNER	BRADFORD	YORK	10.15 York - Bradford (11.44)
3	128 16.24 Leeds - Bradford (17.04)	**COMPOSITE CORRIDOR (21/32)**	LNER	BRADFORD	YORK	10.15 York - Bradford (11.44)
4	128 16.24 Leeds - Bradford (17.04)	**THIRD CORRIDOR (64)**	LNER	BRADFORD	YORK	10.15 York - Bradford (11.44)
5	128 16.24 Leeds - Bradford (17.04)	**BRAKE THIRD CORRIDOR (32)**	LNER	BRADFORD	YORK	10.15 York - Bradford (11.44)

Leeds City was the principal conduit in the West Riding for through running between the LMS and LNER systems although little advantage was taken of the fact that Leeds City was a through station.   The LNW, who made an end-on connection with the North Eastern, ran no more than a handful of Newcastle - Liverpool trains through Leeds (and a proportion of these reversed in Leeds in order to travel via Harrogate as opposed to Church Fenton) whilst the Midland ran into the terminal section of Leeds City and used the fact as an excuse to run as few trains as possible through the LNW part of the station and onto the North Eastern.   What through running there was ran to and from Bradford, Forster Square and the entire programme, such as it was, owed almost its entire existence to pregrouping efforts rather than any post-1914 planning exertions.   The working of the through service was divided between the NER and the Midland and brought the sight of LNER engines and stock into Forster Square on a regular basis.   (The two did not always remain together and occasional Midland trains - the 07.35 ex Bristol was an example - were worked between Leeds and Bradford by LNER D49 4-4-0's).   In order to give a through service to York for business needs, a train of LNER corridor stock - quite a luxury in an area accustomed to non-corridor local trains - was berthed overnight at Bradford to form the 06.42 stopping train from Forster Square.   Worked by a Manningham 2-6-4T, both engine and coaches returned to Bradford with the 10.15 ex York.   Later in the decade the service was completely revised by being extended from York to Newcastle (arrive 10.55) via Durham.

	C/W Previous working	Vehicle	Type	From	To	Next working
		07.00 SHEFFIELD to ST PANCRAS (10.32)				
1	117 14.00 St Pancras - Nottingham (16.17)	**FIRST CORRIDOR (36)**	LMS	NOTTINGHAM	ST PANCRAS	14.00 St Pancras - Nottingham (16.17)
2	117 14.00 St Pancras - Nottingham (16.17)	**FIRST OPEN (42)**	BR	NOTTINGHAM	ST PANCRAS	14.00 St Pancras - Nottingham (16.17)
3	117 14.00 St Pancras - Nottingham (16.17)	**RESTAURANT THIRD (30)**	LMS	NOTTINGHAM	ST PANCRAS	14.00 St Pancras - Nottingham (16.17)
4	14 18.33 St Pancras - Sheffield (21.53)	**BRAKE THIRD CORRIDOR (24)**	BR	SHEFFIELD	ST PANCRAS	14.00 St Pancras - Bradford (19.26)
5	14 18.33 St Pancras - Sheffield (21.53)	**THIRD CORRIDOR (48)**	BR	SHEFFIELD	ST PANCRAS	14.00 St Pancras - Bradford (19.26)
6	14 18.33 St Pancras - Sheffield (21.53)	**THIRD CORRIDOR (48)**	BR	SHEFFIELD	ST PANCRAS	14.00 St Pancras - Bradford (19.26)
7	14 18.33 St Pancras - Sheffield (21.53)	**THIRD CORRIDOR (48)**	BR	SHEFFIELD	ST PANCRAS	14.00 St Pancras - Bradford (19.26)
8	14 18.33 St Pancras - Sheffield (21.53)	**COMPOSITE CORRIDOR (24/18)**	BR	SHEFFIELD	ST PANCRAS	14.00 St Pancras - Bradford (19.26)
9	14 18.33 St Pancras - Sheffield (21.53)	**COMPOSITE CORRIDOR (24/18)**	BR	SHEFFIELD	ST PANCRAS	14.00 St Pancras - Bradford (19.26)
10	14 18.33 St Pancras - Sheffield (21.53)	**BRAKE THIRD CORRIDOR (24)**	LMS	SHEFFIELD	ST PANCRAS	14.00 St Pancras - Bradford (19.26)

The notion, popular in later times, of rising in the middle of the night to get to London at the time offices started to open had not taken root by the 1950's and urgent business travel either used a sleeping car service where one existed or caught a morning express which would reach London in time for lunch and an afternoon of work.   It should be added that the majority of businessmen of the day viewed such exertions as excessive and would have a good breakfast and visit the office before catching a London train at around ten in the morning.

Both the main routes from Sheffield to London vied for the early business market: the Great Central with the 07.50 'Master Cutler' from Victoria to Marylebone and the Midland with the untitled 07.00.   With the Master Cutler taking eleven minutes longer to reach London, it might be thought that the Midland train would be the service of preference but there were several reasons why the seasoned business travellers preferred the Great Central route.   In the first place the Master Cutler had a restaurant service for the entire journey whereas the Midland train lacked any such facilities until reaching Nottingham, seventy minutes after leaving Sheffield.   The Marylebone service made less stops - it called at only Nottingham, Leicester and Rugby - while the 07.00 called at Chesterfield, Alfreton, Nottingham and Manton; the Nottingham stop often seeming interminable as the engine came off, picked up the dining set from the bay and attached it to the front of the express.   The allowance of five minutes for this gyration was ambitious and if the train was not delayed at Nottingham it would either fall foul of the 07.50 Leicester - Peterborough at Oakham or the 09.06 Bedford - St Pancras.   At any rate the train did not have a good reputation for timekeeping whereas the Master Cutler was invariably in Marylebone in good time.   The stock returned intact as the 14.00 St Pancras to Nottingham and Bradford.

	C/W Previous working	Vehicle	Type	From	To	Next working
		08.05 DERBY to ST PANCRAS (10.45)				
1	32 20.10 St Pancras - Derby (23.40)	**BRAKE THIRD CORRIDOR (24)**	BR	DERBY	ST PANCRAS	20.10 St Pancras - Derby (23.40)
2	32 20.10 St Pancras - Derby (23.40)	**THIRD CORRIDOR (48)**	BR	DERBY	ST PANCRAS	20.10 St Pancras - Derby (23.40)
3	32 20.10 St Pancras - Derby (23.40)	**COMPOSITE CORRIDOR (24/18)**	BR	DERBY	ST PANCRAS	20.10 St Pancras - Derby (23.40)
4	32 20.10 St Pancras - Derby (23.40)	**FIRST CORRIDOR (42)**	BR	DERBY	ST PANCRAS	20.10 St Pancras - Derby (23.40)
5	32 20.10 St Pancras - Derby (23.40)	**THIRD CORRIDOR (48)**	BR	DERBY	ST PANCRAS	20.10 St Pancras - Derby (23.40)
6	32 20.10 St Pancras - Derby (23.40)	**BRAKE THIRD CORRIDOR (24)**	BR	DERBY	ST PANCRAS	20.10 St Pancras - Derby (23.40)
7	32 20.10 St Pancras - Derby (23.40)	**THIRD CORRIDOR (42)**	LMS	DERBY	ST PANCRAS	20.10 St Pancras - Derby (23.40)
8	32 20.10 St Pancras - Derby (23.40)	**THIRD CORRIDOR (42)**	LMS	DERBY	ST PANCRAS	20.10 St Pancras - Derby (23.40)
9	32A 14.15 St Pancras - Derby (16.52)	**BRAKE THIRD CORRIDOR (24)**	LMS	DERBY	ST PANCRAS	14.15 St Pancras - Derby (16.52)

Although Derby was both the headquarters and crossroads of the Midland railway, its population was only half that of near-by Nottingham and since the latter exceeded a quarter of a million, it is not surprising that it had the greater claim for consideration in the distribution of express services to London.   Derby, in fact, was seen as little more than an intermediate station on the line of route to Manchester and, in contrast to the policies of later times, the trains that ran from Sheffield to London via Derby were few in number and limited to the night hours.   Such was the importance of Nottingham that one of the Manchester - London trains, after calling at Derby, diverted from the main line to run via Trent, Nottingham and Melton.

For all that, Derby was important enough to warrant a business train of its own to London and the 08.05 filled the breach between the 06.18 indirect service and the first up Manchester express which did not leave Derby until 09.00.   The 08.05 was a reasonably fast express and averaged just under 50 mph with stops at Sawley Junction, Kegworth, Loughborough, Leicester, Market Harborough and Kettering.   The last lap was especially rapid with Kettering to St Pancras being covered at exactly mile a minute which was quite exceptional for the Midland although to achieve this very tight timing the operators acted with considerable caution by running the train under special limit conditions and restricting the load to two vehicles less than the eleven normally allowed to a 5XP 4-6-0.   Unfortunately this caution left no room for dining facilities which was an extraordinary omission in one of the best expresses on the system and for a time passenger had to look to their own means for sustenance until mid-1955 when - probably as a result of journeys made by a hungry operating hierarchy rather than passenger complaints - a dining car was added to the train's formation.

After being released from the West of England express that it has just brought in from the North, Jubilee 4-6-0 45626 'Seychelles' of Derby runs tender first from Temple Meads, Bristol, to Barrow Road Loco.

The importance of Bradford to the Midland's passenger strategy was not immediately obvious from Forster Square's rather gloomy interior yet it was from this location that numerous through trains for London and Bristol were prepared daily. Since these expresses reversed at Leeds, large engines were the exception to the rule at Forster Square where Compound 4-4-0's and 4MT 2-6-4 tanks were the general order of the day. Taken on 29th April 1952, the service on the right is a stopping train for Leeds City headed by Compound 41045 (Lancaster) whilst in the opposite platform 2P 2-4-2T 50636 (Manningham) waits to leave with a Skipton service. (V.R. Webster/ Kidderminster Railway Museum).

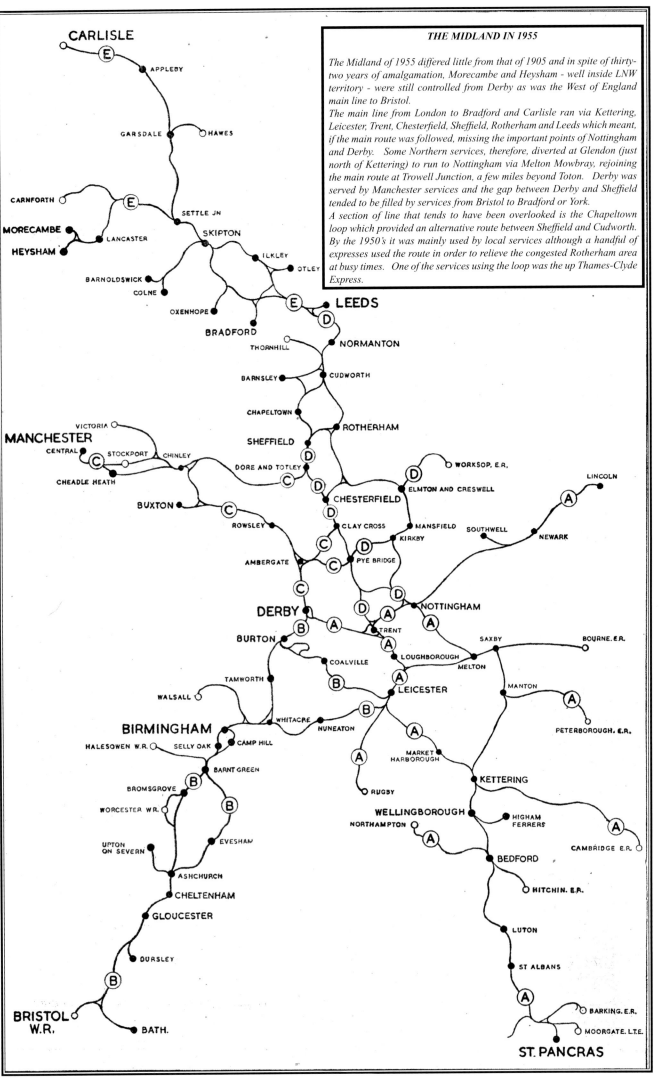

The Midland of 1955 differed little from that of 1905 and in spite of thirty-two years of amalgamation, Morecambe and Heysham - well inside LNW territory - were still controlled from Derby as was the West of England main line to Bristol.

The main line from London to Bradford and Carlisle ran via Kettering, Leicester, Trent, Chesterfield, Sheffield, Rotherham and Leeds which meant, if the main route was followed, missing the important points of Nottingham and Derby. Some Northern services, therefore, diverted at Glendon (just north of Kettering) to run to Nottingham via Melton Mowbray, rejoining the main route at Trowell Junction, a few miles beyond Toton. Derby was served by Manchester services and the gap between Derby and Sheffield tended to be filled by services from Bristol to Bradford or York.

A section of line that tends to have been overlooked is the Chapeltown loop which provided an alternative route between Sheffield and Cudworth. By the 1950's it was mainly used by local services although a handful of expresses used the route in order to relieve the congested Rotherham area at busy times. One of the services using the loop was the up Thames-Clyde Express.

07.35 BRISTOL to BRADFORD (13.58)

	C/W	Previous working	Vehicle	Type	From	To	Next working
1	85	20.55 Bradford - Bristol (04.33)	BRAKE THIRD CORRIDOR (24)	LMS	BRISTOL	BRADFORD	20.55 Bradford - Bristol (04.33)
2	85	20.55 Bradford - Bristol (04.33)	COMPOSITE CORRIDOR (18/24)	LMS	BRISTOL	BRADFORD	20.55 Bradford - Bristol (04.33)
3	85	20.55 Bradford - Bristol (04.33)	THIRD CORRIDOR (42)	LMS	BRISTOL	BRADFORD	20.55 Bradford - Bristol (04.33)
4	43	16.45 Bradford - Bristol (00.03)	FULL BRAKE	LMS	BRISTOL	BRADFORD	16.45 Bradford - Bristol (00.03)
5	43	16.45 Bradford - Bristol (00.03)	THIRD CORRIDOR (42)	LMS	BRISTOL	BRADFORD	16.45 Bradford - Bristol (00.03)
6	43	16.45 Bradford - Bristol (00.03)	COMPOSITE CORRIDOR (18/24)	LMS	BRISTOL	BRADFORD	16.45 Bradford - Bristol (00.03)
7	43	16.45 Bradford - Bristol (00.03)	COMPOSITE CORRIDOR (18/24)	LMS	BRISTOL	BRADFORD	16.45 Bradford - Bristol (00.03)
8	43	16.45 Bradford - Bristol (00.03)	THIRD CORRIDOR (42)	LMS	BRISTOL	BRADFORD	16.45 Bradford - Bristol (00.03)
9	43	16.45 Bradford - Bristol (00.03)	BRAKE THIRD CORRIDOR (24)	LMS	BRISTOL	BRADFORD	16.45 Bradford - Bristol (00.03)
10	43A	16.45 Bradford - Derby (19.29)	RESTAURANT BUFFET (24)	LMS	DERBY	BRADFORD	16.45 Bradford - Derby (19.29)

The running of the Midland's West of England expresses can best be described as uniform rather than exciting since almost all the day trains took within a few minutes of four and a half hours to cover the 166 miles between Bristol and Sheffield: an average speed of less than 40 mph. The distinction between a fast train and an express did not exist and not even the much-publicised Devonian stood out from the rank and file. In fact the untitled 07.35 from Bristol was, by the margin of a few minutes, the fastest of the cross-country expresses since it reached Sheffield from Bristol in four minutes under the four and a half hour yardstick. The reason for this apparent lack of enterprise stemmed from the fact that Bristol did not of itself normally produce enough traffic for one train and therefore even the most prestigious of the route's trains had to canvass what traffic they could by stopping at every point of significance. Station times at Mangotsfield, Gloucester and Cheltenham plus the delays engendered by Bromsgrove and Birmingham New Street were all features that conspired to lengthen overall times whilst, in addition, trains of more than 12 coaches hauled by a 5XP 4-6-0 (11 for a Black 5) had to stop outside Bristol for banking assistance up Fishponds bank.

To compound the miseries of travel, passengers had to sit without food or drink for the three and a half hours that it took to reach Derby; an extraordinary omission on what should have been seen as an important service, not only because it ran through from Bristol to Bradford but because it made a useful connection at Sheffield with the down Thames-Clyde Express.

06.57 CLEETHORPES - BIRMINGHAM (11.13)

	C/W	Previous working	Vehicle	Type	From	To	Next working
1	87	16.50 Birmingham - Cleethorpes	BRAKE THIRD CORRIDOR (24)	LMS	CLEETHORPES	BIRMINGHAM	12.15 Birmingham - Gloucester
2	87	16.50 Birmingham - Cleethorpes	THIRD CORRIDOR (42)	LMS	CLEETHORPES	BIRMINGHAM	12.15 Birmingham - Gloucester
3	87	16.50 Birmingham - Cleethorpes	COMPOSITE CORRIDOR (18/24)	LMS	CLEETHORPES	BIRMINGHAM	12.15 Birmingham - Gloucester
4	87	16.50 Birmingham - Cleethorpes	THIRD CORRIDOR (42)	LMS	CLEETHORPES	BIRMINGHAM	12.15 Birmingham - Gloucester
5	87	16.50 Birmingham - Cleethorpes	BRAKE THIRD CORRIDOR (24)	LMS	CLEETHORPES	BIRMINGHAM	12.15 Birmingham - Gloucester

On a railway system that radiated from London, most cross-country services tended to be rather secondary affairs whilst a through working on a series of otherwise unrelated routes was a wonder to behold. The Southern, for example, operated a train from Brighton to Cardiff and although the service had little to commend it in the way of speed or facilities; the fact it ran counter to the general Waterloo - Exeter flow marked it out as a train of distinction. Such was the case with the Cleethorpes - Birmingham service; the more so as Cleethorpes, right out on a limb of the Great Central, seemed to be a curious choice for a through service since the Black Country and Humberside were not known to have very much in common.

Obscure or not, the service brought to New Street the unique sight of an LNER B1 4-6-0; the Immingham-based engine working through from Cleethorpes and being serviced at Bourneville before working back with the 16.50 return service. Rather surprisingly the carriage stock was not ex-LNER but LMS since the two sets of coaches were involved, both being based in Gloucester. The working commenced with the 13.51 Gloucester to Birmingham and went on to Cleethorpes with the 16.50 from New Street. The following day the set returned in the 06.57 Cleethorpes - Birmingham and regained Gloucester in the 12.15 stopping train from New Street. It was thus possible to watch the unusual spectacle of an LNER B1 4-6-0 making way for a Midland 4-4-0 Compound and vice-versa.

08.15 ST PANCRAS to MANCHESTER CENTRAL (13.02)

	C/W	Previous working	Vehicle	Type	From	To	Next working
1	25	17.55 Manchester - St Pancras (22.52)	FULL BRAKE	LMS	ST PANCRAS	MANCHESTER	17.55 Manchester - St Pancras (22.52)
2	25	17.55 Manchester - St Pancras (22.52)	BRAKE THIRD CORRIDOR (24)	LMS	ST PANCRAS	MANCHESTER	17.55 Manchester - St Pancras (22.52)
3	25	17.55 Manchester - St Pancras (22.52)	THIRD CORRIDOR (42)	LMS	ST PANCRAS	MANCHESTER	17.55 Manchester - St Pancras (22.52)
4	25	17.55 Manchester - St Pancras (22.52)	THIRD CORRIDOR (42)	LMS	ST PANCRAS	MANCHESTER	17.55 Manchester - St Pancras (22.52)
5	25	17.55 Manchester - St Pancras (22.52)	THIRD OPEN (56)	LMS	ST PANCRAS	MANCHESTER	17.55 Manchester - St Pancras (22.52)
6	25	17.55 Manchester - St Pancras (22.52)	FIRST CORRIDOR (36)	LMS	ST PANCRAS	MANCHESTER	17.55 Manchester - St Pancras (22.52)
7	25	17.55 Manchester - St Pancras (22.52)	COMPOSITE CORRIDOR (18/24)	LMS	ST PANCRAS	MANCHESTER	17.55 Manchester - St Pancras (22.52)
8	25	17.55 Manchester - St Pancras (22.52)	BRAKE THIRD CORRIDOR (24)	LMS	ST PANCRAS	MANCHESTER	17.55 Manchester - St Pancras (22.52)
9	28C	16.00 Manchester - St Pancras (20.47)	THIRD CORRIDOR (42)	LMS	ST PANCRAS	MANCHESTER	16.00 Manchester - St Pancras (20.47)
10	25A	15.32 Derby - St Pancras (18.11)	RESTAURANT CAR (12/18)	LMS	ST PANCRAS	DERBY	15.32 Derby - St Pancras (18.11)
11	25A	15.32 Derby - St Pancras (18.11)	THIRD OPEN (56)	LMS	ST PANCRAS	DERBY	15.32 Derby - St Pancras (18.11)

The tentative moves made by British Railways during the 1950's to test the waters of business travel were not enthusiastically supported by the Midland who believed that business traffic from the home counties and Leicester to Manchester was adequately catered for by the (restaurantless) 04.18 ex St Pancras. The Great Northern put on a 07.50 flyer from Kings Cross which reached Leeds at 11.23 whilst on the North Western it was possible to get to Manchester in a shade over four hours by the 08.30 ex Euston. The Midland, in some ways the most conservative of railways and almost wholly preoccupied with goods and mineral traffic, took little note of these developments and limited its business service to the 08.15 St Pancras to Manchester; a train which only just warranted the description express since it served all major stations en route except, perhaps a little unaccountably since it was one of the more important points south of Leicester, Bedford. An hour slower than it might have been, the 08.15 was not much of a magnet for business travellers heading to Manchester who had less than five hours - not very long for the transaction of business - in the city before returning south by the last express of the day from Manchester Central. (Not that this service - the return working of the 08.15 - was any more of an attraction than the down train since it covered the 190 miles in all but five hours, devoid of any catering facilities whatsoever).

Dining facilities on the 08.15 did little to enhance the service since the restaurant car provided did not serve anything like a full range of meals and instead operated as a buffet, serving snacks, coffee and sandwiches. The catering section was removed at Derby and returned to London in the 13.50 from Manchester whilst the rear coach was transferred at Manchester to the 10.15 ex St Pancras to strengthen to 16.00 Manchester to London.

07.35 NOTTINGHAM to BRISTOL (12.00)

	C/W	Previous working	Vehicle	Type	From	To	Next working
1	46	17.30 St Pancras - Nottingham (20.47)	BRAKE THIRD CORRIDOR (24)	LMS	NOTTINGHAM	BRISTOL	01.10 Bristol - Sheffield (06.48)
2	46	17.30 St Pancras - Nottingham (20.47)	THIRD CORRIDOR (42)	LMS	NOTTINGHAM	BRISTOL	01.10 Bristol - Sheffield (06.48)
3	46	17.30 St Pancras - Nottingham (20.47)	COMPOSITE CORRIDOR (18/24)	LMS	NOTTINGHAM	BRISTOL	01.10 Bristol - Sheffield (06.48)
4	46	17.30 St Pancras - Nottingham (20.47)	COMPOSITE CORRIDOR (18/24)	LMS	NOTTINGHAM	BRISTOL	01.10 Bristol - Sheffield (06.48)
5	46	17.30 St Pancras - Nottingham (20.47)	THIRD CORRIDOR (42)	LMS	NOTTINGHAM	BRISTOL	01.10 Bristol - Sheffield (06.48)
6	153A	17.30 St Pancras - Nottingham (20.47)	THIRD CORRIDOR (42)	LMS	NOTTINGHAM	BRISTOL	16.45 Bristol - Derby (20.22)
7	42A	17.30 St Pancras - Nottingham (20.47)	THIRD CORRIDOR (42)	LMS	NOTTINGHAM	BRISTOL	01.10 Bristol - Sheffield (06.48)
8	46	17.30 St Pancras - Nottingham (20.47)	BRAKE THIRD CORRIDOR (24)	LMS	NOTTINGHAM	BRISTOL	01.10 Bristol - Sheffield (06.48)
9	980	20.10 Newcastle - Derby (06.00)	FULL BRAKE	LMS	DERBY	BIRMINGHAM	16.10 Birmingham - Bristol (21.00)
10	983	20.33 West Hartlepool - Derby (06.00)	FULL BRAKE	LMS	DERBY	BIRMINGHAM	16.10 Birmingham - Bristol (21.00)
11	981	21.00 Durham - Derby (06.00)	PMV	LMS	DERBY	BIRMINGHAM	16.10 Birmingham - Bristol (21.00)
12	982	02.08 York - Derby (06.00)	FULL BRAKE	LMS	DERBY	BIRMINGHAM	

One of the more curious aspects of the Midland timetable was the fact in spite of serving the very large centres of Bristol, Birmingham and Nottingham, only the most half-hearted of efforts was made to connect all three. For the most part the West of England line seemed reserved for services from Bradford or York and passengers from Nottingham were, in the majority of cases, required to change trains at Derby.

The exception was the 07.43 from Nottingham which ran via Trent Junction and the Chaddesden curve to Derby, stopping thereafter at all the major intermediate stations including Worcester and some (Kings Norton, Stonehouse and Berkeley Road) that were not. It would be pleasing to think that the train existed in order to prevent a proportion of Nottingham's passengers the inconvenience of changing at Derby but in fact the train operated to fill the West of England breech before the arrival of trains from the North and since it was convenient to use a set of London stock, the train ran from Nottingham. In this connection it is significant to note that there was no corresponding working from Bristol to Nottingham and in fact the London train from which the 07.43 was derived worked into St Pancras from Sheffield. On reaching Temple Meads, the main section of the 07.43 spent the afternoon and evening in Lawrence Hill sidings before forming the 01.10 Bristol - Sheffield and the 07.50 Sheffield to Bradford.

At Derby the train attached four parcels vehicles for Birmingham that had been brought in from the North East by the 02.55 Leeds to Kings Norton. Three of the vehicles later went forward by the 13.50 Derby - Bristol Parcels.

08.28 NOTTINGHAM to ST PANCRAS (11.25)

	C/W	Previous working	Vehicle	Type	From	To	Next working
1	47	16.45 St Pancras - Nottingham (19.48)	BRAKE THIRD CORRIDOR (24)	LMS	NOTTINGHAM	ST PANCRAS	16.45 St Pancras - Nottingham (19.48)
2	47	16.45 St Pancras - Nottingham (19.48)	THIRD CORRIDOR (42)	LMS	NOTTINGHAM	ST PANCRAS	16.45 St Pancras - Nottingham (19.48)
3	47	16.45 St Pancras - Nottingham (19.48)	THIRD CORRIDOR (42)	LMS	NOTTINGHAM	ST PANCRAS	16.45 St Pancras - Nottingham (19.48)
4	47	16.45 St Pancras - Nottingham (19.48)	THIRD CORRIDOR (42)	LMS	NOTTINGHAM	ST PANCRAS	16.45 St Pancras - Nottingham (19.48)
5	47	16.45 St Pancras - Nottingham (19.48)	THIRD CORRIDOR (42)	LMS	NOTTINGHAM	ST PANCRAS	16.45 St Pancras - Nottingham (19.48)
6	47	16.45 St Pancras - Nottingham (19.48)	THIRD CORRIDOR (42)	LMS	NOTTINGHAM	ST PANCRAS	16.45 St Pancras - Nottingham (19.48)
7	47	16.45 St Pancras - Nottingham (19.48)	COMPOSITE CORRIDOR (18/24)	LMS	NOTTINGHAM	ST PANCRAS	16.45 St Pancras - Nottingham (19.48)
8	47	16.45 St Pancras - Nottingham (19.48)	COMPOSITE CORRIDOR (18/24)	LMS	NOTTINGHAM	ST PANCRAS	16.45 St Pancras - Nottingham (19.48)
9	47	16.45 St Pancras - Nottingham (19.48)	THIRD CORRIDOR (42)	LMS	NOTTINGHAM	ST PANCRAS	16.45 St Pancras - Nottingham (19.48)
10	47	16.45 St Pancras - Nottingham (19.48)	BRAKE THIRD CORRIDOR (24)	LMS	NOTTINGHAM	ST PANCRAS	16.45 St Pancras - Nottingham (19.48)

While through business traffic from Nottingham to London was served by the 07.00 Sheffield - St Pancras (08.20 from Nottingham with only one stop), intermediate stations on the Melton line were given the 08.28 semi-fast from Nottingham which called at all major points to Luton before reaching London in just under three hours from Nottingham. For a train of its type, it conveyed quite a heavy load and the high proportion of third class seating without any dining facilities testifies to the fact that much of its trade consisted of day-trip traffic to London. Its running had to be closely watched since after making seven stops it left Luton only eight minutes ahead of the 07.20 Manchester to London - a difference that narrowed to 6 minutes by Hendon.

The carriage working was unremarkable in that the stock, which remained in the working on a daily basis, returned from St Pancras as an afternoon semi-fast.

07.20 MANCHESTER CENTRAL to ST PANCRAS (11.31)

	C/W	Previous working	Vehicle	Type	From	To	Next working
1	23	16.15 St Pancras - Manchester (20.47)	BRAKE THIRD CORRIDOR (24)	LMS	MANCHESTER	ST PANCRAS	14.15 St Pancras - Manchester (18.35)
2	23	16.15 St Pancras - Manchester (20.47)	COMPOSITE CORRIDOR (18/24)	LMS	MANCHESTER	ST PANCRAS	14.15 St Pancras - Manchester (18.35)
3	23	16.15 St Pancras - Manchester (20.47)	FIRST CORRIDOR (36)	LMS	MANCHESTER	ST PANCRAS	14.15 St Pancras - Manchester (18.35)
4	23	16.15 St Pancras - Manchester (20.47)	RESTAURANT FIRST (24)	LMS	MANCHESTER	ST PANCRAS	14.15 St Pancras - Manchester (18.35)
5	23	16.15 St Pancras - Manchester (20.47)	THIRD OPEN (56)	LMS	MANCHESTER	ST PANCRAS	14.15 St Pancras - Manchester (18.35)
6	23	16.15 St Pancras - Manchester (20.47)	THIRD CORRIDOR (42)	LMS	MANCHESTER	ST PANCRAS	14.15 St Pancras - Manchester (18.35)
7	23	16.15 St Pancras - Manchester (20.47)	THIRD CORRIDOR (42)	LMS	MANCHESTER	ST PANCRAS	14.15 St Pancras - Manchester (18.35)
8	23	16.15 St Pancras - Manchester (20.47)	BRAKE THIRD CORRIDOR (24)	LMS	MANCHESTER	ST PANCRAS	14.15 St Pancras - Manchester (18.35)
9	24B	16.15 St Pancras - Derby (19.01)	FIRST CORRIDOR	LMS	DERBY	ST PANCRAS	16.15 St Pancras - Derby (19.01)

Whilst the acquisition of two routes from Manchester to London had resulted in much of the thunder being stolen from the Midland, it was refreshing during the 1950's to see that some elements of the St Pancras service retained some of its former qualities. The principal business train left London Road at 07.55 and ran to Euston in three and a half hours; a timing that the Midland was unable to match given the need to call several time en route if a respectable payload was to be carried. For all the advantages of the West Coast route, the Midland's corresponding service was allowed to keep its place in the timetable and, moreover, ran to a schedule that was only twelve minutes slower than it had been in the days before 1914. Some of its Edwardian elements - the Loughborough slip coach and the through coach from Burton attached at Leicester - had long since disappeared whilst a number of stops had been added but it was still very much an express of the first order with a full restaurant car and a relatively high proportion of first class seating. Due to leave Derby at the popular time of 09.00, further first class accommodation was required and a First Corridor was added to the rear of the train; a facility that complicated matters somewhat at St Pancras since the Manchester portion of the train returned north at 14.15 whilst the Derby FK had to be placed on the rear of the 16.15 St Pancras - Manchester to meet the high demand for first class travel at that time of day.

The full nine-coach formation could have been worked through from Manchester since the 293 ton load was within the limit laid down for a 5XP 4-6-0 over the Peak section but the operators preferred to keep the load to within the 275 tons permitted to a 5MT on special limit timings and therefore the train was pared to eight vehicles for the difficult section between Manchester and Derby.

09.00 'THE WAVERLEY' ST PANCRAS to EDINBURGH WAVERLEY (19.15)

C/W		Previous working	Vehicle	Type	From	To	Next working
1	5	10.05 Edinburgh - St Pancras (20.45)	BRAKE THIRD CORRIDOR (24)	BR	ST PANCRAS	EDINBURGH	10.05 Edinburgh - St Pancras (20.45)
2	5	10.05 Edinburgh - St Pancras (20.45)	THIRD CORRIDOR (48)	BR	ST PANCRAS	EDINBURGH	10.05 Edinburgh - St Pancras (20.45)
3	5	10.05 Edinburgh - St Pancras (20.45)	THIRD CORRIDOR (48)	BR	ST PANCRAS	EDINBURGH	10.05 Edinburgh - St Pancras (20.45)
4	5	10.05 Edinburgh - St Pancras (20.45)	THIRD CORRIDOR (48)	BR	ST PANCRAS	EDINBURGH	10.05 Edinburgh - St Pancras (20.45)
5	5	10.05 Edinburgh - St Pancras (20.45)	THIRD CORRIDOR (48)	BR	ST PANCRAS	EDINBURGH	10.05 Edinburgh - St Pancras (20.45)
6	5	10.05 Edinburgh - St Pancras (20.45)	RESTAURANT THIRD (30)	LMS	ST PANCRAS	EDINBURGH	10.05 Edinburgh - St Pancras (20.45)
7	5	10.05 Edinburgh - St Pancras (20.45)	FIRST CORRIDOR (42)	BR	ST PANCRAS	EDINBURGH	10.05 Edinburgh - St Pancras (20.45)
8	5	10.05 Edinburgh - St Pancras (20.45)	COMPOSITE CORRIDOR (24/18)	BR	ST PANCRAS	EDINBURGH	10.05 Edinburgh - St Pancras (20.45)
9	5	10.05 Edinburgh - St Pancras (20.45)	BRAKE THIRD CORRIDOR (24)	BR	ST PANCRAS	EDINBURGH	10.05 Edinburgh - St Pancras (20.45)
10	5A	12.11 Sheffield - St Pancras (15.39)	COMPOSITE CORRIDOR (18/24)	LMS	ST PANCRAS	NOTTINGHAM (11.25)	17.50 Nottingham - Sheffield (20.00)

Although the journey was somewhat longer than the seven hours of the 10.00 ex Kings Cross, the Midland's Waverley was beyond question the most scenic of the routes from London to Edinburgh; the first third of the way being straight down the centre of the country to Leeds via Nottingham and Sheffield followed by the Long Drag over Ais Gill to Carlisle where the express was handed over to the North British for the final hundred-mile slog over the mountainous border counties. Apart from a trailing coach that ran only between London and Nottingham, the service ran intact between St Pancras and Edinburgh and returned to London the following day at 10.05 from the Waverley. Formed in the main by BR standard stock, a feature not always seen as an improvement on the faster sections of line, the principal blot on the train's horizon was the downgrading of the restaurant facilities to a buffet service even though a full-blown restaurant car was provided.

09.05 ST PANCRAS to LEICESTER (11.40)

C/W	Previous working	Vehicle	Type	From	To	Next working
1		THIRD CORRIDOR (42)	LMS	ST PANCRAS	LEICESTER	
2		THIRD CORRIDOR (42)	LMS	ST PANCRAS	LEICESTER	
3		THIRD CORRIDOR (42)	LMS	ST PANCRAS	LEICESTER	
4	16.25 Leicester - St Pancras (19.00)	THIRD CORRIDOR (42)	LMS	ST PANCRAS	LEICESTER	16.25 Leicester - St Pancras (19.00)
5	16.25 Leicester - St Pancras (19.00)	THIRD CORRIDOR (42)	LMS	ST PANCRAS	LEICESTER	16.25 Leicester - St Pancras (19.00)
6	16.25 Leicester - St Pancras (19.00)	BRAKE THIRD CORRIDOR (32)	LMS	ST PANCRAS	LEICESTER	16.25 Leicester - St Pancras (19.00)
7	16.25 Leicester - St Pancras (19.00)	COMPOSITE CORRIDOR (18/32)	LMS	ST PANCRAS	LEICESTER	16.25 Leicester - St Pancras (19.00)
8	16.25 Leicester - St Pancras (19.00)	BRAKE THIRD CORRIDOR (32)	LMS	ST PANCRAS	LEICESTER	16.25 Leicester - St Pancras (19.00)
9		COMPOSITE CORRIDOR (18/24)	LMS	ST PANCRAS	BEDFORD	
10		COMPOSITE CORRIDOR (18/24)	LMS	ST PANCRAS	BEDFORD	

Strictly speaking the semi-fast trains from St Pancras to Leicester have no place in this book since they were regarded as purely local services, however to ignore them completely would be to leave an unmistakable hole in the subject of Midland express services. The object of the 09.05 was to provide a connection at Leicester from the major intermediate stations into the 10.00 St Pancras - Glasgow and it is a measure of the popularity of the arrangement that no less than ten coaches were deemed necessary although two of these were shed before the hard running north of Bedford commenced. Running into Leicester only eighteen minutes ahead of the Thames-Clyde, the Black 5 4-6-0 booked to the train had its work cut out, the service being set to Limited Load timings to ensure that the connection was made.

On Summer Saturdays the connection at Leicester was dispensed with, the 09.05 being extended through to Glasgow (St Enoch).

10.00 'THE THAMES-CLYDE EXPRESS' ST PANCRAS to GLASGOW ST ENOCH (19.41)

C/W		Previous working	Vehicle	Type	From	To	Next working
1	1	09.20 Glasgow - St Pancras (19.28)	BRAKE THIRD CORRIDOR (24)	BR	ST PANCRAS	GLASGOW	09.20 Glasgow - St Pancras (19.28)
2	1	09.20 Glasgow - St Pancras (19.28)	THIRD CORRIDOR (48)	BR	ST PANCRAS	GLASGOW	09.20 Glasgow - St Pancras (19.28)
3	1	09.20 Glasgow - St Pancras (19.28)	THIRD CORRIDOR (48)	BR	ST PANCRAS	GLASGOW	09.20 Glasgow - St Pancras (19.28)
4	1	09.20 Glasgow - St Pancras (19.28)	THIRD CORRIDOR (48)	BR	ST PANCRAS	GLASGOW	09.20 Glasgow - St Pancras (19.28)
5	1	09.20 Glasgow - St Pancras (19.28)	THIRD OPEN (56)	LMS	ST PANCRAS	GLASGOW	09.20 Glasgow - St Pancras (19.28)
6	1	09.20 Glasgow - St Pancras (19.28)	KITCHEN CAR	LMS	ST PANCRAS	GLASGOW	09.20 Glasgow - St Pancras (19.28)
7	1	09.20 Glasgow - St Pancras (19.28)	FIRST OPEN (42)	LMS	ST PANCRAS	GLASGOW	09.20 Glasgow - St Pancras (19.28)
8	1	09.20 Glasgow - St Pancras (19.28)	COMPOSITE CORRIDOR (24/18)	BR	ST PANCRAS	GLASGOW	09.20 Glasgow - St Pancras (19.28)
9	1	09.20 Glasgow - St Pancras (19.28)	COMPOSITE CORRIDOR (24/18)	BR	ST PANCRAS	GLASGOW	09.20 Glasgow - St Pancras (19.28)
10	1	09.20 Glasgow - St Pancras (19.28)	BRAKE THIRD CORRIDOR (24)	BR	ST PANCRAS	GLASGOW	09.20 Glasgow - St Pancras (19.28)

Although taking two and a half hours more than the 10.00 Royal Scot from Euston, the Thames-Clyde was still an incomparable way of travelling from London to Glasgow and, next to the Waverley, was one of the best ways of passing a day on British Railways. Unlike the latter which ran via Melton and Nottingham, the Thames-Clyde ran down the backbone of the system via Leicester and Trent to reach Sheffield within ten minutes of the prewar three-hour yardstick after having gained twenty-three minutes on the Edinburgh train. The gap between the two trains would have narrowed to less than forty minutes by Leeds but the operators, wishing to keep a respectable interval between successive Anglo-Scottish departures from Leeds, decelerated the Glasgow train by the insertion of nine minutes recovery between Cudworth and Normanton.

Running from London to Leeds behind a 5XP 4-6-0, the train reversed at Leeds to go forward behind a Holbeck rebuilt 7P 4-6-0, the latter working through to Glasgow. The composition of the train remained unaltered throughout the 426-mile journey but had a full brake attached at Glasgow for the return journey. In common with the Waverley, BR Mark 1 stock was used other than in the three-coach dining section. A unanswered question is begged by the fact that the Thames-Clyde offered full restaurant facilities whilst the Waverley had only a buffet.

The Compound 4-4-0's disappeared from the mainstream of Midland affairs from the early 1950's with the appearance of the BR 5MT 4-6-0's although they retained an active presence at Bedford until 1954 when their role in the London suburban workings was taken over, initially, by BR Standard 2-6-4T's and, from 1955, by BR 4MT 4-6-0's. From that time their only regular appearance - often shared with a 4MT 2-6-0 - was on the 15.20 stopping train from St Pancras to Kettering. Compound 41054 of Bedford approaches St Albans with a stopping train for St Pancras - a service that includes a rather remarkable clerestory coach.

On one of its first Midland workings, Britannia Pacific 70042 'Lord Roberts' pulls away from Loughborough with the 16.25 Manchester to St Pancras on the 14 June 19 having just been transferred to Kentish Town from Stratford (GE). The bridge over the third coach carries the Great Central Marylebone - Manchester main line.

Birmingham was not a place where one expected to see LNER locomotives at work and the postwar creation of a direct service from Cleethorpes worked throughout by an Immingham B1 4-6-0 was a talking point for some years.   The service arrived in New Street at 11.13 after being routed via Nottingham, Leicester and Nuneaton; the engine being serviced on Bourneville loco before returning with the 16.50 Birmingham - Cleethorpes.   Rather strangely, the stock of the train followed a completely different pattern by going forward from Birmingham as a local train to Gloucester and not returning to Cleethorpes until the following day.   Immingham B1 4-6-0 61195 sets off light for Bourneville on 20th October 1956 after arriving in New Street with the 06.57 ex Cleethorpes.

the early 1960's Type 4 2500hp diesel-electrics were flooding the Midland system, their workings including the West of England services between Derby and Bristol ...d by 1962 is was becoming very difficult to find a Midland express service on which steam could be guaranteed.   The best bet at this time were irregular trains which ...d yet to be diagrammed to diesels, one such being the 10.20 (Fridays Only) Bristol - Sheffield which is seen making a fairly smoky start from Temple Meads behind ...bilee 4-6-0 45573 'Newfoundland' in 1962.

08.06 SHEFFIELD to GLOUCESTER (12.31)

C/W	Previous working	Vehicle	Type	From	To	Next working
1	132 19.42 Derby - Sheffield (21.18)	BRAKE THIRD CORRIDOR (32)	LMS	SHEFFIELD	GLOUCESTER	13.51 Gloucester - Birmingham (15.59)
2	132 19.42 Derby - Sheffield (21.18)	COMPOSITE CORRIDOR (18/24)	LMS	SHEFFIELD	GLOUCESTER	13.51 Gloucester - Birmingham (15.59)
3	132 19.42 Derby - Sheffield (21.18)	BRAKE THIRD CORRIDOR (32)	LMS	SHEFFIELD	GLOUCESTER	13.51 Gloucester - Birmingham (15.59)
4	133 22.10 Derby - Sheffield (23.28)	THIRD CORRIDOR (42)	LMS	SHEFFIELD	WORCESTER	16.25 Worcester - Derby (19.18)
5	133 22.10 Derby - Sheffield (23.28)	THIRD CORRIDOR (42)	LMS	SHEFFIELD	WORCESTER	16.25 Worcester - Derby (19.18)
6	133 22.10 Derby - Sheffield (23.28)	THIRD CORRIDOR (42)	LMS	SHEFFIELD	WORCESTER	16.25 Worcester - Derby (19.18)
7	133 22.10 Derby - Sheffield (23.28)	BRAKE COMPOSITE CORRIDOR (12/24)	LMS	SHEFFIELD	WORCESTER	16.25 Worcester - Derby (19.18)

In some respects, the counterpoint to the 07.54 Worcester - York, the 08.06 ex Sheffield was a stopping train dressed as an express since there were few stations in the 166-mile journey that it ignored; the first stages even including Dore and Totley and Dronfield: stations that normally saw nothing more grand than the occasional Derby or Nottingham stopping train. In reality, the service was a series of local trains merged to give the appearance of something more grand and although the operation may have saved a little empty stock and shunting work at Derby and Birmingham, there must have been quite a few through passengers who wondered, as the train paused at stations such as Repton & Willington, Wilnecote and Kingsbury, what sort of an express they were travelling on. Those who were better advised or could read a timetable, hung back at Sheffield and picked up the 07.30 Bradford to Bristol which left Sheffield seventy-nine minutes after the 08.06 but reached Cheltenham only ten minutes later.

The service consisted of two three-coach sets of stock which separated at Worcester to make their separate ways back to Sheffield later in the day.

07.15 BRADFORD to ST PANCRAS (12.25)

C/W	Previous working	Vehicle	Type	From	To	Next working
1	19 15.15 St Pancras - Bradford (20.50)	BRAKE THIRD CORRIDOR (24)	BR	BRADFORD	ST PANCRAS	15.15 St Pancras - Bradford (20.50)
2	19 15.15 St Pancras - Bradford (20.50)	THIRD CORRIDOR (48)	BR	BRADFORD	ST PANCRAS	15.15 St Pancras - Bradford (20.50)
3	19 15.15 St Pancras - Bradford (20.50)	THIRD CORRIDOR (48)	BR	BRADFORD	ST PANCRAS	15.15 St Pancras - Bradford (20.50)
4	19 15.15 St Pancras - Bradford (20.50)	THIRD CORRIDOR (48)	BR	BRADFORD	ST PANCRAS	15.15 St Pancras - Bradford (20.50)
5	19 15.15 St Pancras - Bradford (20.50)	COMPOSITE CORRIDOR (24/18)	BR	BRADFORD	ST PANCRAS	15.15 St Pancras - Bradford (20.50)
6	19 15.15 St Pancras - Bradford (20.50)	COMPOSITE CORRIDOR (24/18)	BR	BRADFORD	ST PANCRAS	15.15 St Pancras - Bradford (20.50)
7	19 15.15 St Pancras - Bradford (20.50)	BRAKE FIRST CORRIDOR (30)	LMS	BRADFORD	ST PANCRAS	15.15 St Pancras - Bradford (20.50)
8	124 15.15 St Pancras - Sheffield (18.58)	RESTAURANT FIRST (24)	LMS	SHEFFIELD	ST PANCRAS	15.15 St Pancras - Sheffield (18.58)
9	124 15.15 St Pancras - Sheffield (18.58)	THIRD OPEN (56)	LMS	SHEFFIELD	ST PANCRAS	15.15 St Pancras - Sheffield (18.58)
10	124 15.15 St Pancras - Sheffield (18.58)	THIRD CORRIDOR (42)	LMS	SHEFFIELD	ST PANCRAS	15.15 St Pancras - Sheffield (18.58)

Shown in order leaving Leeds

The position of Bradford in relation to London brought to the front one of the more absurd results of state ownership. At just over five hours, the Midland route took about an hour longer than the Great Northern from Bradford Exchange which, of course, meant that through travel to London from either Leeds or Bradford was the exception rather than the rule. Under a more flexible regime, the Midland might have been able to compete with lower fares or in some other way but competitive tactics lay at odds with the philosophy of nationalisation which resulted in the Midland's London expresses running as fast local trains between Bradford and Sheffield. Bradford also suffered the disadvantage of being on a branch from Leeds where all trains had to reverse. Great Northern trains from Bradford Exchange, on the other hand, were able to run direct to London via Wakefield and thus avoided the additional distance to Leeds and the time taken by a reversal.

In Midland terms, the 07.15 was an excellent service, especially after leaving Sheffield where it collected a three-coach restaurant set and connected with the 09.07 to St Pancras via Nottingham. After leaving Chesterfield, the 07.15 ran straight up the Erewash Valley to call at Leicester and Luton before reaching London at 12.25, fifty-two minutes after the arrival of the corresponding GN train, the 07.30 Bradford Exchange to Kings Cross.

No alterations were made to the formation in London and the train returned complete as the 15.15 St Pancras to Sheffield and Bradford.

09.09 SHEFFIELD to ST PANCRAS (13.21)

C/W	Previous working	Vehicle	Type	From	To	Next working
1	51 17.25 Bradford - Sheffield (19.23)	BRAKE THIRD CORRIDOR (24)	LMS	SHEFFIELD	ST PANCRAS	17.30 St Pancras - Nottingham (20.47)
2	51 17.25 Bradford - Sheffield (19.23)	THIRD CORRIDOR (42)	LMS	SHEFFIELD	ST PANCRAS	17.30 St Pancras - Nottingham (20.47)
3	51 17.25 Bradford - Sheffield (19.23)	COMPOSITE CORRIDOR (18/24)	LMS	SHEFFIELD	ST PANCRAS	17.30 St Pancras - Nottingham (20.47)
4	51 17.25 Bradford - Sheffield (19.23)	COMPOSITE CORRIDOR (18/24)	LMS	SHEFFIELD	ST PANCRAS	17.30 St Pancras - Nottingham (20.47)
5	51 17.25 Bradford - Sheffield (19.23)	THIRD CORRIDOR (42)	LMS	SHEFFIELD	ST PANCRAS	17.30 St Pancras - Nottingham (20.47)
6	51 17.25 Bradford - Sheffield (19.23)	BRAKE THIRD CORRIDOR (24)	LMS	SHEFFIELD	ST PANCRAS	17.30 St Pancras - Nottingham (20.47)

Conveying only half the tonnage taken by many trains, the 09.09 ex Sheffield rekindled memories of the little-and-often policy of the former Midland Railway, not only because of its light load but because it was the second train to leave Sheffield for London in eleven minutes. Few Sheffield passengers used the 09.06 as a London service since it was preceded by the 07.15 Bradford - London Restaurant Car express which ran via Trent and Leicester and reached London a good hour earlier. For the first stage of its journey the 09.09 acted as a Nottingham connection out of the 07.15 and thereafter continued as a semi-fast to St Pancras via Melton Mowbray.

It was a curiously light train for a London service and every third class seat was usually occupied by the time Bedford was reached. The return working was made at the height of the evening rush hour and in order to cope the set had to be increased in size to ten coaches. An interesting aside to what seemed to be a rather undistinguished working was the fact that the day after working the 09.09 ex Sheffield, the coaching set transferred to the West of England route by working the 07.43 Nottingham - Bristol.

08.45 BRISTOL to NEWCASTLE (16.57)

	C/W	Previous working	Vehicle	Type	From	To	Next working
		MONDAYS, WEDNESDAYS & FRIDAYS ONLY					
1	57	08.15 Newcastle - Bristol (16.02)	BRAKE THIRD CORRIDOR (24)	LMS	BRISTOL	NEWCASTLE	08.15 Newcastle - Bristol (16.02)
2	57	08.15 Newcastle - Bristol (16.02)	THIRD CORRIDOR (42)	LMS	BRISTOL	NEWCASTLE	08.15 Newcastle - Bristol (16.02)
3	57	08.15 Newcastle - Bristol (16.02)	COMPOSITE CORRIDOR (18/24)	LMS	BRISTOL	NEWCASTLE	08.15 Newcastle - Bristol (16.02)
4	57	08.15 Newcastle - Bristol (16.02)	RESTAURANT THIRD (30)	LMS	BRISTOL	NEWCASTLE	08.15 Newcastle - Bristol (16.02)
5	57	08.15 Newcastle - Bristol (16.02)	BRAKE THIRD CORRIDOR (24)	LMS	BRISTOL	NEWCASTLE	08.15 Newcastle - Bristol (16.02)
6	59	08.30 Cardiff - Gloucester	BRAKE THIRD CORRIDOR (32)	GWR	GLOUCESTER	NEWCASTLE	08.15 Newcastle - Cardiff
7	59	08.30 Cardiff - Gloucester	THIRD CORRIDOR (64)	GWR	GLOUCESTER	NEWCASTLE	08.15 Newcastle - Cardiff
8	59	08.30 Cardiff - Gloucester	COMPOSITE CORRIDOR (24/24)	GWR	GLOUCESTER	NEWCASTLE	08.15 Newcastle - Cardiff
9	59	08.30 Cardiff - Gloucester	THIRD CORRIDOR (64)	GWR	GLOUCESTER	NEWCASTLE	08.15 Newcastle - Cardiff
10	59	08.30 Cardiff - Gloucester	THIRD CORRIDOR (64)	GWR	GLOUCESTER	NEWCASTLE	08.15 Newcastle - Cardiff
11	59	08.30 Cardiff - Gloucester	THIRD CORRIDOR (64)	GWR	GLOUCESTER	NEWCASTLE	08.15 Newcastle - Cardiff
12	59	08.30 Cardiff - Gloucester	BRAKE THIRD CORRIDOR (32)	GWR	GLOUCESTER	NEWCASTLE	08.15 Newcastle - Cardiff
		TUESDAYS & THURSDAYS ONLY					
1	58	08.15 Newcastle - Bristol (16.02)	BRAKE THIRD CORRIDOR (24)	BR	BRISTOL	NEWCASTLE	08.15 Newcastle - Bristol (16.02)
2	58	08.15 Newcastle - Bristol (16.02)	THIRD CORRIDOR (48)	BR	BRISTOL	NEWCASTLE	08.15 Newcastle - Bristol (16.02)
3	58	08.15 Newcastle - Bristol (16.02)	COMPOSITE CORRIDOR (24/18)	LNER	BRISTOL	NEWCASTLE	08.15 Newcastle - Bristol (16.02)
4	58	08.15 Newcastle - Bristol (16.02)	RESTAURANT UNCLASSED (24)	BR	BRISTOL	NEWCASTLE	08.15 Newcastle - Bristol (16.02)
5	58	08.15 Newcastle - Bristol (16.02)	BRAKE THIRD CORRIDOR (24)	BR	BRISTOL	NEWCASTLE	08.15 Newcastle - Bristol (16.02)
6	60	08.30 Cardiff - Gloucester	BRAKE THIRD CORRIDOR (24)	BR	GLOUCESTER	NEWCASTLE	08.15 Newcastle - Cardiff
7	60	08.30 Cardiff - Gloucester	THIRD CORRIDOR (48)	BR	GLOUCESTER	NEWCASTLE	08.15 Newcastle - Cardiff
8	60	08.30 Cardiff - Gloucester	COMPOSITE CORRIDOR (24/18)	BR	GLOUCESTER	NEWCASTLE	08.15 Newcastle - Cardiff
9	60	08.30 Cardiff - Gloucester	THIRD CORRIDOR (48)	BR	GLOUCESTER	NEWCASTLE	08.15 Newcastle - Cardiff
10	60	08.30 Cardiff - Gloucester	THIRD CORRIDOR (42)	LNER	GLOUCESTER	NEWCASTLE	08.15 Newcastle - Cardiff
11	60	08.30 Cardiff - Gloucester	THIRD CORRIDOR (42)	LNER	GLOUCESTER	NEWCASTLE	08.15 Newcastle - Cardiff
12	60	08.30 Cardiff - Gloucester	BRAKE THIRD CORRIDOR (24)	BR	GLOUCESTER	NEWCASTLE	08.15 Newcastle - Cardiff

Note: All BR Standard Stock allocated to the NER

Shown in order of leaving Gloucester

Although its West of England main line came very close to the Welsh border, little interest was shown by the Midland in running through services to South Wales, not the least of the reasons being the fact that access to Cardiff could only be achieved by running over the Swindon - Gloucester - Severn Tunnel Junction line of the Great Western which meant a complex and difficult liaison between Derby and Paddington and the various district offices involved. Neither 1923 nor 1948 did very much in bringing the railways any closer to each other. In spite of these difficulties, 1952 saw the introduction of the through coaches between Cardiff and Newcastle, a joint LM/GW/NE operation in which one set of coaches was provided by Newcastle whilst another was shared between Cardiff and Bristol. Interestingly the LNER set consisted almost entirely of BR Mark 1 vehicles whilst the other was formed of LMS and GWR stock. The decision to run the Newcastle service as a combined Cardiff and Bristol service posed a considerable problem regarding the combining of the portions at Gloucester since there were only very limited connections between the two systems. The solution arrived at was to run the Bristol section into Gloucester Central (GW) via Standish Junction where it combined with the section from Cardiff, the Bristol coaches changing direction as a result. The motive power were, to say the least, interesting since they involved a Midland 2P from Bristol to Gloucester, a 43xx 2-6-0 (later a Castle 4-6-0 or Britannia 4-6-2) between Cardiff and Gloucester with the usual 5XP 4-6-0 on the main section of the journey. The last leg from Heaton to Newcastle was handled by a Newcastle (Heaton) A3 Pacific.

Although the train was a tolerably good instance of cross-country working, it had its weak points. It did not cater particularly well for passengers going to Scotland; at Newcastle a connection was made with the down Queen of Scots to Edinburgh Glasgow whilst those who objected to the Pullman supplement had to spend over two and a quarter hours waiting for the Heart of Midlothian to arrive. With a slightly earlier start and some adjustment of times - was it really essential to stop the train at Mangotsfield, Tamworth, Burton and Chesterfield? - it should have been possible to have reached Sheffield in time to connect with the down Thames-Clyde Express.

Although a restaurant car was included in the Cardiff portion and ran through to Newcastle, it was staffed and operated as a buffet car.

10.15 ST PANCRAS to MANCHESTER CENTRAL (14.32)

	C/W	Previous working	Vehicle	Type	From	To	Next working
1	29	16.00 Manchester - St Pancras (20.34)	BRAKE THIRD CORRIDOR (24)	BR	ST PANCRAS	MANCHESTER	16.00 Manchester - St Pancras (20.34)
2	29	16.00 Manchester - St Pancras (20.34)	COMPOSITE CORRIDOR (24/18)	BR	ST PANCRAS	MANCHESTER	16.00 Manchester - St Pancras (20.34)
3	29	16.00 Manchester - St Pancras (20.34)	THIRD CORRIDOR (48)	BR	ST PANCRAS	MANCHESTER	16.00 Manchester - St Pancras (20.34)
4	29	16.00 Manchester - St Pancras (20.34)	THIRD OPEN (64)	BR	ST PANCRAS	MANCHESTER	16.00 Manchester - St Pancras (20.34)
5	29	16.00 Manchester - St Pancras (20.34)	KITCHEN BUFFET	LMS	ST PANCRAS	MANCHESTER	16.00 Manchester - St Pancras (20.34)
6	29	16.00 Manchester - St Pancras (20.34)	BRAKE THIRD CORRIDOR (24)	LMS	ST PANCRAS	MANCHESTER	16.00 Manchester - St Pancras (20.34)
7	29	16.00 Manchester - St Pancras (20.34)	COMPOSITE CORRIDOR (18/24)	LMS	ST PANCRAS	MANCHESTER	16.00 Manchester - St Pancras (20.34)
8	29	16.00 Manchester - St Pancras (20.34)	COMPOSITE CORRIDOR (18/24)	LMS	ST PANCRAS	MANCHESTER	16.00 Manchester - St Pancras (20.34)
9	29	16.00 Manchester - St Pancras (20.34)	BRAKE THIRD CORRIDOR (24)	LMS	ST PANCRAS	MANCHESTER	16.00 Manchester - St Pancras (20.34)
10	29A	15.35 Derby - St Pancras (18.14)	COMPOSITE CORRIDOR (18/24)	LMS	ST PANCRAS	DERBY	15.35 Derby - St Pancras (18.14)

Leaving at the time of day when demand was at its highest, the 10.15 was - by the narrowest of margins - the fastest Manchester service of the day and was also notable for making a very fast turn-round in Manchester before returning as the 16.00 back to London. Unlike the preceding 08.15, it retained its dining service throughout but at the cost of shedding a coach at Derby in order to keep the train to within the 310-ton special limit loading for the Peak District section. Unfortunately the resulting nine-coach train had insufficient accommodation for the popular 16.00 Manchester to London and was strengthened by a vehicle that had come down with the 08.15 from St Pancras. The ten-coach formation was then over the limit for an unaided Jubilee 4-6-0 but to save the expense and trouble of providing a 2P 4-4-0 pilot to Derby, the train was downgraded from Special Limit to Limited Load, the few minutes difference being within the capacity of a 5XP 4-6-0.

07.24 MANCHESTER CENTRAL to DERBY (10.01)

C/W	Previous working	Vehicle	Type	From	To	Next working
1	30	18.40 St Pancras - Manchester (23.08)	BRAKE THIRD CORRIDOR (24)	LMS	MANCHESTER	DERBY	12.05 Derby - St Pancras (15.12)
2	30	18.40 St Pancras - Manchester (23.08)	COMPOSITE CORRIDOR (18/24)	LMS	MANCHESTER	DERBY	12.05 Derby - St Pancras (15.12)
3	30	18.40 St Pancras - Manchester (23.08)	COMPOSITE CORRIDOR (18/24)	LMS	MANCHESTER	DERBY	12.05 Derby - St Pancras (15.12)
4	30	18.40 St Pancras - Manchester (23.08)	BRAKE THIRD CORRIDOR (24)	LMS	MANCHESTER	DERBY	12.05 Derby - St Pancras (15.12)

Even though there sometimes used the same type of stock, generally local and express services belonged to two entirely separate camps; a fact that made the handful of trains that crossed the boundary objects of particular fascination. One such was the 07.24 from Manchester Central which was remarkable only for calling at every station (except Derby, Nottingham Road which only operated for short periods during the rush hours) between Manchester and Derby and taking over two and a half hours to complete the journey. If any of its passengers gave any thought to what the train did after reaching Derby, few would guess that it spent the remainder of the day engaged in express work, firstly by providing part of the stock for the 12.05 Derby to St Pancras - the service that often used the early BR diesels when they were operating on the Midland - and secondly by forming the Manchester section of the late-evening business express from London.

07.30 BRADFORD to BRISTOL (13.37)

C/W	Previous working	Vehicle	Type	From	To	Next working
1	40	07.50 Sheffield - Bradford (09.55)	BRAKE THIRD CORRIDOR (24)	LMS	BRADFORD	BRISTOL	16.45 Bristol - York (23.02)
2	40A	21.45 Leeds - Bradford (22.33)	THIRD CORRIDOR (42)	LMS	BRADFORD	BRISTOL	16.45 Bristol - York (23.02)
3	40A	21.45 Leeds - Bradford (22.33)	THIRD CORRIDOR (42)	LMS	BRADFORD	BRISTOL	16.45 Bristol - York (23.02)
4	40	07.50 Sheffield - Bradford (09.55)	THIRD CORRIDOR (42)	LMS	BRADFORD	BRISTOL	16.45 Bristol - York (23.02)
5	40	07.50 Sheffield - Bradford (09.55)	COMPOSITE CORRIDOR (18/24)	LMS	BRADFORD	BRISTOL	16.45 Bristol - York (23.02)
6	40	07.50 Sheffield - Bradford (09.55)	COMPOSITE CORRIDOR (18/24)	LMS	BRADFORD	BRISTOL	16.45 Bristol - York (23.02)
7	40	07.50 Sheffield - Bradford (09.55)	THIRD CORRIDOR (42)	LMS	BRADFORD	BRISTOL	16.45 Bristol - York (23.02)
8	40	07.50 Sheffield - Bradford (09.55)	BRAKE THIRD CORRIDOR (24)	LMS	BRADFORD	BRISTOL	16.45 Bristol - York (23.02)
9	153	16.45 Bristol - Derby (20.21)	RESTAURANT THIRD (30)	LMS	DERBY	BRISTOL	16.45 Bristol - Derby (20.21)
10	153	16.45 Bristol - Derby (20.21)	THIRD CORRIDOR (42)	LMS	DERBY	BRISTOL	16.45 Bristol - Derby (20.21)

South of Derby the Midland's West of England trains were a pretty stirring sight and probably represented the high point of British cross-country services, not that that is saying a great deal. North of Derby the picture was often rather less impressive and the 07.30 Bradford - Bristol was no exception since it was booked to stop every twenty minutes or so between Leeds and Chesterfield with seven minutes being granted at Sheffield to allow a pair of London trains to get well ahead. After Derby, where a strengthening coach and a restaurant car (working as a buffet) was attached, the running became more express-like with stops being confined to the larger of the intermediate stations. Bristol was reached just in time to connect with the 11.10 Swansea - Penzance (20.25); the stock being taken out to Lawrence Hill to be cleaned before returning to Temple Meads for the 16.45 Bristol to York.

09.00 MANCHESTER CENTRAL to ST PANCRAS (14.00)

C/W	Previous working	Vehicle	Type	From	To	Next working
1	24	14.15 St Pancras - Manchester (18.35)	BRAKE THIRD CORRIDOR (24)	LMS	MANCHESTER	ST PANCRAS	16.15 St Pancras - Manchester (20.47)
2	24	14.15 St Pancras - Manchester (18.35)	COMPOSITE CORRIDOR (18/24)	LMS	MANCHESTER	ST PANCRAS	16.15 St Pancras - Manchester (20.47)
3	24C	16.15 St Pancras - Manchester (20.47)	COMPOSITE CORRIDOR (18/24)	LMS	MANCHESTER	ST PANCRAS	16.15 St Pancras - Manchester (20.47)
4	24	14.15 St Pancras - Manchester (18.35)	FIRST CORRIDOR (36)	LMS	MANCHESTER	ST PANCRAS	16.15 St Pancras - Manchester (20.47)
5	24	14.15 St Pancras - Manchester (18.35)	RESTAURANT FIRST (24)	LMS	MANCHESTER	ST PANCRAS	16.15 St Pancras - Manchester (20.47)
6	24	14.15 St Pancras - Manchester (18.35)	THIRD OPEN (56)	LMS	MANCHESTER	ST PANCRAS	16.15 St Pancras - Manchester (20.47)
7	24	14.15 St Pancras - Manchester (18.35)	THIRD CORRIDOR (42)	LMS	MANCHESTER	ST PANCRAS	16.15 St Pancras - Manchester (20.47)
8	24	14.15 St Pancras - Manchester (18.35)	THIRD CORRIDOR (42)	LMS	MANCHESTER	ST PANCRAS	16.15 St Pancras - Manchester (20.47)
9	24	14.15 St Pancras - Manchester (18.35)	BRAKE THIRD CORRIDOR (24)	LMS	MANCHESTER	ST PANCRAS	16.15 St Pancras - Manchester (20.47)
10	101	09.39 Buxton - Millers Dale (09.48)	BRAKE COMPOSITE CORRIDOR (12/21)	LMS	MILLERS DALE	ST PANCRAS	14.15 St Pancras - Manchester (18.35)
11	24A	16.45 Bristol - Derby (20.22)	THIRD CORRIDOR (42)	LMS	DERBY	ST PANCRAS	17.32 St Pancras - Nottingham (20.47)

Although the 07.20 from the Central was the principal morning London express, it was too early a departure for many and the 09.00 ex Manchester was equally well-used although it was scarcely the most direct of trains since it ran from Derby to Kettering via Nottingham and Melton instead of the direct route via Leicester. It was also a heavy train by Midland standards, its 5XP 4-6-0 taking nine vehicles over the Peak to Millers Dale where the daily Buxton - London coach was added. At Derby an eleventh vehicle - which had worked in from Bristol the previous evening - was added. The return service was the 16.15 St Pancras to Manchester; the Buxton coach being left behind until the following day when it was reunited with the others in the 14.15 from London to Manchester. The main portion alternated daily between the 14.15 and 16.15 expresses from St Pancras.

08.46 BRADFORD to SCARBOROUGH (11.14)

C/W	Previous working	Vehicle	Type	From	To	Next working
1	41	16.22 Scarborough - Bradford	BRAKE THIRD CORRIDOR (24)	LMS	BRADFORD	SCARBOROUGH	16.22 Scarborough - Bradford
2	41	16.22 Scarborough - Bradford	THIRD CORRIDOR (42)	LMS	BRADFORD	SCARBOROUGH	16.22 Scarborough - Bradford
3	41	16.22 Scarborough - Bradford	COMPOSITE CORRIDOR (18/24)	LMS	BRADFORD	SCARBOROUGH	16.22 Scarborough - Bradford
4	41	16.22 Scarborough - Bradford	COMPOSITE CORRIDOR (18/24)	LMS	BRADFORD	SCARBOROUGH	16.22 Scarborough - Bradford
5	41	16.22 Scarborough - Bradford	THIRD CORRIDOR (42)	LMS	BRADFORD	SCARBOROUGH	16.22 Scarborough - Bradford
6	41	16.22 Scarborough - Bradford	THIRD CORRIDOR (42)	LMS	BRADFORD	SCARBOROUGH	16.22 Scarborough - Bradford
7	41	16.22 Scarborough - Bradford	THIRD CORRIDOR (42)	LMS	BRADFORD	SCARBOROUGH	16.22 Scarborough - Bradford
8	41	16.22 Scarborough - Bradford	THIRD CORRIDOR (42)	LMS	BRADFORD	SCARBOROUGH	16.22 Scarborough - Bradford
9	41	16.22 Scarborough - Bradford	THIRD CORRIDOR (42)	LMS	BRADFORD	SCARBOROUGH	16.22 Scarborough - Bradford
10	41	16.22 Scarborough - Bradford	BRAKE THIRD CORRIDOR (24)	LMS	BRADFORD	SCARBOROUGH	16.22 Scarborough - Bradford

At any time between April and October, the slightest glimmer of sunshine would sow the seeds for a day at Scarborough, the North-East's most popular resort, amongst enough local families to fill a good-sized trains and for this reason the 08.46 was diagrammed for no less than ten coaches. The train was also part of the Leeds rush-hour whilst loadings between York and Leeds were usually high so a solid formation was called for in any event. Some problems arose with the motive power arrangements since the operating department called for a class 5 engine whilst Manningham had nothing larger than either a Compound 4-4-0 or a 2-6-4 tank. The solution arrived at was to use the Holbeck 5MT 4-6-0 which arrived with the 06.55 Leeds - Bradford, returning it on the 12.38 Scarborough to Leeds. The 16.22 from Scarborough, the return service of the 08.46, was worked to Bradford by a Neville Hill B1 4-6-0.

10.15 GLOUCESTER to WORCESTER (11.20)

	C/W Previous working	Vehicle	Type	From	To	Next working
1	52A 17.15 Sheffield - Gloucester (21.49)	BRAKE THIRD CORRIDOR (24)	LMS	GLOUCESTER	WORCESTER	07.45 Worcester - York (12.50)
2	52A 17.15 Sheffield - Gloucester (21.49)	THIRD CORRIDOR (42)	LMS	GLOUCESTER	WORCESTER	07.45 Worcester - York (12.50)
3	52A 17.15 Sheffield - Gloucester (21.49)	COMPOSITE CORRIDOR (18/24)	LMS	GLOUCESTER	WORCESTER	07.45 Worcester - York (12.50)
4	52A 17.15 Sheffield - Gloucester (21.49)	COMPOSITE CORRIDOR (18/24)	LMS	GLOUCESTER	WORCESTER	07.45 Worcester - York (12.50)
5	52A 17.15 Sheffield - Gloucester (21.49)	THIRD CORRIDOR (42)	LMS	GLOUCESTER	WORCESTER	07.45 Worcester - York (12.50)
6	52A 17.15 Sheffield - Gloucester (21.49)	THIRD CORRIDOR (42)	LMS	GLOUCESTER	WORCESTER	07.45 Worcester - York (12.50)
7	52A 17.15 Sheffield - Gloucester (21.49)	THIRD CORRIDOR (42)	LMS	GLOUCESTER	WORCESTER	07.45 Worcester - York (12.50)
8	52A 17.15 Sheffield - Gloucester (21.49)	BRAKE THIRD CORRIDOR (24)	LMS	GLOUCESTER	WORCESTER	07.45 Worcester - York (12.50)

In spite of its commercial importance, Gloucester did not feature prominently in the passenger workings of the Midland and Eastgate was little more than a calling point for expresses on the Bristol - Derby route. Most of the services originating at Gloucester were local trains to Birmingham or Bristol, some of which attracted considerable attention during the late 1950's by being the preserve of the surviving Compound 4-4-0's. The very few main line services that terminated in the area were somewhat haphazardly arranged with an unbalanced 17.15 Sheffield to Gloucester and 07.45 Worcester to York. The two workings were brought together by the rather strange business of leaving the stock in the area for an entire day and using it for an hour in a local train between Gloucester and Worcester with the result that three sets of stock were used in the complete cycle when with a little adjustment of the carriage workings, two might have sufficed.

10.40 ST PANCRAS to LEICESTER (13.32)

	C/W Previous working	Vehicle	Type	From	To	Next working
1		THIRD CORRIDOR (42)	LMS	ST PANCRAS	LEICESTER	14.35 Leicester - Nottingham (15.36)
2	18.15 Nottingham - St Pancras (21.56)	BRAKE THIRD CORRIDOR (32)	LMS	ST PANCRAS	LEICESTER	14.35 Leicester - Nottingham (15.36)
3	18.15 Nottingham - St Pancras (21.56)	COMPOSITE CORRIDOR (18/32)	LMS	ST PANCRAS	LEICESTER	14.35 Leicester - Nottingham (15.36)
4	18.15 Nottingham - St Pancras (21.56)	BRAKE THIRD CORRIDOR (32)	LMS	ST PANCRAS	LEICESTER	14.35 Leicester - Nottingham (15.36)
5	18.15 Nottingham - St Pancras (21.56)	BRAKE THIRD CORRIDOR (32)	LMS	ST PANCRAS	BEDFORD	18.06 Bedford - Kettering (18.52)
6	18.15 Nottingham - St Pancras (21.56)	COMPOSITE CORRIDOR (18/32)	LMS	ST PANCRAS	BEDFORD	18.06 Bedford - Kettering (18.52)
7	18.15 Nottingham - St Pancras (21.56)	BRAKE THIRD CORRIDOR (32)	LMS	ST PANCRAS	BEDFORD	18.06 Bedford - Kettering (18.52)
8		THIRD CORRIDOR (42)	LMS	ST PANCRAS	BEDFORD	18.06 Bedford - Kettering (18.52)

A stopping train which, like the 09.05 ex St Pancras, was technically a local train, the 10.40 ran in connection with the 11.45 St Pancras to Bradford. Far less of an express than the 09.05, the 10.40 dropped half its load at Bedford partly to provide stock for an evening local to Nottingham via Kettering and partly to make life easier on the run over Sharnbrook, and then degenerated into a class B local from Kettering calling at all stations to Leicester. The leading section of the train formed a stopping train from Leicester to Nottingham (where it married up to the previous day's Bedford section) via Trent and returned to London as the 18.15 semi-fast.

10.20 BRISTOL to NEWCASTLE (18.30)

	C/W Previous working	Vehicle	Type	From	To	Next working
		OPERATES ON MONDAYS, WEDNESDAYS & FRIDAYS ONLY				
1	64 12.37 Newcastle - Bristol (20.23)	BRAKE THIRD CORRIDOR (24)	BR	BRISTOL	NEWCASTLE	12.37 Newcastle - Bristol (20.23)
2	64 12.37 Newcastle - Bristol (20.23)	THIRD CORRIDOR (48)	BR	BRISTOL	NEWCASTLE	12.37 Newcastle - Bristol (20.23)
3	64 12.37 Newcastle - Bristol (20.23)	THIRD CORRIDOR (48)	BR	BRISTOL	NEWCASTLE	12.37 Newcastle - Bristol (20.23)
4	64 12.37 Newcastle - Bristol (20.23)	THIRD CORRIDOR (48)	BR	BRISTOL	NEWCASTLE	12.37 Newcastle - Bristol (20.23)
5	64 12.37 Newcastle - Bristol (20.23)	THIRD CORRIDOR (48)	BR	BRISTOL	NEWCASTLE	12.37 Newcastle - Bristol (20.23)
6	64 12.37 Newcastle - Bristol (20.23)	THIRD CORRIDOR (48)	BR	BRISTOL	NEWCASTLE	12.37 Newcastle - Bristol (20.23)
7	64 12.37 Newcastle - Bristol (20.23)	THIRD OPEN (64)	BR	BRISTOL	NEWCASTLE	12.37 Newcastle - Bristol (20.23)
8	64 12.37 Newcastle - Bristol (20.23)	RESTAURANT COMPOSITE (12/18)	LMS	BRISTOL	NEWCASTLE	12.37 Newcastle - Bristol (20.23)
9	64 12.37 Newcastle - Bristol (20.23)	FIRST CORRIDOR (42)	BR	BRISTOL	NEWCASTLE	12.37 Newcastle - Bristol (20.23)
10	64 12.37 Newcastle - Bristol (20.23)	BRAKE THIRD CORRIDOR (24)	BR	BRISTOL	NEWCASTLE	12.37 Newcastle - Bristol (20.23)
		Note. All BR Standard stock allocated to the LMR (Bristol)				
		OPERATES ON TUESDAYS & THURSDAYS ONLY				
1	65 12.37 Newcastle - Bristol (20.23)	BRAKE THIRD CORRIDOR (24)	BR	BRISTOL	NEWCASTLE	12.37 Newcastle - Bristol (20.23)
2	65 12.37 Newcastle - Bristol (20.23)	THIRD CORRIDOR (48)	BR	BRISTOL	NEWCASTLE	12.37 Newcastle - Bristol (20.23)
3	65 12.37 Newcastle - Bristol (20.23)	THIRD CORRIDOR (48)	BR	BRISTOL	NEWCASTLE	12.37 Newcastle - Bristol (20.23)
4	65 12.37 Newcastle - Bristol (20.23)	THIRD CORRIDOR (48)	BR	BRISTOL	NEWCASTLE	12.37 Newcastle - Bristol (20.23)
5	65 12.37 Newcastle - Bristol (20.23)	THIRD CORRIDOR (48)	BR	BRISTOL	NEWCASTLE	12.37 Newcastle - Bristol (20.23)
6	65 12.37 Newcastle - Bristol (20.23)	THIRD CORRIDOR (48)	BR	BRISTOL	NEWCASTLE	12.37 Newcastle - Bristol (20.23)
7	65 12.37 Newcastle - Bristol (20.23)	THIRD OPEN (48)	LNER	BRISTOL	NEWCASTLE	12.37 Newcastle - Bristol (20.23)
8	65 12.37 Newcastle - Bristol (20.23)	RESTAURANT FIRST (18)	LNER	BRISTOL	NEWCASTLE	12.37 Newcastle - Bristol (20.23)
9	65 12.37 Newcastle - Bristol (20.23)	FIRST CORRIDOR (24)	BR	BRISTOL	NEWCASTLE	12.37 Newcastle - Bristol (20.23)
10	65 12.37 Newcastle - Bristol (20.23)	BRAKE THIRD CORRIDOR (24)	BR	BRISTOL	NEWCASTLE	12.37 Newcastle - Bristol (20.23)
		Note: All BR Standard Stock allocated to the NER				

The second through Newcastle service of the day from Bristol, the 10.20 Bristol - Newcastle was also a joint venture and, like the 08.45 ex Temple Meads, consisted of two alternating NER and an LMR sets of coaches. Unfortunately for the purist, neither set was easy to distinguish from the other since both were formed of BR Mark 1 stock. The easiest way to spot the difference, apart from looking at the carriage numbers, was by the dining cars which both pre-dated British Railways. (In this connection it is interesting to note how much the catering accomodation varied. The NER provided 66 seats whilst the LM had nearly half as much again at 94).

Having a straightforward run, unlike the 08.45, through the Gloucester district and by running non-stop between Birmingham and Burton, the 10.20 was almost half an hour faster to Sheffield than the earlier train although the advantage was lost on the North Eastern sector since the 10.20 was routed via Stockton, West Hartlepool and Sunderland whilst the 08.45 followed the main line through Darlington and Durham.

The variety of motive power employed was almost as varied as that of the earlier train and although the 10.20 did not have the extremes of a 2P and a Gresley Pacific, it was unusual in being worked forward from Sheffield by an LNER V2 instead of being taken over the S&K Joint, as was usual, by an LMS 4-6-0. The V2 did not remain long with the train and was exchanged at York for a Heaton-based A1 Pacific.

On the West of England road a Black 5 on limited load timings could only be expected to maintain running times with up to eleven vehicles. Anything beyond that and either loss of time had to be accepted by the operators or a pilot provided. In the above view, the latter course has been chosen as a Compound 4-4-0 double-heads a Black Fiv 4-6-0 on a West of England relief at Clay Mills, near Burton on Trent.

12.15 BIRMINGHAM to GLOUCESTER (14.21)

	C/W	Previous working	Vehicle	Type	From	To	Next working
1	87	06.57 Cleethorpes - Birmingham (11.13)	**BRAKE THIRD CORRIDOR (24)**	LMS	**BIRMINGHAM**	**GLOUCESTER**	13.51 Gloucester - Birmingham (15.59)
2	87	06.57 Cleethorpes - Birmingham (11.13)	**THIRD CORRIDOR (42)**	LMS	**BIRMINGHAM**	**GLOUCESTER**	13.51 Gloucester - Birmingham (15.59)
3	87	06.57 Cleethorpes - Birmingham (11.13)	**COMPOSITE CORRIDOR (18/24)**	LMS	**BIRMINGHAM**	**GLOUCESTER**	13.51 Gloucester - Birmingham (15.59)
4	87	06.57 Cleethorpes - Birmingham (11.13)	**THIRD CORRIDOR (42)**	LMS	**BIRMINGHAM**	**GLOUCESTER**	13.51 Gloucester - Birmingham (15.59)
5	87	06.57 Cleethorpes - Birmingham (11.13)	**BRAKE THIRD CORRIDOR (24)**	LMS	**BIRMINGHAM**	**GLOUCESTER**	13.51 Gloucester - Birmingham (15.59)

Instances of an LNER B1 handing over to a Midland 4-4-0 Compound were, to say the least, rare but the unlikely exchange was a daily feature of operations at Birmingham New Street as the set of coaches which arrived with the 06.57 from Cleethorpes went forward an hour later as the 12.15 Gloucester stopping train. The Immingham B1 4-6-0 which arrived from Cleethorpes had not at that time been cleared for passage west of Kings Norton and therefore the 12.15 had to be given another engine; in this case the Compound 4-4-0 which had worked in with the 07.50 ex Gloucester. The B1 retired light to Bourneville shed to be made ready for the 16.50 Birmingham - Cleethorpes.

10.10 SHEFFIELD to BIRMINGHAM (12.09)

	C/W	Previous working	Vehicle	Type	From	To	Next working
1	68	14.38 Birmingham - Sheffield (16.33)	**BRAKE THIRD CORRIDOR (24)**	LMS	**SHEFFIELD**	**BIRMINGHAM**	**12.42 Birmingham - B'mouth (17.32)**
2	68	14.38 Birmingham - Sheffield (16.33)	**COMPOSITE CORRIDOR (18/24)**	LMS	**SHEFFIELD**	**BIRMINGHAM**	**12.42 Birmingham - B'mouth (17.32)**
3	50	16.15 York - Sheffield (18.06)	**BRAKE THIRD CORRIDOR (24)**	LMS	**SHEFFIELD**	**BIRMINGHAM**	08.05 Birmingham - Newcastle (13.03)
4	50	16.15 York - Sheffield (18.06)	**THIRD CORRIDOR (42)**	LMS	**SHEFFIELD**	**BIRMINGHAM**	08.05 Birmingham - Newcastle (13.03)
5	50	16.15 York - Sheffield (18.06)	**COMPOSITE CORRIDOR (18/24)**	LMS	**SHEFFIELD**	**BIRMINGHAM**	08.05 Birmingham - Newcastle (13.03)
6	50	16.15 York - Sheffield (18.06)	**COMPOSITE CORRIDOR (18/24)**	LMS	**SHEFFIELD**	**BIRMINGHAM**	08.05 Birmingham - Newcastle (13.03)
7	50	16.15 York - Sheffield (18.06)	**THIRD CORRIDOR (42)**	LMS	**SHEFFIELD**	**BIRMINGHAM**	08.05 Birmingham - Newcastle (13.03)
8	50	16.15 York - Sheffield (18.06)	**BRAKE THIRD CORRIDOR (24)**	LMS	**SHEFFIELD**	**BIRMINGHAM**	08.05 Birmingham - Newcastle (13.03)

Looking for all the world like any other Midland semi-fast service, the 10.10 from Sheffield conveyed a pair of through coaches for Bournemouth and was therefore a close relative to the Pines Express; the service which took the section forward from Birmingham. The main six-coach section of the service was part of the celebrated cyclic working which took it all over the system; its next working being the morning Birmingham - Newcastle express.

On Mondays and Fridays during the summer a substitute set of nine vehicles was employed, all of which ran through to Bournemouth to return as the 09.30 (Friday) and 09.55 (Saturday) Bournemouth to Sheffield.

09.12 BRADFORD to ST PANCRAS (14.15)

	C/W	Previous working	Vehicle	Type	From	To	Next working
1	18	16.50 St Pancras - Bradford (22.42)	**BRAKE THIRD CORRIDOR (24)**	BR	**BRADFORD**	**ST PANCRAS**	16.50 St Pancras - Bradford (22.42)
2	18	16.50 St Pancras - Bradford (22.42)	**COMPOSITE CORRIDOR (24/18)**	BR	**BRADFORD**	**ST PANCRAS**	16.50 St Pancras - Bradford (22.42)
3	18	16.50 St Pancras - Bradford (22.42)	**BRAKE FIRST CORRIDOR (30)**	LMS	**BRADFORD**	**ST PANCRAS**	16.50 St Pancras - Bradford (22.42)
4	18	16.50 St Pancras - Bradford (22.42)	**FIRST CORRIDOR (36)**	LMS	**BRADFORD**	**ST PANCRAS**	16.50 St Pancras - Bradford (22.42)
5	18	16.50 St Pancras - Bradford (22.42)	**FIRST OPEN (42)**	BR	**BRADFORD**	**ST PANCRAS**	16.50 St Pancras - Bradford (22.42)
6	18	16.50 St Pancras - Bradford (22.42)	**KITCHEN CAR**	LMS	**BRADFORD**	**ST PANCRAS**	16.50 St Pancras - Bradford (22.42)
7	18	16.50 St Pancras - Bradford (22.42)	**THIRD OPEN (64)**	BR	**BRADFORD**	**ST PANCRAS**	16.50 St Pancras - Bradford (22.42)
8	18	16.50 St Pancras - Bradford (22.42)	**THIRD CORRIDOR (48)**	BR	**BRADFORD**	**ST PANCRAS**	16.50 St Pancras - Bradford (22.42)
9	18	16.50 St Pancras - Bradford (22.42)	**THIRD CORRIDOR (48)**	BR	**BRADFORD**	**ST PANCRAS**	16.50 St Pancras - Bradford (22.42)
10	18	16.50 St Pancras - Bradford (22.42)	**BRAKE THIRD CORRIDOR (24)**	BR	**BRADFORD**	**ST PANCRAS**	16.50 St Pancras - Bradford (22.42)

Shown in order leaving Leeds

Had there been a strand of justice in BR's train-naming policy, the 09.12 ex Bradford would certainly have been a beneficiary since not only wa it the fastest Bradford train of the day but it ran from Leeds to London with no more than three stops and with its return service, achieved the very high carriage utilisation of 424 miles per day. The service was further noteworthy since the entire working was covered intact; the dining section working throughout and not being attached, as was often done, at Sheffield. The set had a remarkably short turn-round at St Pancras - no alteration to the formation was made - before returning north with the 16.50 to Bradford.

From 1943 until 1957 the only section of the Midland to see class 7P 4-6-0's regularly at work was the Leeds - Carlisle section; Holbeck having an allocation of eight engines to work three daily turns between Leeds and Glasgow. Rebuilt Royal Scot 4-6-0 46133 'The Green Howards' passes Skipton with the down Thames-Clyde Express in October 1954. These engines were allowed to haul fifty-five tons more than a 5XP 4-6-0 between Leeds and Carlisle.

	C/W Previous working	Vehicle	Type	From	To	Next working
		15.10 SHEFFIELD to HULL				
1	129 09.15 Hull - Sheffield (11.03)	**NON-CORRIDOR THIRD (80)**	LNER	SHEFFIELD	HULL	09.15 Hull - Sheffield (11.03)
2	129 09.15 Hull - Sheffield (11.03)	**BRAKE THIRD CORRIDOR (24)**	LNER	SHEFFIELD	HULL	09.15 Hull - Sheffield (11.03)
3	129 09.15 Hull - Sheffield (11.03)	**THIRD CORRIDOR (64)**	LNER	SHEFFIELD	HULL	09.15 Hull - Sheffield (11.03)
4	129 09.15 Hull - Sheffield (11.03)	**THIRD CORRIDOR (64)**	LNER	SHEFFIELD	HULL	09.15 Hull - Sheffield (11.03)
5	129 09.15 Hull - Sheffield (11.03)	**COMPOSITE CORRIDOR (21/32)**	LNER	SHEFFIELD	HULL	09.15 Hull - Sheffield (11.03)
6	129 09.15 Hull - Sheffield (11.03)	**BRAKE THIRD CORRIDOR (24)**	LNER	SHEFFIELD	HULL	09.15 Hull - Sheffield (11.03)

Although there had once been two Midland-based services between Sheffield and Hull, the majority of workings under BR ran from Sheffield Victoria via Doncaster and, it has to be said, were not particularly numerous. One of the services had shut down as early as 1932; this being the Hull & Barnsley route which had diverged at Cudworth and had consisted of three through daily services between Hull (Cannon Street) and Sheffield Midland. The surviving working into Sheffield Midland was a North Eastern service involving a Hull D49 4-4-0 and six LNER vehicles which left Hull at 09.15 and returned from Sheffield at 15.10 after connecting with the 10.15 Bristol - Newcastle. In addition to the basic formation of five corridor vehicles, an LNER non-corridor strengthening coach was conveyed next to the engine for the benefit of school traffic which joined the service at Mexborough and Doncaster.

	C/W Previous working	Vehicle	Type	From	To	Next working
		12.40 KINGS NORTON to BIRMINGHAM				
1	90 09.00 Yarmouth - Birmingham (15.38)	**THIRD CORRIDOR (42)**	LMS	KINGS NORTON	BIRMINGHAM	13.45 Birmingham - Yarmouth
2	90 09.00 Yarmouth - Birmingham (15.38)	**THIRD CORRIDOR (42)**	LMS	KINGS NORTON	BIRMINGHAM	13.45 Birmingham - Yarmouth
3	90 09.00 Yarmouth - Birmingham (15.38)	**BRAKE COMPOSITE CORRIDOR (12/24)**	LMS	KINGS NORTON	BIRMINGHAM	13.45 Birmingham - Yarmouth
4	91 09.30 Norwich - Birmingham (15.38)	**THIRD CORRIDOR (42)**	LMS	KINGS NORTON	BIRMINGHAM	13.45 Birmingham - Yarmouth
5	91 09.30 Norwich - Birmingham (15.38)	**BRAKE COMPOSITE CORRIDOR (12/24)**	LMS	KINGS NORTON	BIRMINGHAM	13.45 Birmingham - Yarmouth
6	89 09.40 Cromer - Birmingham (15.38)	**THIRD CORRIDOR (42)**	LMS	KINGS NORTON	BIRMINGHAM	13.45 Birmingham - Cromer
7	89 09.40 Cromer - Birmingham (15.38)	**BRAKE COMPOSITE CORRIDOR (12/24)**	LMS	KINGS NORTON	BIRMINGHAM	13.45 Birmingham - Cromer
8	89 09.40 (Sats) Cromer - Birmingham (15.38)	**THIRD CORRIDOR (42)**	LMS	KINGS NORTON	BIRMINGHAM	13.45 Birmingham - Cromer
9	89 09.40 (Sats) Cromer - Birmingham (15.38)	**THIRD CORRIDOR (42)**	LMS	KINGS NORTON	BIRMINGHAM	13.45 Birmingham - Cromer

New Street (Midland) was a most curious place and whilst it served a (nominal) third of one of Britain's largest conurbations, the number of services originating from the station was almost laughably small. The reason for this was that the station was small and cramped with very little in the way of facilities for dealing with empty stock whilst an engine running round a train could tie half of New Street up for an uncomfortable length of time. Many trains were berthed at Kings Norton, five miles towards Bristol, and to keep events moving smoothly it was normal practice for trains to Derby and Leicester to be worked in by their train engine - prepared in the majority of cases at Bourneville - from Kings Norton. An occasional variation on this theme occurred when instead of running the stock empty it was used to work a passenger service; this being the case with the 13.45 M&GN express Birmingham to Great Yarmouth and Cromer which started its working as the 12.40 local train from Kings Norton to Birmingham. A similar procedure applied to westbound trains, many of which originated in Saltley carriage sidings.

	C/W Previous working	Vehicle	Type	From	To	Next working
		16.24 LEEDS to BRADFORD (17.04)				
1	128A 15.10 York - Leeds (15.50)	**BRAKE THIRD CORRIDOR (32)**	LNER	LEEDS	BRADFORD	06.42 Bradford - York (08.19(
2	128A 15.10 York - Leeds (15.50)	**THIRD CORRIDOR (64)**	LNER	LEEDS	BRADFORD	06.42 Bradford - York (08.19(
3	128A 15.10 York - Leeds (15.50)	**COMPOSITE CORRIDOR (21/32)**	LNER	LEEDS	BRADFORD	06.42 Bradford - York (08.19(
4	128A 15.10 York - Leeds (15.50)	**THIRD CORRIDOR (64)**	LNER	LEEDS	BRADFORD	06.42 Bradford - York (08.19(
5	128A 15.10 York - Leeds (15.50)	**BRAKE THIRD CORRIDOR (32)**	LNER	LEEDS	BRADFORD	06.42 Bradford - York (08.19(

This was an LNER set of coaches that worked into Forster Square to provide the stock for the next morning's through service to York and at the same time performed a useful function during the evening rush-hour by operating a service between Leeds and Bradford which had a part better chance of running to time than the greater part of the Leeds/Bradford service which was operated by through trains from the south. Without the 16.24, passengers would have had to rely on the 16.40 Leeds to Bradford which was the 11.45 ex St Pancras and therefore likely, after five hours and two hundred miles of running, to be somewhat erratic in its time-keeping.

12.05 DERBY to ST PANCRAS (15.12)

	C/W Previous working	Vehicle	Type	From	To	Next working
1	119 18.40 St Pancras - Derby (21.22)	BRAKE THIRD CORRIDOR (24)	LMS	DERBY	ST PANCRAS	18.40 St Pancras - Derby (21.22)
2	119 18.40 St Pancras - Derby (21.22)	THIRD OPEN (56)	LMS	DERBY	ST PANCRAS	18.40 St Pancras - Derby (21.22)
3	119 18.40 St Pancras - Derby (21.22)	THIRD OPEN (64)	BR	DERBY	ST PANCRAS	18.40 St Pancras - Derby (21.22)
4	119 18.40 St Pancras - Derby (21.22)	RESTAURANT FIRST (24)	LMS	DERBY	ST PANCRAS	18.40 St Pancras - Derby (21.22)
5	119 18.40 St Pancras - Derby (21.22)	COMPOSITE CORRIDOR (18/24)	LMS	DERBY	ST PANCRAS	18.40 St Pancras - Derby (21.22)
6	119 18.40 St Pancras - Derby (21.22)	THIRD CORRIDOR (42)	LMS	DERBY	ST PANCRAS	18.40 St Pancras - Derby (21.22)
7	119 18.40 St Pancras - Derby (21.22)	THIRD CORRIDOR (42)	LMS	DERBY	ST PANCRAS	18.40 St Pancras - Derby (21.22)
8	30 07.24 Manchester - Derby (10.01)	BRAKE THIRD CORRIDOR (24)	LMS	DERBY	ST PANCRAS	18.40 St Pancras - Manchester (23.05)
9	30 07.24 Manchester - Derby (10.01)	COMPOSITE CORRIDOR (18/24)	LMS	DERBY	ST PANCRAS	18.40 St Pancras - Manchester (23.05)
10	30 07.24 Manchester - Derby (10.01)	COMPOSITE CORRIDOR (18/24)	LMS	DERBY	ST PANCRAS	18.40 St Pancras - Manchester (23.05)
11	30 07.24 Manchester - Derby (10.01)	BRAKE THIRD CORRIDOR (24)	LMS	DERBY	ST PANCRAS	18.40 St Pancras - Manchester (23.05)

The rule observed by every main line terminus that there should be a London departure at about ten in the morning had a major objector in the form of Manchester Central whose St Pancras service was broken by a gap of almost five hours after the departure of the 09.00 which itself was scarcely a fast express since it was routed via Derby, Trent and Nottingham. With competing services to Euston and Marylebone, Manchester could perhaps forgo one of its London workings but the intermediate stations could not and therefore a service was started from Derby at 12.05, picking up the strands of what might have been a ten o'clock departure from Manchester.

The connection with Manchester was not entirely fanciful since four of the eleven vehicles in the 12.05 started the day as the 07.24 stopping train from Manchester; being attached to the remaining seven vehicles after arriving in Derby. The return working was the 18.40 St Pancras to Manchester although only the four vehicles which worked the 07.24 slow actually completed the journey to Manchester.

A semi-fast rather than an express, the 12.05 was noted for being the test-bed for any of the early BR diesels that were being examined by the workshops staff and during the mid-1950's it was by no means unusual to find the train being worked by the Fell diesel-mechanical 10100 or a pair of SR locomotives, usually 10201 and 10202, working in multiple. When this happened instead of working the booked return working, the 19.10 London to Derby via Nottingham, the diesels would usually perform a very quick turn-round in St Pancras and leave with the 16.15 Manchester.

10.25 'PINES EXPRESS' MANCHESTER (LONDON RD) to BOURNEMOUTH (17.32)

	C/W Previous working	Vehicle	Type	From	To	Next working
1	68 10.10 Sheffield - Birmingham (12.09)	BRAKE THIRD CORRIDOR (24)	LMS	MANCHESTER (LR)	BOURNEMOUTH	09.45 Bournemouth - Sheffield
2	68 10.10 Sheffield - Birmingham (12.09)	COMPOSITE CORRIDOR (18/24)	LMS	MANCHESTER (LR)	BOURNEMOUTH	09.45 Bournemouth - Sheffield
3	72 09.45 Bournemouth - Liverpool (16.50)	BRAKE THIRD CORRIDOR (24)	LMS	LIVERPOOL (LS)	BOURNEMOUTH	09.45 Bournemouth - Liverpool (16.50)
4	72 09.45 Bournemouth - Liverpool (16.50)	COMPOSITE CORRIDOR (18/24)	LMS	LIVERPOOL (LS)	BOURNEMOUTH	09.45 Bournemouth - Liverpool (16.50)
5	74 09.45 Bournemouth - Manchester Mayfield (16.35)	BRAKE THIRD CORRIDOR (24)	LMS	MANCHESTER (LR)	BOURNEMOUTH	09.45 Bournemouth - Manchester Mayfield (16.35)
6	74 09.45 Bournemouth - Manchester Mayfield (16.35)	COMPOSITE OPEN (18/18)	LMS	MANCHESTER (LR)	BOURNEMOUTH	09.45 Bournemouth - Manchester Mayfield (16.35)
7	74 09.45 Bournemouth - Manchester Mayfield (16.35)	RESTAURANT THIRD (30)	LMS	MANCHESTER (LR)	BOURNEMOUTH	09.45 Bournemouth - Manchester Mayfield (16.35)
8	74 09.45 Bournemouth - Manchester Mayfield (16.35)	THIRD OPEN (56)	LMS	MANCHESTER (LR)	BOURNEMOUTH	09.45 Bournemouth - Manchester Mayfield (16.35)
9	74 09.45 Bournemouth - Manchester Mayfield (16.35)	THIRD CORRIDOR (42)	LMS	MANCHESTER (LR)	BOURNEMOUTH	09.45 Bournemouth - Manchester Mayfield (16.35)
10	74 09.45 Bournemouth - Manchester Mayfield (16.35)	COMPOSITE CORRIDOR (18/24)	LMS	MANCHESTER (LR)	BOURNEMOUTH	09.45 Bournemouth - Manchester Mayfield (16.35)
11	74 09.45 Bournemouth - Manchester Mayfield (16.35)	BRAKE COMPOSITE CORR (18/21)	LMS	MANCHESTER (LR)	BOURNEMOUTH	09.45 Bournemouth - Manchester Mayfield (16.35)

Given that the Midland had its own route between Manchester and Birmingham and was part owner of the section between Bath and Broadstone (Bournemouth), the Pines Express might have made more sense had it started at Manchester Central and run to Birmingham via Derby before continuing forward to Dorset. For some years prior to 1914, the Midland had run through coaches, usually on the rear of a London train as far as Derby, to from Manchester to Bristol but the initiative for the Pines came from the LNWR in 1910 with a proposal that a through Manchester - Bournemouth service should be jointly run; the LNW running the service as far as Birmingham, where it was to run into the Midland side of New Street, with the Midland working the train beyond. The approach by the LNWR was prompted by the newly introduced Birkenhead - Bournemouth service of the GWR and the fear that the upgrading of the Shrewsbury - Paddington route might induce further competitive measures. The Midland entered into the arrangement with the result that the Pines Express ran for more than fifty years without significant change although in its final few years it was rerouted to run via Oxford and Basingstoke following the closure of the Somerset & Dorset line.

The service (during the 1950's) consisted of three sections, the principal of which was the seven coach dining set which ran between Manchester and Bournemouth. A two-coach subsidiary section from Liverpool was attached at Crewe whilst a portion from Sheffield joined the train at Birmingham. Running the train to Birmingham via Crewe saved about half an hour although for the Midland diehards who were unable to bring themselves to use London Road, a connection was available from Manchester Central by using the 09.00 express to Derby.

09.15 HULL to SHEFFIELD MIDLAND (11.03)

	C/W Previous working	Vehicle	Type	From	To	Next working
1	129 15.10 Sheffield - Hull (17.10)	BRAKE THIRD CORRIDOR (24)	LNER	HULL	SHEFFIELD	15.10 Sheffield - Hull (17.10)
2	129 15.10 Sheffield - Hull (17.10)	COMPOSITE CORRIDOR (21/32)	LNER	HULL	SHEFFIELD	15.10 Sheffield - Hull (17.10)
3	129 15.10 Sheffield - Hull (17.10)	THIRD CORRIDOR (64)	LNER	HULL	SHEFFIELD	15.10 Sheffield - Hull (17.10)
4	129 15.10 Sheffield - Hull (17.10)	THIRD CORRIDOR (64)	LNER	HULL	SHEFFIELD	15.10 Sheffield - Hull (17.10)
5	129 15.10 Sheffield - Hull (17.10)	BRAKE THIRD CORRIDOR (24)	LNER	HULL	SHEFFIELD	15.10 Sheffield - Hull (17.10)
6	129 15.10 Sheffield - Hull (17.10)	NON-CORRIDOR THIRD (80)	LNER	HULL	SHEFFIELD	15.10 Sheffield - Hull (17.10)

Hull occupied a strange position in terms of railway connections and shared with many towns of significance on the East coast the sense of being served under sufferance. One only has to look at the examples of Grimsby, Saltburn, Middlesbrough, Stockton and Sunderland to realise that if one lived away from a straight line between London and Newcastle, the chances of a decent train service were slight. Hull, however, was in a position worse than most since its parent company, the North Eastern, tended to regard it as being off the beaten track since the geography of the situation made it rather difficult to run fast trains to and from Newcastle without performing something of a dogs leg. Through trains to London consisted of a handful of through coaches run rather grudgingly via Goole and Doncaster. Ironically the best providers of trains from Hull were the LNWR and the Great Central who both ran through services to Manchester and Liverpool via their respective routes.

The occasional Great Central service to Sheffield was useful but had the disadvantage of running to Sheffield Victoria where connections to the West Midlands, South Wales and the West of England were less satisfactory than those offered by the neighbouring Midland Railway and passengers for Birmingham, for example, were obliged to transfer from one station to another at Sheffield. During the war the matter was considerably improved by the introduction of a through service between Hull and Sheffield Midland, the principal object being to provide a connection into the up Devonian and thus allow passengers for Birmingham,. Bristol and the West a far easier journey.

The train was an LNER initiative and continued to operate throughout BR days. Formed of six LNER corridor coaches, the service made a strange sight in Sheffield Midland, not least because it was booked to be worked by a Hull (Botanic Gardens) D49 4-4-0. Engine and coaches returned at 15.10 after connecting with the 10.20 Sheffield - Newcastle.

11.45 ST PANCRAS to BRADFORD (17.15)

	C/W	Previous working	Vehicle	Type	From	To	Next working
1	17	11.50 Bradford - St Pancras (17.52)	THIRD CORRIDOR (48)	BR	ST PANCRAS	BRADFORD	11.50 Bradford - St Pancras (17.52)
2	17	11.50 Bradford - St Pancras (17.52)	BRAKE THIRD CORRIDOR (24)	BR	ST PANCRAS	BRADFORD	11.50 Bradford - St Pancras (17.52)
3	17	11.50 Bradford - St Pancras (17.52)	THIRD CORRIDOR (48)	BR	ST PANCRAS	BRADFORD	11.50 Bradford - St Pancras (17.52)
4	17	11.50 Bradford - St Pancras (17.52)	THIRD CORRIDOR (48)	BR	ST PANCRAS	BRADFORD	11.50 Bradford - St Pancras (17.52)
5	17	11.50 Bradford - St Pancras (17.52)	THIRD CORRIDOR (48)	BR	ST PANCRAS	BRADFORD	11.50 Bradford - St Pancras (17.52)
6	17	11.50 Bradford - St Pancras (17.52)	THIRD OPEN (64)	BR	ST PANCRAS	BRADFORD	11.50 Bradford - St Pancras (17.52)
7	17	11.50 Bradford - St Pancras (17.52)	KITCHEN CAR	LMS	ST PANCRAS	BRADFORD	11.50 Bradford - St Pancras (17.52)
8	17	11.50 Bradford - St Pancras (17.52)	FIRST OPEN (42)	BR	ST PANCRAS	BRADFORD	11.50 Bradford - St Pancras (17.52)
9	17	11.50 Bradford - St Pancras (17.52)	FIRST CORRIDOR (42)	BR	ST PANCRAS	BRADFORD	11.50 Bradford - St Pancras (17.52)
10	17	11.50 Bradford - St Pancras (17.52)	COMPOSITE CORRIDOR (24/18)	BR	ST PANCRAS	BRADFORD	11.50 Bradford - St Pancras (17.52)
11	17	11.50 Bradford - St Pancras (17.52)	BRAKE THIRD CORRIDOR (24)	BR	ST PANCRAS	BRADFORD	11.50 Bradford - St Pancras (17.52)

The 11.45 was the postwar version of the former midday St Pancras - Glasgow express, truncated at Leeds and extended to Bradford Forster Square, the Midland's principal terminus in the West Riding. It was an awkward train to find coaching stock for since it left London forty minutes before the first arrival from Bradford reached London, preventing a return working in the same day. Two sets of stock were therefore necessary for the service; one working the 11.45 from St Pancras whilst the other formed the corresponding mid-day express from Bradford.

Rather curiously, since the train spanned only the lunchtime hours and reached Bradford too early for a service of dinner, the three-coach dining set - with full restaurant facilities including a Kitchen-only car - worked throughout and was not removed, as was often the case, at an intermediate point. The 14.00 and 15.15 Bradford expresses from St Pancras, for example, shed their dining sections at Nottingham and Sheffield respectively.

Insofar as competition with British Railways existed, the 11.45 competed with the Great Northern for Leeds and Bradford traffic and received little quarter from the East Coast who not only ran the 12.05 Queen of Scots Pullman (15.19 into Leeds Central) but operated an ordinary express at 13.18 which reached Bradford Exchange only half an hour after the arrival of the Midland train. Unfortunately the increased weight of postwar Midland trains and the lack of inertia brought on by state ownership meant that the days when Leeds could be reached in less than four hours from St Pancras were a matter of history.

09.45 'PINES EXPRESS' BOURNEMOUTH WEST to MANCHESTER MAYFIELD (16.35)

	C/W	Previous working	Vehicle	Type	From	To	Next working
1	73	10.25 Manchester - Bournemouth (17.32)	BRAKE COMPOSITE CORRIDOR (12/21)	LMS	BOURNEMOUTH	MANCHESTER	10.25 Manchester - Bournemouth (17.32)
2	73	10.25 Manchester - Bournemouth (17.32)	COMPOSITE CORRIDOR (18/24)	LMS	BOURNEMOUTH	MANCHESTER	10.25 Manchester - Bournemouth (17.32)
3	73	10.25 Manchester - Bournemouth (17.32)	THIRD CORRIDOR (42)	LMS	BOURNEMOUTH	MANCHESTER	10.25 Manchester - Bournemouth (17.32)
4	73	10.25 Manchester - Bournemouth (17.32)	THIRD OPEN (56)	LMS	BOURNEMOUTH	MANCHESTER	10.25 Manchester - Bournemouth (17.32)
5	73	10.25 Manchester - Bournemouth (17.32)	RESTAURANT THIRD (30)	LMS	BOURNEMOUTH	MANCHESTER	10.25 Manchester - Bournemouth (17.32)
6	73	10.25 Manchester - Bournemouth (17.32)	COMPOSITE OPEN (18/18)	LMS	BOURNEMOUTH	MANCHESTER	10.25 Manchester - Bournemouth (17.32)
7	73	10.25 Manchester - Bournemouth (17.32)	BRAKE THIRD CORRIDOR (24)	LMS	BOURNEMOUTH	MANCHESTER	10.25 Manchester - Bournemouth (17.32)
8	72	10.15 Liverpool - Bournemouth (17.32)	BRAKE THIRD CORRIDOR (24)	LMS	BOURNEMOUTH	LIVERPOOL	10.15 Liverpool - Bournemouth (17.32)
9	72	10.15 Liverpool - Bournemouth (17.32)	COMPOSITE CORRIDOR (18/24)	LMS	BOURNEMOUTH	LIVERPOOL	10.15 Liverpool - Bournemouth (17.32)
10	69	10.10 Sheffield - Bournemouth (17.32)	BRAKE THIRD CORRIDOR (24)	LMS	BOURNEMOUTH	BIRMINGHAM	14.38 Birmingham - Sheffield (16.33)
11	69	10.10 Sheffield - Bournemouth (17.32)	COMPOSITE CORRIDOR (18/24)	LMS	BOURNEMOUTH	BIRMINGHAM	14.38 Birmingham - Sheffield (16.33)

Shown in the order of running between Bath and Birmingham

Traffic from Bournemouth - which thanks to the Somerset & Dorset Joint was partly Midland territory - could be turned on or off like a tap. On summer Saturdays train after train would run across the Mendips; queue up to reverse in Bath before joining the West of England main line at Mangotsfield - a service so heavy that ingenuity was often strained to the limit to find engines for it. During the rest of the year the flood subsided into a trickle that consisted only of the Pines Express to Manchester and a slow train from Bournemouth to Gloucester.

The 09.45 Bournemouth to Manchester - the Pines - was operated jointly with the LNW and provided one of the few instances of a service which crossed from one side of New Street to the other. (One half of New Street station was operated by the LNW and the other by the Midland and though both halves had the appearance of being the same station, they might have been a mile apart for all the notice they took of each other). Arriving at 14.23, the Midland 5MT 4-6-0 which had worked the train from Bath made way for a Longsight 5XP and, when the main portion of the train had departed, shunted the rear two coaches onto the 14.38 express for Sheffield, the empty stock for which preceded the Pines by ten minutes from Kings Norton. It is interesting to note that the Pines, whose loadings were quite poor at certain times of the year, was granted full dining facilities whilst services that were perennially busy, such as the early morning business trains from Birmingham to Bradford and York had nothing. However, in spite of its name and status, no room for the service could be found in Manchester, London Road and instead the service was sidetracked to the adjacent Mayfield station.

14.38 BIRMINGHAM to SHEFFIELD (16.33)

	C/W	Previous working	Vehicle	Type	From	To	Next working
1	69A	14.03 ECS Kings Norton - Birmingham (14.15)	BRAKE THIRD CORRIDOR (32)	LMS	BIRMINGHAM	SHEFFIELD	19.05 Sheffield - Birmingham (21.05)
2	69A	14.03 ECS Kings Norton - Birmingham (14.15)	COMPOSITE CORRIDOR (18/32)	LMS	BIRMINGHAM	SHEFFIELD	19.05 Sheffield - Birmingham (21.05)
3	69A	14.03 ECS Kings Norton - Birmingham (14.15)	BRAKE THIRD CORRIDOR (32)	LMS	BIRMINGHAM	SHEFFIELD	19.05 Sheffield - birmingham (21.05)
4	69	09.45 Bournemouth - Birmingham (14.23)	BRAKE THIRD CORRIDOR (24)	LMS	BIRMINGHAM	SHEFFIELD	10.10 Sheffield - Birmingham (12.09)
5	69	09.45 Bournemouth - Birmingham (14.23)	COMPOSITE CORRIDOR (18/24)	LMS	BIRMINGHAM	SHEFFIELD	10.10 Sheffield - Birmingham (12.09)

The 14.38 ex Birmingham consisted of the through Sheffield coaches from the Pines Express padded out with a trio of local vehicles in case local demand outstripped the two Bournemouth coaches. Since the 14.38 was the first express to leave in the Derby direction for an hour and a half and preceded the up Devonian by only half an hour, it was a safe bet that accommodation over and above that offered by the two Pines coaches would be needed. Although it did not convey the name of the Pines, the 14.38 ran as an express should and, calling only at Burton, Derby and Chesterfield, reached Sheffield in one hour fifty-five minutes from Birmingham, in the same time - bar a paltry minute - as the following Devonian.

On reaching Sheffield, the stock was taken to Heeley carriage sidings where the Bournemouth coaches were set aside for the next day's 10.10 to Birmingham and the Pines Express to Bournemouth. The three local coaches returned to Birmingham that same evening as a strengthening section in the 15.57 Newcastle express.

09.25 'DEVONIAN' BRADFORD to PAIGNTON (19.25)

	C/W	Previous working	Vehicle	Type	From	To	Next working
1	33	09.15 Paignton - Bradford (19.09)	BRAKE THIRD CORRIDOR (24)	LMS	BRADFORD	PAIGNTON	09.15 Paignton - Bradford (19.09)
2	33	09.15 Paignton - Bradford (19.09)	THIRD CORRIDOR (48)	BR	BRADFORD	PAIGNTON	09.15 Paignton - Bradford (19.09)
3	33	09.15 Paignton - Bradford (19.09)	THIRD CORRIDOR (48)	BR	BRADFORD	PAIGNTON	09.15 Paignton - Bradford (19.09)
4	33	09.15 Paignton - Bradford (19.09)	COMPOSITE CORRIDOR (24/18)	BR	BRADFORD	PAIGNTON	09.15 Paignton - Bradford (19.09)
5	33	09.15 Paignton - Bradford (19.09)	BRAKE THIRD CORRIDOR (24)	BR	BRADFORD	PAIGNTON	09.15 Paignton - Bradford (19.09)
6	35	08.45 Plymouth - Bradford (19.09)	BRAKE THIRD CORRIDOR (24)	BR	BRADFORD	NEWTON ABBOT	19.30 Newton Abbot - Plymouth (20.45)
7	35	08.45 Plymouth - Bradford (19.09)	THIRD OPEN (64)	BR	BRADFORD	NEWTON ABBOT	19.30 Newton Abbot - Plymouth (20.45)
8	35	08.45 Plymouth - Bradford (19.09)	RESTAURANT COMPOSITE (12/18)	LMS	BRADFORD	NEWTON ABBOT	19.30 Newton Abbot - Plymouth (20.45)
9	35	08.45 Plymouth - Bradford (19.09)	COMPOSITE CORRIDOR (24/18)	BR	BRADFORD	NEWTON ABBOT	19.30 Newton Abbot - Plymouth (20.45)
10	35	08.45 Plymouth - Bradford (19.09)	THIRD CORRIDOR (48)	BR	BRADFORD	NEWTON ABBOT	19.30 Newton Abbot - Plymouth (20.45)
11	35	08.45 Plymouth - Bradford (19.09)	BRAKE THIRD CORRIDOR (24)	BR	BRADFORD	NEWTON ABBOT	19.30 Newton Abbot - Plymouth (20.45)

Shown in order leaving Leeds

Although several named services graced the Great Northern Bradford Exchange station, Forster Square possessed only one: the Devonian which, as its title suggested, ran to the West of England. Speed, alas, was not amongst the criteria for bestowing a name since the train stopped at a variety of places - Normanton, Cudworth and Rotherham, etc - that would normally expect to be graced by a titled express and in fact the name was selected simply because the train strayed beyond Bristol, the usual terminating point of Midland West of England trains. In pre-war days the service had consisted of three coaches that had been transferred at Bristol from an ordinary Midland express to an equally ordinary GWR service and somehow during the war the service had expanded into a full-blown train and had remained as such ever since.

Leaving Sheffield nearly two hours after starting from Bradford, the Devonian assumed a more express-like mantle through Derby and Birmingham, preceding the 08.15 Newcastle - Bristol by no more than a couple of block sections. Later in the journey the running of the two trains reversed when the Devonian left the main line at Stoke Works Junction to call at Worcester, a diversion that allowed the Newcastle train to overtake and - despite having to reverse in Gloucester Central where it dropped its Cardiff section - reach Bristol eight minutes earlier. At Newton Abbot, the Devonian divided with the leading five coaches proceeding down the Torbay branch to Paignton whilst the remainder followed the 15.30 Paddington - Penzance from Newton Abbot as a stopping train to Plymouth.

08.15 NEWCASTLE to BRISTOL (16.02)

	C/W	Previous working	Vehicle	Type	From	To	Next working
			Mondays, Wednesdays and Fridays				
1	60	08.30 Cardiff - Newcastle (16.57)	BRAKE THIRD CORRIDOR (24)	BR (NER)	NEWCASTLE	CARDIFF	08.30 Cardiff - Newcastle (16.57)
2	60	08.30 Cardiff - Newcastle (16.57)	THIRD CORRIDOR (42)	BR (NER)	NEWCASTLE	CARDIFF	08.30 Cardiff - Newcastle (16.57)
3	60	08.30 Cardiff - Newcastle (16.57)	THIRD CORRIDOR (42)	BR (NER)	NEWCASTLE	CARDIFF	08.30 Cardiff - Newcastle (16.57)
4	60	08.30 Cardiff - Newcastle (16.57)	THIRD CORRIDOR (48)	BR (NER)	NEWCASTLE	CARDIFF	08.30 Cardiff - Newcastle (16.57)
5	60	08.30 Cardiff - Newcastle (16.57)	COMPOSITE CORRIDOR (24/18)	BR (NER)	NEWCASTLE	CARDIFF	08.30 Cardiff - Newcastle (16.57)
6	60	08.30 Cardiff - Newcastle (16.57)	THIRD CORRIDOR (48)	BR (NER)	NEWCASTLE	CARDIFF	08.30 Cardiff - Newcastle (16.57)
7	60	08.30 Cardiff - Newcastle (16.57)	BRAKE THIRD CORRIDOR (24)	BR (NER)	NEWCASTLE	CARDIFF	08.30 Cardiff - Newcastle (16.57)
8	58	08.45 Bristol - Newcastle (16.57)	BRAKE THIRD CORRIDOR (24)	BR (NER)	NEWCASTLE	BRISTOL	08.45 Bristol - Newcastle (16.57)
9	58	08.45 Bristol - Newcastle (16.57)	RESTAURANT BUFFET (24)	LNER	NEWCASTLE	BRISTOL	08.45 Bristol - Newcastle (16.57)
10	58	08.45 Bristol - Newcastle (16.57)	COMPOSITE CORRIDOR (24/18)	BR (NER)	NEWCASTLE	BRISTOL	08.45 Bristol - Newcastle (16.57)
11	58	08.45 Bristol - Newcastle (16.57)	THIRD CORRIDOR (48)	BR (NER)	NEWCASTLE	BRISTOL	08.45 Bristol - Newcastle (16.57)
12	58	08.45 Bristol - Newcastle (16.57)	BRAKE THIRD CORRIDOR (24)	BR (NER)	NEWCASTLE	BRISTOL	08.45 Bristol - Newcastle (16.57)
			Tuesdays and Thursdays				
1	59	08.30 Cardiff - Newcastle (16.57)	BRAKE THIRD CORRIDOR (32)	GW	NEWCASTLE	CARDIFF	08.30 Cardiff - Newcastle (16.57)
2	59	08.30 Cardiff - Newcastle (16.57)	THIRD CORRIDOR (64)	GW	NEWCASTLE	CARDIFF	08.30 Cardiff - Newcastle (16.57)
3	59	08.30 Cardiff - Newcastle (16.57)	THIRD CORRIDOR (64)	GW	NEWCASTLE	CARDIFF	08.30 Cardiff - Newcastle (16.57)
4	59	08.30 Cardiff - Newcastle (16.57)	THIRD CORRIDOR (64)	GW	NEWCASTLE	CARDIFF	08.30 Cardiff - Newcastle (16.57)
5	59	08.30 Cardiff - Newcastle (16.57)	COMPOSITE CORRIDOR (24/24)	GW	NEWCASTLE	CARDIFF	08.30 Cardiff - Newcastle (16.57)
6	59	08.30 Cardiff - Newcastle (16.57)	THIRD CORRIDOR (64)	GW	NEWCASTLE	CARDIFF	08.30 Cardiff - Newcastle (16.57)
7	59	08.30 Cardiff - Newcastle (16.57)	BRAKE THIRD CORRIDOR (32)	GW	NEWCASTLE	CARDIFF	08.30 Cardiff - Newcastle (16.57)
8	57	08.45 Bristol - Newcastle (16.57)	BRAKE THIRD CORRIDOR (24)	LMS	NEWCASTLE	BRISTOL	08.45 Bristol - Newcastle (16.57)
9	57	08.45 Bristol - Newcastle (16.57)	RESTAURANT BUFFET (30)	LMS	NEWCASTLE	BRISTOL	08.45 Bristol - Newcastle (16.57)
10	57	08.45 Bristol - Newcastle (16.57)	COMPOSITE CORRIDOR (18/24)	LMS	NEWCASTLE	BRISTOL	08.45 Bristol - Newcastle (16.57)
11	57	08.45 Bristol - Newcastle (16.57)	THIRD CORRIDOR (42)	LMS	NEWCASTLE	BRISTOL	08.45 Bristol - Newcastle (16.57)
12	57	08.45 Bristol - Newcastle (16.57)	BRAKE THIRD CORRIDOR (24)	LMS	NEWCASTLE	BRISTOL	08.45 Bristol - Newcastle (16.57)

A very popular train and one that served both South Wales and the West of England although the utility of the latter might have been improved had it been extended to Paignton or Plymouth. (The chief obstacle to such an improvement, in addition to the rather tenuous communications between the Midland and ex-GWR, was the problem of returning the vehicles to Bristol by 08.45 the following morning: not an easy task given that Plymouth was some three hours away). The service had operated for many years as a Bristol train but in the early 1950s a Cardiff section was added which complicated the working of the train since it had to be run into the GWR station at Gloucester which while it facilitated the working of the Cardiff coaches, meant that the Bristol section had to reverse and, as a consequence, had to be given a fresh engine. Whilst this caused the Bristol arrival to be forty minutes later than had been the case, the variety of motive power used was impressive to say the least since the train started its journey behind a Heaton A1 Pacific which worked as far as York where it gave way to a V2 2-6-2 for the 46-mile leg via Church Fenton and the Swinton & Knottingley Joint to Sheffield, the Midland Railway being joined by the connection between Dearne Junction and Wath Road Junction. (The dispersal of trains from York to the stations in Sheffield was overwhelmingly in the Midland's favour and of the thirteen daily trains only three ran to Sheffield Victoria). A 5XP 4-6-0 ran the train from Sheffield to Gloucester from where a BR 4MT 4-6-0 worked the South Wales portion to Cardiff whilst a Compound 4-4-0 worked the Bristol coaches over the thirty-seven miles to Temple Meads.

The service required two 12-coach sets of stock; one based at Heaton, Newcastle, and consisting of eleven BR Mk1 Standard coaches and an LNER restaurant which acted as a buffet car. The opposing set was of greater interest since the five Bristol-based coaches were LMS vehicles whilst the seven that were based at Canton, Cardiff, were of Great Western design. Despite the route's traditional connection with Bristol, the emphasis of the Newcastle service leaned towards Cardiff and from 1957 the Bristol portion was reduced from five to three coaches when the dining section was diverted to run to and from Cardiff.

12.50 ST PANCRAS to LEICESTER (15.25)

	C/W	Previous working	Vehicle	Type	From	To	Next working
1	27	06.40 Nottingham - St Pancras (09.55)	THIRD CORRIDOR (48)	BR	ST PANCRAS	LEICESTER	15.35 Leicester - Nottingham (16.22)
2	27	06.40 Nottingham - St Pancras (09.55)	THIRD CORRIDOR (48)	BR	ST PANCRAS	LEICESTER	15.35 Leicester - Nottingham (16.22)
3	27	06.40 Nottingham - St Pancras (09.55)	BRAKE THIRD CORRIDOR (24)	BR	ST PANCRAS	LEICESTER	15.35 Leicester - Nottingham (16.22)
4	27	06.40 Nottingham - St Pancras (09.55)	COMPOSITE CORRIDOR (24/18)	BR	ST PANCRAS	LEICESTER	15.35 Leicester - Nottingham (16.22)
5	27	06.40 Nottingham - St Pancras (09.55)	COMPOSITE CORRIDOR (24/18)	BR	ST PANCRAS	LEICESTER	15.35 Leicester - Nottingham (16.22)
6	27	06.40 Nottingham - St Pancras (09.55)	THIRD OPEN (56)	LMS	ST PANCRAS	LEICESTER	15.35 Leicester - Nottingham (16.22)
7	27	06.40 Nottingham - St Pancras (09.55)	RESTAURANT THIRD (30)	LMS	ST PANCRAS	LEICESTER	15.35 Leicester - Nottingham (16.22)
8	27	06.40 Nottingham - St Pancras (09.55)	FIRST OPEN (42)	LMS	ST PANCRAS	LEICESTER	15.35 Leicester - Nottingham (16.22)
9	27	06.40 Nottingham - St Pancras (09.55)	FIRST OPEN (42)	LMS	ST PANCRAS	LEICESTER	15.35 Leicester - Nottingham (16.22)
10	27	06.40 Nottingham - St Pancras (09.55)	BRAKE THIRD CORRIDOR (24)	LMS	ST PANCRAS	LEICESTER	15.35 Leicester - Nottingham (16.22)

Whilst advertised as a London - Leicester service, the train actually continued, via Loughborough and Trent, to Nottingham; a feature obscured by the timetable since it was overtaken by the 14.00 St Pancras to Bradford which ran via Melton and reached Nottingham five minutes ahead of the 12.50. This particular piece of timetable compilation gave the observer the strange sight of two London expresses, both hauled by 5XP Jubilee 4-6-0's, arriving from opposite directions.

Although equipped with a fully fledged restaurant car and a high proportion of first class accomodation, the 12.50 was (apart from its 5XP 4-6-0) little more than a run-of-the mill semi-fast and called at all principal points to Leicester, taking almost two and a half hours to cover the 99-mile distance. After a ten minute pause in London Road, the service degenerated even further by adding Kegworth - not a location normally associated with express services - to the list of stations served. The reason for such an august ensemble forming a rather secondary service was that it was a convenient way of returning the stock of the morning Nottingham to London business express.

16.22 SCARBOROUGH to BRADFORD (19.00)

	C/W	Previous working	Vehicle	Type	From	To	Next working
1	41	08.46 Bradford - Scarborough	BRAKE THIRD CORRIDOR (24)	LMS	SCARBOROUGH	BRADFORD	08.46 Bradford - Scarborough
2	41	08.46 Bradford - Scarborough	THIRD CORRIDOR (42)	LMS	SCARBOROUGH	BRADFORD	08.46 Bradford - Scarborough
3	41	08.46 Bradford - Scarborough	THIRD CORRIDOR (42)	LMS	SCARBOROUGH	BRADFORD	08.46 Bradford - Scarborough
4	41	08.46 Bradford - Scarborough	THIRD CORRIDOR (42)	LMS	SCARBOROUGH	BRADFORD	08.46 Bradford - Scarborough
5	41	08.46 Bradford - Scarborough	THIRD CORRIDOR (42)	LMS	SCARBOROUGH	BRADFORD	08.46 Bradford - Scarborough
6	41	08.46 Bradford - Scarborough	THIRD CORRIDOR (42)	LMS	SCARBOROUGH	BRADFORD	08.46 Bradford - Scarborough
7	41	08.46 Bradford - Scarborough	COMPOSITE CORRIDOR (18/24)	LMS	SCARBOROUGH	BRADFORD	08.46 Bradford - Scarborough
8	41	08.46 Bradford - Scarborough	COMPOSITE CORRIDOR (18/24)	LMS	SCARBOROUGH	BRADFORD	08.46 Bradford - Scarborough
9	41	08.46 Bradford - Scarborough	THIRD CORRIDOR (42)	LMS	SCARBOROUGH	BRADFORD	08.46 Bradford - Scarborough
10	41	08.46 Bradford - Scarborough	BRAKE THIRD CORRIDOR (24)	LMS	SCARBOROUGH	BRADFORD	08.46 Bradford - Scarborough

Popular in the summer when it was used by scores of families returning to the West Riding after a day by the sea, the 16.22 also served as a late evening rush-hour service between Leeds and Bradford. It was also the first of a trio of interesting arrivals at Forster Square, being closely followed by the Devonian and the 14.00 from St Pancras: twenty-eight coaches in less than half an hour. Of these the Scarborough was probably the most avidly watched for since it was worked throughout by a Neville Hill B1 4-6-0 and the sight of an LNER engine at Forster Square, whilst more commonplace than had been the case a few years earlier, was still guaranteed to provoke excitement amongst local observers. The ten-coach set used in the service was Bradford-based and worked out with the 08.46 Bradford to Scarborough.

09.15 'DEVONIAN' PAIGNTON to BRADFORD (19.09)

	C/W	Previous working	Vehicle	Type	From	To	Next working
1	36	08.45 Plymouth - Bristol (12.21)	BRAKE THIRD CORRIDOR (24)	BR	BRISTOL	BRADFORD	09.25 Bradford - Bristol (16.00)
2	36	08.45 Plymouth - Bristol (12.21)	THIRD CORRIDOR (48)	BR	BRISTOL	BRADFORD	09.25 Bradford - Bristol (16.00)
3	36	08.45 Plymouth - Bristol (12.21)	COMPOSITE CORRIDOR (24/18)	BR	BRISTOL	BRADFORD	09.25 Bradford - Bristol (16.00)
4	36	08.45 Plymouth - Bristol (12.21)	RESTAURANT COMPOSITE (12/18)	LMS	BRISTOL	BRADFORD	09.25 Bradford - Bristol (16.00)
5	36	08.45 Plymouth - Bristol (12.21)	THIRD OPEN (64)	BR	BRISTOL	BRADFORD	09.25 Bradford - Bristol (16.00)
6	36	08.45 Plymouth - Bristol (12.21)	BRAKE THIRD CORRIDOR (24)	BR	BRISTOL	BRADFORD	09.25 Bradford - Bristol (16.00)
7	34	09.15 Paignton - Bristol (12.21)	BRAKE THIRD CORRIDOR (24)	BR	BRISTOL	BRADFORD	09.25 Bradford - Bristol (16.00)
8	34	09.15 Paignton - Bristol (12.21)	COMPOSITE CORRIDOR (24/18)	BR	BRISTOL	BRADFORD	09.25 Bradford - Bristol (16.00)
9	34	09.15 Paignton - Bristol (12.21)	BRAKE THIRD CORRIDOR (24)	BR	BRISTOL	BRADFORD	09.25 Bradford - Bristol (16.00)
10	34	09.15 Paignton - Bristol (12.21)	BRAKE THIRD CORRIDOR (24)	BR	BRISTOL	BRADFORD	09.25 Bradford - Bristol (16.00)
11	34	09.15 Paignton - Bristol (12.21)	BRAKE THIRD CORRIDOR (24)	BR	BRISTOL	BRADFORD	09.25 Bradford - Bristol (16.00)

The fact that of all the Midland trains from Derby to Bristol, only one ventured across the boundary into Great Western territory was an extraordinary comment on the sanctity of railway boundaries years after the companies who borders they marked had ceased to be. This exception was the Devonian which, under an agreement between the LMS and GWR, had conveyed three Great Western coaches from Bristol to Bradford; the trio starting their journey at Paignton and making their way in the 08.45 Plymouth - Manchester to Bristol where they were shunted across to the 12.30 Bristol to Bradford. The service was suspended during the war but when revived appeared as a through train from both Plymouth and Paignton, combining at Newton Abbot and continuing forward from Temple Meads as the 12.30 Bristol to Bradford.

Given the distinction of a name, a restaurant car and a journey length of 324 miles - slightly further than St Pancras to Carlisle - the service was not distinguished in terms of speed. It was not a slow train but its running times north of Bristol were little different from those of the other Midland West of England expresses; indeed the anonymous 10.20 Bristol to Newcastle was seven minutes faster to Sheffield although the difference was due to the Devonian leaving Bristol over the Great Western exit via Stapleton Road and Westerleigh rather than the normal Mangotsfield route, a diversion that cost thirteen minutes. The purpose was to allow Midland crews to retain knowledge of the alternative route whilst, inter alia, the 10.35 Penzance - Wolverhampton was routed via Mangotsfield so that Great Western crews remained familiar with the Midland.

15.20 GLOUCESTER to BOURNEMOUTH WEST (19.23)

	C/W Previous working	Vehicle	Type	From	To	Next working
1	88A 10.35 Bristol - Gloucester (12.05)	COMPOSITE CORRIDOR (18/24)	LMS	GLOUCESTER	BOURNEMOUTH	11.40 Bournemouth - Gloucester (14.50)
2	88A 10.35 Bristol - Gloucester (12.05)	BRAKE THIRD CORRIDOR (32)	LMS	GLOUCESTER	BOURNEMOUTH	11.40 Bournemouth - Gloucester (14.50)
3	88A 10.35 Bristol - Gloucester (12.05)	COMPOSITE CORRIDOR (18/32)	LMS	GLOUCESTER	BOURNEMOUTH	11.40 Bournemouth - Gloucester (14.50)
4	88A 10.35 Bristol - Gloucester (12.05)	BRAKE THIRD CORRIDOR (32)	LMS	GLOUCESTER	BOURNEMOUTH	11.40 Bournemouth - Gloucester (14.50)

Except on summer Saturdays when all roads led to Bournemouth, through travel between the Midland Railway and the Somerset & Dorset was almost entirely absent. There was one through train - the Pines Express - from the North - and one local and in all other cases passengers had to alight at Mangotsfield and pick up a Bristol - Bath stopping train. The local was the 15.20 Gloucester to Bournemouth which connected with the 09.25 Bradford - Paignton 'Devonian' thus allowing the latter to omit the usual Mangotsfield call.

The 15.20 was a good service so far as Bath was concerned which was as far as most through passengers went. So good was the service that it had a faster booking - by four minutes - between Gloucester and Yate than either the Devonian or the Pines Express although to ensure that it reached Bath in time to catch its path over the single line of the Somerset & Dorset, the 15.20's schedule was padded out with nine minutes recovery time. South of Bath the service fell into step with the usual pattern of joint line working by calling at most stations beyond Shepton Mallet and in spite of its promising start, the overall time between Gloucester and Bournemouth was twenty-eight minutes greater than that of the Pines.

The train was worked by two sets of four coaches, one based at Bournemouth and the other at Bristol; both following a two-day cycle which on the first day covered the 10.35 Bristol - Gloucester stopping train and the 15.20 Gloucester - Bournemouth and on the second reversed the process by working the 11.40 Bournemouth - Gloucester and the 15.55 Gloucester - Bristol.

On summer Fridays the formation was altered as part of the arrangements to see that Bournemouth received an adequate supply of rolling stock for the week-end working and a seven coach set (7 = TK, TK, BTK, TK, CK, TK, BTK) was placed into the diagram by Bristol in order to form the 10.05 Bournemouth West - Cleethorpes the following day. Similarly, on summer Mondays the normal four-coach formation was augmented by two corridor thirds, a composite corridor and a brake third corridor to maintain the level of stock at Bournemouth for the following weekend.

10.30 BRADFORD to ST PANCRAS (15.42)

	C/W Previous working	Vehicle	Type	From	To	Next working
1	15 14.00 St Pancras - Bradford (19.26)	BRAKE THIRD CORRIDOR (24)	BR	BRADFORD	ST PANCRAS	18.33 St Pancras - Sheffield (21.53)
2	15A 07.50 Sheffield - Bradford (09.55)	THIRD CORRIDOR (48)	BR	BRADFORD	ST PANCRAS	17.30 St Pancras - Nottingham (17.32)
3	15 14.00 St Pancras - Bradford (19.26)	THIRD CORRIDOR (48)	BR	BRADFORD	ST PANCRAS	18.33 St Pancras - Sheffield (21.53)
4	15 14.00 St Pancras - Bradford (19.26)	THIRD CORRIDOR (48)	BR	BRADFORD	ST PANCRAS	18.33 St Pancras - Sheffield (21.53)
5	15 14.00 St Pancras - Bradford (19.26)	COMPOSITE CORRIDOR (24/18)	BR	BRADFORD	ST PANCRAS	18.33 St Pancras - Sheffield (21.53)
6	15 14.00 St Pancras - Bradford (19.26)	COMPOSITE CORRIDOR (24/18)	BR	BRADFORD	ST PANCRAS	18.33 St Pancras - Sheffield (21.53)
7	15 14.00 St Pancras - Bradford (19.26)	BRAKE THIRD CORRIDOR (24)	LMS	BRADFORD	ST PANCRAS	18.33 St Pancras - Sheffield (21.53)
8	15 14.00 St Pancras - Bradford (19.26)	THIRD CORRIDOR (42)	LMS	BRADFORD	ST PANCRAS	18.33 St Pancras - Sheffield (21.53)
9	126 18.33 St Pancras - Sheffield (21.53)	RESTAURANT FIRST (24)	LMS	SHEFFIELD	ST PANCRAS	18.33 St Pancras - Sheffield (21.53)
10	126 18.33 St Pancras - Sheffield (21.53)	THIRD OPEN (56)	LMS	SHEFFIELD	ST PANCRAS	18.33 St Pancras - Sheffield (21.53)
11	126 18.33 St Pancras - Sheffield (21.53)	COMPOSITE CORRIDOR (18/24)	LMS	SHEFFIELD	ST PANCRAS	18.33 St Pancras - Sheffield (21.53)

Shown in order leaving Leeds

For fast running the 10.30 Bradford to St Pancras was almost in the same class as the 09.12, both trains coming as close to mile-a-minute bookings as one was likely to get on the Midland. The earlier train was required to average 56 mph between Leicester and London - not an easy task for a moderately-sized engine with 10 coaches over quite a hilly route. The same 56 mph running was demanded of the 10.30 on the last leg between Kettering and London, the preceding stage of the journey having been slightly different from that of the earlier service, the 10.30 leaving the main line at Trowell Junction to run via Nottingham and Melton Mowbray. The load was one coach heavier to compensate for diversion away from the hilly section between Leicester to Kettering.

The Bradford-based element of the train, a six-coach set of BR Standard vehicles, worked to a two-day cyclic diagram because the 10.30 reached London too late to return to the West Riding the same day. Instead, it returned to Sheffield as the 18.33 from St Pancras and formed the 07.05 Sheffield to London the following morning. Later in the day it completed the cycle with the 14.00 St Pancras to Bradford. The three coach dining section maintained the same duty each weekday: going up with the 10.30 Bradford - London from Sheffield and returning in the 18.33. One of the Third Corridor vehicles was shunted out at St Pancras and transferred to the 17.32 Nottingham express.

13.35 NOTTINGHAM to ST PANCRAS (17.05)

	C/W Previous working	Vehicle	Type	From	To	Next working
1	49A 19.10 St Pancras - Nottingham (21.40)	BRAKE THIRD CORRIDOR (24)	LMS	NOTTINGHAM	ST PANCRAS	19.10 St Pancras - Nottingham (21.40)
2	49A 19.10 St Pancras - Nottingham (21.40)	THIRD CORRIDOR (42)	LMS	NOTTINGHAM	ST PANCRAS	19.10 St Pancras - Nottingham (21.40)
3	49A 19.10 St Pancras - Nottingham (21.40)	THIRD OPEN (56)	LMS	NOTTINGHAM	ST PANCRAS	19.10 St Pancras - Nottingham (21.40)
4	49A 19.10 St Pancras - Nottingham (21.40)	CAFÉ CAR	LMS	NOTTINGHAM	ST PANCRAS	19.10 St Pancras - Nottingham (21.40)
5	49 06.18 Derby - Nottingham (07.06)	BRAKE THIRD CORRIDOR (24)	LMS	NOTTINGHAM	ST PANCRAS	19.10 St Pancras - Derby (22.15)
6	49 06.18 Derby - Nottingham (07.06)	THIRD CORRIDOR (42)	LMS	NOTTINGHAM	ST PANCRAS	19.10 St Pancras - Derby (22.15)
7	49 06.18 Derby - Nottingham (07.06)	COMPOSITE CORRIDOR (18/24)	LMS	NOTTINGHAM	ST PANCRAS	19.10 St Pancras - Derby (22.15)
8	49 06.18 Derby - Nottingham (07.06)	COMPOSITE CORRIDOR (18/24)	LMS	NOTTINGHAM	ST PANCRAS	19.10 St Pancras - Derby (22.15)
9	49 06.18 Derby - Nottingham (07.06)	THIRD CORRIDOR (42)	LMS	NOTTINGHAM	ST PANCRAS	19.10 St Pancras - Derby (22.15)
10	49 06.18 Derby - Nottingham (07.06)	BRAKE THIRD CORRIDOR (24)	LMS	NOTTINGHAM	ST PANCRAS	19.10 St Pancras - Derby (22.15)

The 13.35 was noted for three qualities. Firstly because of the inclusion in its formation of a cafeteria car, secondly because it was routed via Trent instead of Melton and thirdly because it called at a number of locations that did not normally deal with express services. Semi-fast trains were rather tedious affairs to ride in for any length of time but the 13.35 excelled itself by calling at Beeston, Trent, Kegworth, Loughborough, Barrow-on-Soar, Sileby and Syston before reaching Leicester. The rest of the journey, after calling at Kibworth, followed the general pattern established for main-line semi-fast services.

There were two sets of stock involved in the working; the main one being a six-coach set which was based in Derby and started its day in the 06.18 Derby - Nottingham local. The second set was a four-coach rake which included the cafeteria car - a recent innovation although most of the vehicles in traffic were converted ambulance or sleeping cars - and was attached in Nottingham carriage sidings to the set that worked in from Derby. Combined, the ten vehicles worked from Nottingham as the 13.35 and returned as the 19.10 St Pancras to Derby, dropping off the cafeteria section at Nottingham, without any change being made to the formation. The two sets remained in the working on a daily basis.

Arguably one of the most handsome classes of engine ever produced, Jubilee 4-6-0 45602 'British Honduras' of Bristol calls at Derby with a Bristol - York express in July 1956.

	C/W	Previous working	Vehicle	Type	From	To	Next working
			14.00 ST PANCRAS to BRADFORD (19.26)				
1	14	07.00 Sheffield - St Pancras (10.32)	**BRAKE THIRD CORRIDOR** (24)	LMS	ST PANCRAS	BRADFORD	10.30 Bradford - St Pancras (15.42)
2	14	07.00 Sheffield - St Pancras (10.32)	**COMPOSITE CORRIDOR** (24/18)	BR	ST PANCRAS	BRADFORD	10.30 Bradford - St Pancras (15.42)
3	14	07.00 Sheffield - St Pancras (10.32)	**COMPOSITE CORRIDOR** (24/18)	BR	ST PANCRAS	BRADFORD	10.30 Bradford - St Pancras (15.42)
4	14	07.00 Sheffield - St Pancras (10.32)	**THIRD CORRIDOR** (48)	BR	ST PANCRAS	BRADFORD	10.30 Bradford - St Pancras (15.42)
5	14	07.00 Sheffield - St Pancras (10.32)	**THIRD CORRIDOR** (48)	BR	ST PANCRAS	BRADFORD	10.30 Bradford - St Pancras (15.42)
6	14	07.00 Sheffield - St Pancras (10.32)	**THIRD CORRIDOR** (48)	BR	ST PANCRAS	BRADFORD	10.30 Bradford - St Pancras (15.42)
7	14	07.00 Sheffield - St Pancras (10.32)	**BRAKE THIRD CORRIDOR** (24)	BR	ST PANCRAS	BRADFORD	10.30 Bradford - St Pancras (15.42)
8	117	08.15 Nottingham - St Pancras (10.32)	**RESTAURANT THIRD** (30)	LMS	ST PANCRAS	NOTTINGHAM	08.15 Nottingham - St Pancras (10.32)
9	117	08.15 Nottingham - St Pancras (10.32)	**FIRST OPEN** (42)	BR	ST PANCRAS	NOTTINGHAM	08.15 Nottingham - St Pancras (10.32)
10	117	08.15 Nottingham - St Pancras (10.32)	**FIRST CORRIDOR** (36)	LMS	ST PANCRAS	NOTTINGHAM	08.15 Nottingham - St Pancras (10.32)

The 14.00 was a train of long standing and which in Midland days had been remarkable for calling at Kentish Town in order to attach a through portion from Dover via the SECR and Ludgate Hill. By BR days through coaches from Kent were becoming a distant memory although the 14.00 remained notable by having the second longest run from St Pancras by running non-stop to Nottingham (where, incidentally, it met the 12.50 ex St Pancras as the latter arrived from the opposite direction). During its five minute stop in Nottingham the three-coach dining section was removed from the rear of the train, its next working being with the 07.00 Sheffield to St Pancras from Nottingham the next morning. The remaining seven coaches did not work to a daily diagram but followed a two-day cyclic working alternating between the 07.00 Sheffield to London, the 10.30 Bradford to St Pancras and the 18.33 St Pancras to Sheffield. The 14.00 was unique in being the only regular service from St Pancras to run from Sheffield to Leeds via Chapeltown as opposed to the normal route via Rotherham.

Jubilee 4-6-0 45607 'Fiji' of Sheffield (Millhouses) restarts the Devonian from Derby in June 1954. In LMS days the service had operated only between Bradford and Bristol but had included a GWR three-coach portion for Paignton which was transferred at Temple Meads to an internal GWR service. After the war and in contrast to the general trend of neglecting the more unusual elements of passenger services, the Devonian was run as a complete through train from Bradford to Newton Abbot; five of the eleven coaches going forward to Paignton and the remainder to Plymouth.

13.45 BIRMINGHAM to YARMOUTH BEACH (19.34)

	C/W	Previous working	Vehicle	Type	From	To	Next working
1	90A	11.26 S. Lynn - Leicester (13.40)	RESTAURANT BUFFET	LMS	LEICESTER	SOUTH LYNN	11.26 S. Lynn - Leicester (13.40)
2	90	12.40 Kings Norton - Birmingham (12.55)	THIRD CORRIDOR (42)	LMS	BIRMINGHAM	YARMOUTH	09.00 Yarmouth - Birmingham (15.38)
3	90	12.40 Kings Norton - Birmingham (12.55)	THIRD CORRIDOR (42)	LMS	BIRMINGHAM	YARMOUTH	09.00 Yarmouth - Birmingham (15.38)
4	90	12.40 Kings Norton - Birmingham (12.55)	BRAKE COMPOSITE CORRIDOR (12/24)	LMS	BIRMINGHAM	YARMOUTH	09.00 Yarmouth - Birmingham (15.38)
5	91	12.40 Kings Norton - Birmingham (12.55)	THIRD CORRIDOR (42)	LMS	BIRMINGHAM	NORWICH	09.30 Norwich - Birmingham (15.38)
6	91	12.40 Kings Norton - Birmingham (12.55)	BRAKE COMPOSITE CORRIDOR (12/24)	LMS	BIRMINGHAM	NORWICH	09.30 Norwich - Birmingham (15.38)
7	89	12.40 Kings Norton - Birmingham (12.55)	THIRD CORRIDOR (42)	LMS	BIRMINGHAM	CROMER	09.40 Cromer - Birmingham (15.38)
8	89	12.40 Kings Norton - Birmingham (12.55)	BRAKE COMPOSITE CORRIDOR (12/24)	LMS	BIRMINGHAM	CROMER	09.40 Cromer - Birmingham (15.38)
9	89	12.40 Kings Norton - Birmingham (12.55)	THIRD CORRIDOR (42)	LMS	BIRMINGHAM	CROMER	09.40 (Sats) Cromer - Birmingham (15.38)
10	89	12.40 Kings Norton - Birmingham (12.55)	THIRD CORRIDOR (42)	LMS	BIRMINGHAM	CROMER	09.40 (Sats) Cromer - Birmingham (15.38)

The Midland & Great Northern was a very insular and self contained railway, few of whose trains ever strayed west of Peterborough or Spalding. The LMS had withdrawn from the joint arrangement in 1937, leaving the line in the hands of the LNER although, rather ironically, it was LMS engines that worked the route after nationalisation; the post-war 4MT 2-6-0's almost enjoying a monopoly of M&GN workings throughout the 1950's. A daily express connection with the Midland was retained in the form of a through train between Great Yarmouth and Birmingham; the service being worked between Yarmouth and Leicester by a B12 4-6-0. Neither the engine nor dining car worked through to Birmingham but came off at Leicester in order to return with the eastbound service the same day. An interesting feature of the 13.45 - which, incidentally, worked into New Street as a local from Kings Norton - was the way in which Cromer was supplied daily with vehicles which were then accumulated for the Saturday service.

12.20 YORK to BRISTOL (18.26)

	C/W	Previous working	Vehicle	Type	From	To	Next working
1	55	16.45 Bristol - York (23.02)	BRAKE THIRD CORRIDOR (24)	LMS	YORK	BRISTOL	14.15 Bristol - York (20.00)
2	55	16.45 Bristol - York (23.02)	THIRD CORRIDOR (42)	LMS	YORK	BRISTOL	14.15 Bristol - York (20.00)
3	55	16.45 Bristol - York (23.02)	COMPOSITE CORRIDOR (18/24)	LMS	YORK	BRISTOL	14.15 Bristol - York (20.00)
4	55	16.45 Bristol - York (23.02)	COMPOSITE CORRIDOR (18/24)	LMS	YORK	BRISTOL	14.15 Bristol - York (20.00)
5	55	16.45 Bristol - York (23.02)	THIRD CORRIDOR (42)	LMS	YORK	BRISTOL	14.15 Bristol - York (20.00)
6	151	16.45 Bristol - York (23.02)	THIRD CORRIDOR (42)	LMS	YORK	BRISTOL	14.15 Bristol - York (20.00)
7	151	16.45 Bristol - York (23.02)	THIRD CORRIDOR (42)	LMS	YORK	BRISTOL	14.15 Bristol - York (20.00)
8	55	16.45 Bristol - York (23.02)	BRAKE THIRD CORRIDOR (24)	LMS	YORK	BRISTOL	14.15 Bristol - York (20.00)

Connecting with the 10.00 Newcastle - Kings Cross 'Northumbrian' and, on the days it ran, the boat train that connected with the overnight sailing from Bergen, it is difficult to think of a cross-country service that competed for importance with the midday service from York to Bristol, especially since it made a connection at Temple Meads with the 16.15 Paddington to Plymouth. (In parenthesis, it has to be pointed out that Newcastle - Plymouth passengers were better advised to remain on the Northumbrian and travel via London since by catching the 17.30 ex Paddington which ran via Westbury, they were able to reach North Road almost an hour ahead of the 16.15. The cross-country route, however, was considerably cheaper).

Despite these circumstances, all of which helped to fill the train, there was nothing in the running of the service that distinguished it from any other Midland West of England service and, worst of all, its passengers had to sit for over six hours divorced from any form of refreshment save the platform trolley at Birmingham - if, that is, they were lucky enough to attract its attention during the six minutes the train spent in New Street.

Apart from a pair of strengthening coaches, the stock of the service followed a five-day cycle that covered several West of England workings: the 14.15 Bristol to York, the 07.30 Bradford to Bristol and the 16.45 Bristol to York, the last pair being worked in the same day. The remainder of the cycle was concerned with short distance working between York and Sheffield and from Sheffield to Bradford.

11.50 BRADFORD to ST PANCRAS (17.52)

	C/W	Previous working	Vehicle	Type	From	To	Next working
1	16	11.45 St Pancras - Bradford (17.15)	BRAKE THIRD CORRIDOR (24)	BR	BRADFORD	ST PANCRAS	11.45 St Pancras - Bradford (17.15)
2	16	11.45 St Pancras - Bradford (17.15)	COMPOSITE CORRIDOR (24/18)	BR	BRADFORD	ST PANCRAS	11.45 St Pancras - Bradford (17.15)
3	16	11.45 St Pancras - Bradford (17.15)	FIRST CORRIDOR (42)	BR	BRADFORD	ST PANCRAS	11.45 St Pancras - Bradford (17.15)
4	16	11.45 St Pancras - Bradford (17.15)	FIRST OPEN (42)	BR	BRADFORD	ST PANCRAS	11.45 St Pancras - Bradford (17.15)
5	16	11.45 St Pancras - Bradford (17.15)	KITCHEN CAR	LMS	BRADFORD	ST PANCRAS	11.45 St Pancras - Bradford (17.15)
6	16	11.45 St Pancras - Bradford (17.15)	THIRD OPEN (64)	BR	BRADFORD	ST PANCRAS	11.45 St Pancras - Bradford (17.15)
7	16	11.45 St Pancras - Bradford (17.15)	THIRD CORRIDOR (48)	BR	BRADFORD	ST PANCRAS	11.45 St Pancras - Bradford (17.15)
8	16	11.45 St Pancras - Bradford (17.15)	THIRD CORRIDOR (48)	BR	BRADFORD	ST PANCRAS	11.45 St Pancras - Bradford (17.15)
9	16	11.45 St Pancras - Bradford (17.15)	THIRD CORRIDOR (48)	BR	BRADFORD	ST PANCRAS	11.45 St Pancras - Bradford (17.15)
10	16	11.45 St Pancras - Bradford (17.15)	BRAKE THIRD CORRIDOR (24)	BR	BRADFORD	ST PANCRAS	11.45 St Pancras - Bradford (17.15)
11	16	11.45 St Pancras - Bradford (17.15)	THIRD CORRIDOR (48)	BR	BRADFORD	ST PANCRAS	11.45 St Pancras - Bradford (17.15)

A curious feature of the Bradford to London service was that it operated in the mornings only, the last through service to St Pancras leaving Forster Square at 11.50. Although it had all the trappings of a principal express, the formation even included a Kitchen car in the three-coach dining section, it took an hour longer to reach London than other trains on the route, mainly because it called at six intermediate stations south of Nottingham. One wonders whether the restaurant car might not have found more profitable employment elsewhere since it did a couple of sittings of luncheon between Leeds and Nottingham but reached London too early to commence a serving of dinner. One useful aid to the 11.50 was that it ran during a four-hour gap in Kings Cross departures and was therefore less prone to GN competition than any other Midland service. An interesting feature of the service was its routing via the Chapeltown loop to avoid clashing in the Rotherham area with the 11.48 York - Sheffield and the 12.20 York - Bristol.

The formation not only remained complete in its entirety throughout the journey but returned intact the following day - also via Nottingham - as the 11.45 St Pancras to Bradford. Although the 11.50 was, as mentioned above, the last through service of the day from Bradford to St Pancras, the fact was not the result of some Midland manana aimed at the West Riding and, of course, a regular service of departures was available from Bradford Exchange to Kings Cross. The reason was that the early and mid afternoon saw the two Midland day Anglo-Scottish trains and these were deemed sufficient to meet the needs of the area. Connections, of course, were available from Bradford whilst the last indirect service of the day to St Pancras was the 16.45 Forster Square to Bristol, connecting at Derby with the 17.55 Manchester - London.

With steam shut off to allow speed to fall for the 60 mph limit at Trent Junction, rebuilt Royal Scot 4-6-0 46137 'The Prince of Wales's Volunteers (South Lancashire)' hurries through Kegworth with a St Pancras - Manchester express on 26th March 1960. Although members of the class had been at work on the Midland since the end of 1957, 46137 was a rare visitor since it was an Edge Hill engine and usually employed between Liverpool and Euston or Liverpool and Leeds. Rebuilt in March 1955, it was the last of the class to be modified although at the time of the photograph it had little main line work left to it, being transferred a short time afterwards to Newton Heath.

	C/W	Previous working	Vehicle	Type	From	To	Next working
			15.35 LEICESTER to NOTTINGHAM (16.22)				
1	27	12.50 St Pancras - Leicester (15.25)	THIRD CORRIDOR (48)	BR	LEICESTER	NOTTINGHAM	06.40 Nottingham - St Pancras (09.55)
2	27	12.50 St Pancras - Leicester (15.25)	THIRD CORRIDOR (48)	BR	LEICESTER	NOTTINGHAM	06.40 Nottingham - St Pancras (09.55)
3	27	12.50 St Pancras - Leicester (15.25)	BRAKE THIRD CORRIDOR (24)	BR	LEICESTER	NOTTINGHAM	06.40 Nottingham - St Pancras (09.55)
4	27	12.50 St Pancras - Leicester (15.25)	COMPOSITE CORRIDOR (24/18)	BR	LEICESTER	NOTTINGHAM	06.40 Nottingham - St Pancras (09.55)
5	27	12.50 St Pancras - Leicester (15.25)	COMPOSITE CORRIDOR (24/18)	BR	LEICESTER	NOTTINGHAM	06.40 Nottingham - St Pancras (09.55)
6	27	12.50 St Pancras - Leicester (15.25)	THIRD OPEN (56)	LMS	LEICESTER	NOTTINGHAM	06.40 Nottingham - St Pancras (09.55)
7	27	12.50 St Pancras - Leicester (15.25)	RESTAURANT THIRD (30)	LMS	LEICESTER	NOTTINGHAM	06.40 Nottingham - St Pancras (09.55)
8	27	12.50 St Pancras - Leicester (15.25)	FIRST OPEN (42)	LMS	LEICESTER	NOTTINGHAM	06.40 Nottingham - St Pancras (09.55)
9	27	12.50 St Pancras - Leicester (15.25)	FIRST OPEN (42)	LMS	LEICESTER	NOTTINGHAM	06.40 Nottingham - St Pancras (09.55)
10	27	12.50 St Pancras - Leicester (15.25)	BRAKE THIRD CORRIDOR (24)	LMS	LEICESTER	NOTTINGHAM	06.40 Nottingham - St Pancras (09.55)

This, ostensibly a local train which ran from Leicester to Nottingham and called at Loughborough, Kegworth and Trent, was actually the last leg of the 12.50 semi-fast from St Pancras which, although terminating in Nottingham, was not shown as a through train as it was overtaken by the 14.00 St Pancras to Bradford which ran via Melton and reached Nottingham five minutes earlier.

	C/W	Previous working	Vehicle	Type	From	To	Next working
			14.15 ST PANCRAS to MANCHESTER CENTRAL (18.35)				
1	23	07.15 Manchester - St Pancras (11.34)	BRAKE THIRD CORRIDOR (24)	LMS	ST PANCRAS	MANCHESTER	09.00 Manchester - St Pancras (14.00)
2	23	07.15 Manchester - St Pancras (11.34)	THIRD CORRIDOR (42)	LMS	ST PANCRAS	MANCHESTER	09.00 Manchester - St Pancras (14.00)
3	23	07.15 Manchester - St Pancras (11.34)	THIRD CORRIDOR (42)	LMS	ST PANCRAS	MANCHESTER	09.00 Manchester - St Pancras (14.00)
4	23	07.15 Manchester - St Pancras (11.34)	THIRD OPEN (56)	LMS	ST PANCRAS	MANCHESTER	09.00 Manchester - St Pancras (14.00)
5	23	07.15 Manchester - St Pancras (11.34)	RESTAURANT FIRST (24)	LMS	ST PANCRAS	MANCHESTER	09.00 Manchester - St Pancras (14.00)
6	23	07.15 Manchester - St Pancras (11.34)	FIRST CORRIDOR (36)	LMS	ST PANCRAS	MANCHESTER	09.00 Manchester - St Pancras (14.00)
7	23	07.15 Manchester - St Pancras (11.34)	COMPOSITE CORRIDOR (18/24)	LMS	ST PANCRAS	MANCHESTER	09.00 Manchester - St Pancras (14.00)
8	23	07.15 Manchester - St Pancras (11.34)	BRAKE THIRD CORRIDOR (24)	LMS	ST PANCRAS	MANCHESTER	09.00 Manchester - St Pancras (14.00)
9	101	09.39 Buxton - St Pancras (14.00)	BRAKE COMPOSITE CORRIDOR (12/21)	LMS	ST PANCRAS	MILLERS DALE	17.56 Millers Dale - Buxton (18.06)
10	32A	08.05 Derby - St Pancras (10.45)	BRAKE THIRD CORRIDOR (24)	LMS	ST PANCRAS	DERBY	08.05 Derby - St Pancras (10.45)

Manchester occupied a curious place in the priorities of the postwar Midland. On the one hand it commanded a series of expresses that were the equal of anything on the system yet on the other a gap of four hours was allowed to elapse after the departure of the 10.15. In LMS days the Midland service was seen as complimentary to that from Euston and there had been a excellent (three hour and thirty-eight minutes) train at 12.30 from St Pancras with, of course, a further choice being available from Marylebone. The war put an end to such duplication of services and in spite of the continuing Great Central service, the London Midland Region failed to recover the expansive view of earlier times.

The 14.15 was the return of the relatively light (eight coach) morning business express from Manchester but with a pair of additional vehicles; one a Brake Third which ran as far as Derby and the other the daily through coach between London and Buxton.

To permit the dining car staff to alternate between an early and middle turn of duty with losing their vehicle and its stores, the carriage set worked to a two-day cycle which covered the 07.15 Manchester - London and the 14.15 London - Manchester on the first day and the 09.00 Manchester - London and the 16.15 London - Manchester on the second.

May 1958 saw Pacifics drafted to the Midland for the first time as a batch of six Britannia Pacifics arrived to reinforce the class 7P Royal Scots that had arrived in November 1957. The Pacifics replaced the 5XP Jubilee 4-6-0's on the Manchester - St Pancras service and complemented the six Royal Scot 4-6-0's at Kentish Town that worked to Sheffield and Leeds from St Pancras. The arrival of the Britannia Pacifics coincided with a reinvigoration of Midland services to Manchester, not the least of the reasons being the impending dislocation of LNW services caused by the 25kv electrification. By 1961 the number of down trains had been increased from five to eight, one of which was a dmu Pullman working, with two of the steam services reaching Manchester in under four hours thanks to the introduction of XL timings and the excising of certain intermediate stops. Above, Britannia 70021 'Morning Star' of Trafford Park runs into Leicester (London Road) with the 07.15 Manchester Central to St Pancras on 14th May 1959.

		13.50 MANCHESTER CENTRAL to ST PANCRAS (18.14)					
	C/W Previous working	Vehicle	Type	From	To	Next working	
1	26 04.18 St Pancras - Manchester (09.46)	BRAKE THIRD CORRIDOR (24)	BR	MANCHESTER	ST PANCRAS	04.18 St Pancras - Manchester (09.46)	
2	26 04.18 St Pancras - Manchester (09.46)	FIRST CORRIDOR (42)	BR	MANCHESTER	ST PANCRAS	04.18 St Pancras - Manchester (09.46)	
3	26 04.18 St Pancras - Manchester (09.46)	COMPOSITE CORRIDOR (24/18)	BR	MANCHESTER	ST PANCRAS	04.18 St Pancras - Manchester (09.46)	
4	26 04.18 St Pancras - Manchester (09.46)	THIRD CORRIDOR (48)	BR	MANCHESTER	ST PANCRAS	04.18 St Pancras - Manchester (09.46)	
5	26 04.18 St Pancras - Manchester (09.46)	THIRD CORRIDOR (42)	LMS	MANCHESTER	ST PANCRAS	04.18 St Pancras - Manchester (09.46)	
6	26 04.18 St Pancras - Manchester (09.46)	BRAKE THIRD CORRIDOR (24)	LMS	MANCHESTER	ST PANCRAS	04.18 St Pancras - Manchester (09.46)	
7	28B 20.10 St Pancras - Derby (23.40)	THIRD CORRIDOR (42)	LMS	DERBY	ST PANCRAS	As Required	
8	29A 10.15 St Pancras - Derby (12.50)	COMPOSITE CORRIDOR (18/24)	LMS	DERBY	ST PANCRAS	10.15 St Pancras - Derby (12.50)	
9	28A 08.15 St Pancras - Derby (11.19)	RESTAURANT (BUFFET) COMPOSITE (12/18)	LMS	DERBY	ST PANCRAS	08.15 St Pancras - Derby (11.19)	
10	28A 08.15 St Pancras - Derby (11.19)	THIRD OPEN (56)	LMS	DERBY	ST PANCRAS	08.15 St Pancras - Derby (11.19)	

The most noticeable sign that the favoured post-war route between Manchester and London traffic was the ex-LNWR to Euston came from the gap of almost five hours in services to St Pancras after the 09.00 departure. In Midland days there had been trains at 10.15, 10.20, 12.00 and 13.50, most of which attached a through section from Liverpool at either Stockport or Chinley but subsequent developments had seen these services wiped away until nothing remained between the 09.00 and 13.50 expresses. Interestingly the stock for the 13.50 - later to be christened 'The Palatine' - arrived and left during this gap; the six-coach set arriving with the 04.18 Newspaper train from St Pancras and being prepared for its return in Manchester Central. By postwar standards the 13.50 was quite a fast train, second only to the 07.20, although its importance was somewhat diminished through consisting of only six coaches sans dining facilities. It was from Derby that the train took on a more serious aspect as the dining section was attached to the rear of the train; an assortment of coaches that had come down from London in the 08.15 and 10.15 services from St Pancras and which raised the weight of the train from 198 to 335 tons. The latter took the load beyond the 310 tons allowed for a Black 5 on Special Limit timings between Leicester and London and although it was just, by fifteen tons, inside the 5XP limit; the margin was too fine and the train was therefore timed to the slower limited load schedule which amounted to about thirteen minutes between Leicester and London.

Apart from the complications involved at Derby in congregating the various parts of the dining portion, there were no particular complexities to the carriage workings; each section working the 04.18 and the 08.15 trains from London each weekday.

11.40 BOURNEMOUTH WEST to GLOUCESTER (14.50)

	C/W Previous working	Vehicle	Type	From	To	Next working
1	88B 15.20 Gloucester - Bournemouth	BRAKE THIRD CORRIDOR (32)	LMS	BOURNEMOUTH	GLOUCESTER	15.20 Gloucester - Bournemouth
2	88B 15.20 Gloucester - Bournemouth	COMPOSITE CORRIDOR (18/32)	LMS	BOURNEMOUTH	GLOUCESTER	15.20 Gloucester - Bournemouth
3	88B 15.20 Gloucester - Bournemouth	BRAKE THIRD CORRIDOR (32)	LMS	BOURNEMOUTH	GLOUCESTER	15.20 Gloucester - Bournemouth
4	88B 15.20 Gloucester - Bournemouth	COMPOSITE CORRIDOR (18/24)	LMS	BOURNEMOUTH	GLOUCESTER	15.20 Gloucester - Bournemouth

With London only two and a half hours away by a frequent series of expresses, the scope for cross-country trains to the north from Bournemouth was rather limited and it is to the Midland's credit that even at the quietest time of year, two through trains were provided which eliminated the need to navigate from Waterloo to St Pancras or to change trains at Bath and Mangotsfield. The greater of the pair was the 09.45 Pines Express to Sheffield, Manchester and Liverpool whilst the other was the 11.40 from Bournemouth which ran to Gloucester in much the same timings as the Pines and connected with the 14.15 Bristol - York, giving an arrival of 20.00 in the latter.

The utility of the 11.40 was somewhat curbed by the fact that a through service via Oxford and Leicester left Bournemouth for York at 11.16 and arrived half an hour earlier than the 14.15 ex Bristol. The passenger in a hurry, however, could ignore both these offerings and reach York in a fraction over seven hours by the 10.30 from Bournemouth Central and the 14.00 Heart of Midlothian from Kings Cross. You paid your money and you made your choice!

Perhaps a more flexible organisation might have noticed the glut of trains and evened things out a little by retarding the 11.40 by a couple of hours but nationalisation brought no more liaison to railway affairs than the grouping had done and each of the parties at Bournemouth carried on as though the other did not exist. One result was that patronage of the 11.40 was such that only four carriages were needed except on Summer Fridays when forces leave requirements saw the train strengthened to eight vehicles and extended to Derby as a relief to the 14.15 Bristol - York. Two four-coach sets were used for the working, one forming the 11.40 Bournemouth - Gloucester and the 15.55 Gloucester - Bristol whilst the other worked the 10.35 Bristol - Gloucester and the 15.20 Gloucester to Bournemouth.

14.15 BRISTOL to YORK (20.00)

	C/W	Previous working	Vehicle	Type	From	To	Next working
1	44	12.00 York - Bristol (18.25)	BRAKE THIRD CORRIDOR (24)	LMS	BRISTOL	YORK	09.42 York - Sheffield (10.56)
2	150	12.00 York - Bristol (18.25)	THIRD CORRIDOR (42)	LMS	BRISTOL	YORK	12.00 York - Bristol (18.25)
3	150	12.00 York - Bristol (18.25)	THIRD CORRIDOR (42)	LMS	BRISTOL	YORK	12.00 York - Bristol (18.25)
4	44	12.00 York - Bristol (18.25)	THIRD CORRIDOR (42)	LMS	BRISTOL	YORK	09.42 York - Sheffield (10.56)
5	44	12.00 York - Bristol (18.25)	COMPOSITE CORRIDOR (18/24)	LMS	BRISTOL	YORK	09.42 York - Sheffield (10.56)
6	44	12.00 York - Bristol (18.25)	COMPOSITE CORRIDOR (18/24)	LMS	BRISTOL	YORK	09.42 York - Sheffield (10.56)
7	44	12.00 York - Bristol (18.25)	THIRD CORRIDOR (42)	LMS	BRISTOL	YORK	09.42 York - Sheffield (10.56)
8	44	12.00 York - Bristol (18.25)	BRAKE THIRD CORRIDOR (24)	LMS	BRISTOL	YORK	09.42 York - Sheffield (10.56)
9	152		THIRD CORRIDOR (42)	LMS	BRISTOL	SHEFFIELD	19.25 Sheffield - Leeds (21.01)
10	152		THIRD CORRIDOR (42)	LMS	BRISTOL	SHEFFIELD	19.25 Sheffield - Leeds (21.01)
11	152A		THIRD CORRIDOR (42)	LMS	BRISTOL	SHEFFIELD	09.08 Sheffield - Bradford (11.04)

The 14.15 ex Bristol was of importance since it connected with the 07.30 Penzance - Manchester via Hereford and therefore gave the first service of the day between Cornwall and Yorkshire since the preceding Devonian left Plymouth too early for connections to arrive from the Duchy. By cross-country standards it was quite a fast train; at a shade under four and a half hours it was amongst the fastest Bristol - Sheffield services whilst in spite of having to change trains at York, it gave a faster service by half an hour to Newcastle than either of the through trains. The other side of the coin was the lack of any catering services whatsoever in an express that was not only popular but spanned the hours when the demand for dinner was assured. The reason for this was the reluctance of the operators to increase the weight of the train to thirteen vehicles given the difficulties at Bromsgrove where twelve coaches was the normal limit for a 5XP and the 0-10-0 banker. This limit was not absolute but a thirteen coach train would have tied up more banking power - three 0-6-0T's or the 0-10-0 and an 0-6-0T - than the operators cared to use at one time. The climb out of Bristol to Fishponds with thirteen vehicles and although the 14.15's schedule was eased by six minutes to allow for it, the LM preferred not to bank if it could be avoided.

The stock of the train consisted of the six vehicles that worked to the celebrated 10-day cycle plus five strengthening coaches. The trailing set of coaches was removed at Sheffield while the remainder went forward to York to form the following day's 12.20 York - Bristol and the 09.42 stopping service from York to Sheffield.

15.15 ST PANCRAS to BRADFORD (20.50)

	C/W	Previous working	Vehicle	Type	From	To	Next working
1	124	09.00 Sheffield - St Pancras (12.25)	COMPOSITE CORRIDOR (18/24)	LMS	ST PANCRAS	SHEFFIELD	09.00 Sheffield - St Pancras (12.25)
2	124	09.00 Sheffield - St Pancras (12.25)	THIRD OPEN (56)	LMS	ST PANCRAS	SHEFFIELD	09.00 Sheffield - St Pancras (12.25)
3	124	09.00 Sheffield - St Pancras (12.25)	RESTAURANT FIRST (24)	LMS	ST PANCRAS	SHEFFIELD	09.00 Sheffield - St Pancras (12.25)
4	19	07.15 Bradford - St Pancras (12.25)	BRAKE FIRST CORRIDOR (30)	LMS	ST PANCRAS	BRADFORD	07.15 Bradford - St Pancras (12.25)
5	19	07.15 Bradford - St Pancras (12.25)	COMPOSITE CORRIDOR (24/18)	BR	ST PANCRAS	BRADFORD	07.15 Bradford - St Pancras (12.25)
6	19	07.15 Bradford - St Pancras (12.25)	COMPOSITE CORRIDOR (24/18)	BR	ST PANCRAS	BRADFORD	07.15 Bradford - St Pancras (12.25)
7	19	07.15 Bradford - St Pancras (12.25)	THIRD CORRIDOR (48)	BR	ST PANCRAS	BRADFORD	07.15 Bradford - St Pancras (12.25)
8	19	07.15 Bradford - St Pancras (12.25)	THIRD CORRIDOR (48)	BR	ST PANCRAS	BRADFORD	07.15 Bradford - St Pancras (12.25)
9	19	07.15 Bradford - St Pancras (12.25)	THIRD CORRIDOR (48)	BR	ST PANCRAS	BRADFORD	07.15 Bradford - St Pancras (12.25)
10	19	07.15 Bradford - St Pancras (12.25)	BRAKE THIRD CORRIDOR (24)	BR	ST PANCRAS	BRADFORD	07.15 Bradford - St Pancras (12.25)

It is easy to forget that not only was the West Coast port of Heysham - 267 miles distant - a Midland possession but that before 1914 through coaches from St Pancras to Morecambe and Heysham were an ordinary part of the everyday ritual with several of the West Riding expresses - of which the 15.15 was one - conveying through coaches. The use made of this facility was not great since the London & North Western had a route that was shorter by thirty-three miles and enabled the journey to be reduced by the best part of an hour and it is probable that the facility was scarcely missed when it disappeared at the time of the grouping. By 1955 such matters were a memory - although a London - Morecambe ticket was still valid via Leeds - and the 15.15 had been pared to ten coaches, seven of which ran to Bradford whilst the remainder came off at Sheffield.

Running via Kettering and Nottingham, most of the 15.15's patronage consisted of Nottingham and Sheffield businessmen since the 15.45 West Riding from Kings Cross reached Bradford Exchange almost an hour and a quarter earlier. The 15.15 did however exchange many of its London passengers at Sheffield for West Riding travellers who transferred from the 14.12 Bristol - York and who were liable to a particularly hungry journey since not only did the Bristol train lack dining facilities but those of the 15.15 were removed at Sheffield. The ten vehicles of the 15.15 repeated their journey each day; the main portion of the service working up with the 07.15 ex Bradford and collecting its dining portion en route during the call at Sheffield.

16.25 LEICESTER to ST PANCRAS (19.00)

	C/W Previous working	Vehicle	Type	From	To	Next working
1	921 23.50 St Pancras - Leicester (02.34)	FULL BRAKE	LMS	LEICESTER	ST PANCRAS	
2	09.05 St Pancras - Leicester (11.40)	THIRD CORRIDOR (42)	LMS	LEICESTER	ST PANCRAS	09.05 St Pancras - Leicester (11.40)
3	09.05 St Pancras - Leicester (11.40)	THIRD CORRIDOR (42)	LMS	LEICESTER	ST PANCRAS	09.05 St Pancras - Leicester (11.40)
4	09.05 St Pancras - Leicester (11.40)	BRAKE THIRD CORRIDOR (32)	LMS	LEICESTER	ST PANCRAS	09.05 St Pancras - Leicester (11.40)
5	09.05 St Pancras - Leicester (11.40)	COMPOSITE CORRIDOR (18/32)	LMS	LEICESTER	ST PANCRAS	09.05 St Pancras - Leicester (11.40)
6	09.05 St Pancras - Leicester (11.40)	BRAKE THIRD CORRIDOR (32)	LMS	LEICESTER	ST PANCRAS	09.05 St Pancras - Leicester (11.40)

A local service and therefore separate from the running of through trains but of some importance since it connected with the 13.50 Manchester to St Pancras and by doing so, allowed the latter to run non-stop from Leicester to London. Whilst this doubtless cheered through passengers from Manchester to London, it had a depressing effect on passengers from Manchester to, for instance, St Albans who found their journey time extended by three-quarters of an hour. Most expresses from Manchester tended to stop at either Bedford, Luton or St Albans in order to give the Home Counties a direct service but the 13.50 - later to be entitled 'The Palatine' - was the exception to the rule.

Sandwiched between the 13.50 ex Manchester and the up Thames Clyde which left Leicester at 17.17, the 16.25 was deliberately lightened to five coaches and a BG in order to see that the Black Five 4-6-0 to which the train was entrusted, could not use overloading as an excuse for poor running. The timing of the service was something of a mixed bag and although run to Limited Load timings, the usual semi-fast stops was augmented by calls at Irchester and Harpenden.

09.20 'THAMES-CLYDE EXPRESS' GLASGOW (ST ENOCH) to ST PANCRAS (19.19)

	C/W Previous working	Vehicle	Type	From	To	Next working
1	945	FULL BRAKE	LMS	GLASGOW	ST PANCRAS	
2	2 10.00 St Pancras - Glasgow	BRAKE THIRD CORRIDOR (24)	BR	GLASGOW	ST PANCRAS	10.00 St Pancras - Glasgow
3	2 10.00 St Pancras - Glasgow	COMPOSITE CORRIDOR (24/18)	BR	GLASGOW	ST PANCRAS	10.00 St Pancras - Glasgow
4	2 10.00 St Pancras - Glasgow	COMPOSITE CORRIDOR (24/18)	BR	GLASGOW	ST PANCRAS	10.00 St Pancras - Glasgow
5	2 10.00 St Pancras - Glasgow	FIRST OPEN (42)	LMS	GLASGOW	ST PANCRAS	10.00 St Pancras - Glasgow
6	2 10.00 St Pancras - Glasgow	KITCHEN CAR	LMS	GLASGOW	ST PANCRAS	10.00 St Pancras - Glasgow
7	2 10.00 St Pancras - Glasgow	THIRD OPEN (56)	LMS	GLASGOW	ST PANCRAS	10.00 St Pancras - Glasgow
8	2 10.00 St Pancras - Glasgow	THIRD CORRIDOR (48)	BR	GLASGOW	ST PANCRAS	10.00 St Pancras - Glasgow
9	2 10.00 St Pancras - Glasgow	THIRD CORRIDOR (48)	BR	GLASGOW	ST PANCRAS	10.00 St Pancras - Glasgow
10	2 10.00 St Pancras - Glasgow	THIRD CORRIDOR (48)	BR	GLASGOW	ST PANCRAS	10.00 St Pancras - Glasgow
11	2 10.00 St Pancras - Glasgow	BRAKE THIRD CORRIDOR (24)	BR	GLASGOW	ST PANCRAS	10.00 St Pancras - Glasgow

Popularly supposed to be the showpiece of the line, the Thames-Clyde was a reminder of the days when the Midland had daily run three through trains (09.20, 11.00 and 13.30) from St Enoch to St Pancras (arriving at 18.30, 20.15 and 22.25 respectively). Time, tide and progress had seen the trio reduced until only the Thames-Clyde remained and while the wonder of a Midland Anglo-Scottish service remained, it cannot be said that the operators quite did all they could to promote the train although, in contrast to some of the Midland's best trains, the dining facilities were second to none with a full Kitchen car being provided to meet the demand for the three main meals that the train's running encompassed. It's Edinburgh counterpart, the Waverley, had as the icing on the cake, an extremely fast timing from Nottingham to London and it would have been fitting had the Thames-Clyde been given a similar tour de force by which to round off its day. Alas, such timings as the Waverley possessed called either for a load of under 350 tons (eleven coaches) or a class 7 engine and the Thames-Clyde could meet neither of these criteria. The weight of the train was five tons over the special limit maximum - the LM was nothing if not a bureaucracy - and therefore it had to run to the slower limited load timings which meant a disappointing eighty-two minute schedule - ten minutes greater than it might have been - for the Kettering - London leg.

This constraint did not apply to the northbound train which ran in special limit timings, the formation having been lightened by leaving out the Full Brake. The remainder of the train alternated between the up and down Thames-Clyde Expresses. To keep clear of the 12.27 Newcastle - Bristol in the vikcinity of Rotherham, the service was diverted over the Chapeltown loop between Cudworth and Sheffield.

14.57 BRADFORD to HULL (17.17)

	C/W Previous working	Vehicle	Type	From	To	Next working
1	130 10.42 Hull - Bradford (12.57)	BRAKE THIRD CORRIDOR (24)	BR/NER	BRADFORD	HULL	10.42 Hull - Bradford (12.57)
2	130 10.42 Hull - Bradford (12.57)	THIRD CORRIDOR (48)	BR/NER	BRADFORD	HULL	10.42 Hull - Bradford (12.57)
3	130 10.42 Hull - Bradford (12.57)	THIRD CORRIDOR (48)	BR/NER	BRADFORD	HULL	10.42 Hull - Bradford (12.57)
4	130 10.42 Hull - Bradford (12.57)	FIRST CORRIDOR (36)	LNER	BRADFORD	HULL	10.42 Hull - Bradford (12.57)
5	130 10.42 Hull - Bradford (12.57)	COMPOSITE CORRIDOR (24/18)	BR/NER	BRADFORD	HULL	10.42 Hull - Bradford (12.57)
6	130 10.42 Hull - Bradford (12.57)	THIRD CORRIDOR (48)	BR/NER	BRADFORD	HULL	10.42 Hull - Bradford (12.57)
7	130 10.42 Hull - Bradford (12.57)	BRAKE THIRD CORRIDOR (24)	BR/NER	BRADFORD	HULL	10.42 Hull - Bradford (12.57)

Trains over the 52-mile stretch between Hull and Leeds were fairly numerous - thirteen a day - yet few, thanks to the complications of having to make arrangements for engines, stock and guards with the successors of the LNW and Midland Railway, ventured west of Leeds City. Ten of the trains confined themselves to Leeds and Hull, two went through to Liverpool whilst the thirteenth ran through to Bradford, Forster Square. Whilst through running between Hull and Bradford was a generally laudable concept, there was a certain surreal element about the 10.42. In the first place it ran in both directions, when demand was at its lowest and although the running in the westbound direction was reasonable - four stops between Hull and Leeds - the return working was deplorably slow with scarcely a station being omitted. Yet for all this, with the exception of the centre vehicle, the train was formed of the latest and most modern stock available! In the course of their lives the British Railways Mark 1 coaches gained more detractors than adherents and it may be that the North Eastern was abnormally prescient in this matter. Not only was the stock North Eastern but so was the motive power with a Neville Hill B1 4-6-0 being used throughout in both directions. In addition to connecting Bradford with Hull the service was also the Bradford connection into the 10.05 'Waverley' Edinburgh - St Pancras.

16.50 BIRMINGHAM to CLEETHORPES (21.28)

C/W	Previous working	Vehicle	Type	From	To	Next working
1	88	13.51 Gloucester - Birmingham (15.59)	BRAKE THIRD CORRIDOR (24)	LMS	BIRMINGHAM	CLEETHORPES	06.57 Cleethorpes - Birmingham (11.13)
2	88	13.51 Gloucester - Birmingham (15.59)	THIRD CORRIDOR (42)	LMS	BIRMINGHAM	CLEETHORPES	06.57 Cleethorpes - Birmingham (11.13)
3	88	13.51 Gloucester - Birmingham (15.59)	COMPOSITE CORRIDOR (18/24)	LMS	BIRMINGHAM	CLEETHORPES	06.57 Cleethorpes - Birmingham (11.13)
4	88	13.51 Gloucester - Birmingham (15.59)	THIRD CORRIDOR (42)	LMS	BIRMINGHAM	CLEETHORPES	06.57 Cleethorpes - Birmingham (11.13)
5	88	13.51 Gloucester - Birmingham (15.59)	BRAKE THIRD CORRIDOR (24)	LMS	BIRMINGHAM	CLEETHORPES	06.57 Cleethorpes - Birmingham (11.13)

The 'Cleethorpes' as it was known was something of a celebrity in the West Midlands since it was the only train apart from the Tamworth - Lincoln mail to run east of Nottingham. Its status was further enhanced by being worked by an LNER B1 4-6-0; the Immingham-based engine arriving at 11.13 with the westbound train and being serviced in the interim on Bourneville loco. The rolling stock did not follow the same pattern but remained in the West Midlands overnight, being used on arrival from Cleethorpes for an stopping train to Gloucester. The balance the following day commenced with the 13.51 Gloucester to Birmingham, a stopping train via Worcester that connected out of the up Devonian, and continued on to Cleethorpes after three quarters of an hour in New Street.

The routing of the train was of almost as much interest as the engine and carriage working since instead of running direct from Birmingham to Nottingham via Derby, a distance of fifty-seven miles for which about eighty minutes would be required, the service was routed via Nuneaton, Leicester and Trent, taking two hours for the additional ten miles. There was no question of avoiding the detour by catching a later train from Birmingham, changing at Derby and joining the Cleethorpes service at Trent or Nottingham since, thanks to a frustratingly clever piece of timetabling, the only direct train to Derby was the 17.15 slow which arrived too late to make a Nottingham connection.

Whether Leicester was of greater commercial benefit than Derby is difficult to say but the Cleethorpes certainly turned up on the Midland main line at an awkward time since it left Leicester at 18.06 to run non-stop to Loughborough, nine minutes behind the down Cricklewood milk empties and ten minutes ahead of the 16.15 London - Manchester. It was not an ideal place for the Leicester driver and his unusual engine to get used to each other.

16.15 ST PANCRAS to MANCHESTER CENTRAL (20.47)

C/W	Previous working	Vehicle	Type	From	To	Next working
1	24A	00.05 Manchester - St Pancras (06.54)	THIRD CORRIDOR (42)	LMS	ST PANCRAS	MANCHESTER	00.05 Manchester - St Pancras (06.54)
2	24	09.00 Manchester - St Pancras (14.00)	BRAKE THIRD CORRIDOR (24)	LMS	ST PANCRAS	MANCHESTER	07.15 Manchester - St Pancras (11.34)
3	24	09.00 Manchester - St Pancras (14.00)	THIRD CORRIDOR (42)	LMS	ST PANCRAS	MANCHESTER	07.15 Manchester - St Pancras (11.34)
4	24	09.00 Manchester - St Pancras (14.00)	THIRD CORRIDOR (42)	LMS	ST PANCRAS	MANCHESTER	07.15 Manchester - St Pancras (11.34)
5	24	09.00 Manchester - St Pancras (14.00)	THIRD OPEN (56)	LMS	ST PANCRAS	MANCHESTER	07.15 Manchester - St Pancras (11.34)
6	24	09.00 Manchester - St Pancras (14.00)	RESTAURANT FIRST (36)	LMS	ST PANCRAS	MANCHESTER	07.15 Manchester - St Pancras (11.34)
7	24	09.00 Manchester - St Pancras (14.00)	FIRST CORRIDOR (36)	LMS	ST PANCRAS	MANCHESTER	07.15 Manchester - St Pancras (11.34)
8	24	09.00 Manchester - St Pancras (14.00)	COMPOSITE CORRIDOR (18/24)	LMS	ST PANCRAS	MANCHESTER	07.15 Manchester - St Pancras (11.34)
9	24C	09.00 Manchester - St Pancras (14.00)	COMPOSITE CORRIDOR (18/24)	LMS	ST PANCRAS	MANCHESTER	09.00 Manchester - St Pancras (14.00)
10	24	09.00 Manchester - St Pancras (14.00)	BRAKE THIRD CORRIDOR (24)	LMS	ST PANCRAS	MANCHESTER	07.15 Manchester - St Pancras (11.34)
11	24B	09.00 Derby - St Pancras (11.31)	FIRST CORRIDOR (36)	LMS	ST PANCRAS	DERBY	09.00 Derby - St Pancras (11.31)

The Midland provided two evening Manchester business expresses; one at 16.15 and the other at 18.40, both taking just under four and a half hours. The neighbouring North Western also ran a pair from Euston, 16.30 and 18.30, reaching Manchester at 20.14 and 21.30 respectively whilst those who thought the Midland slow by comparison were welcome to take the 18.15 from Marylebone and get to Manchester at 23.24.

The eight-coach main body of the 16.15 alternated with the 14.15 ex St Pancras each day in order to balance out the hours of the dining car staff whilst a pair of coaches remained in the 16.15 on a daily basis. One of these was a Third Corridor which came up in the overnight service from Manchester whilst the other was a Composite Corridor which came out of the set at Manchester to be added to the 14.15 ex St Pancras prior to returning as the 09.00 to London. Not only did this involve a considerable amount of shunting at Cornbrook carriage sidings but meant some energetic station work at St Pancras since the inward train arrived at 14.00 with the through Buxton Brake Composite second from rear which had to be removed and put to one side for the following day's 14.15 express. At the same time a First Corridor for Derby that had arrived in the 07.20 ex Manchester had to be attached to the rear of the train. It was a lot to do in not much more than an hour.

One item of unintended entertainment arose in the London suburbs as the 16.15 overhauled the 15.50 St Pancras - Harpenden local; the latter normally being overtaken in the vicinity of Radlett. With a good 2-6-4T and a driver who could rise to an occasion it was not unknown for the local to overhaul the 5XP at least once, giving the passengers of both trains the fascinating view of a steam engine working at full cry.

16.25 ST PANCRAS to KETTERING (18.06)

C/W	Previous working	Vehicle	Type	From	To	Next working
1	47	18.30 Kettering - Nottingham (19.51)	BRAKE THIRD CORRIDOR (24)	LMS	ST PANCRAS	KETTERING	18.27 Kettering - Nottingham (19.48)
2	47	18.30 Kettering - Nottingham (19.51)	THIRD CORRIDOR (42)	LMS	ST PANCRAS	KETTERING	18.27 Kettering - Nottingham (19.48)
3	47	08.28 Nottingham - St Pancras (11.25)	THIRD CORRIDOR (42)	LMS	ST PANCRAS	KETTERING	18.27 Kettering - Nottingham (19.48)
4	47	08.28 Nottingham - St Pancras (11.25)	THIRD CORRIDOR (42)	LMS	ST PANCRAS	KETTERING	18.27 Kettering - Nottingham (19.48)
5	47	08.28 Nottingham - St Pancras (11.25)	THIRD CORRIDOR (42)	LMS	ST PANCRAS	KETTERING	18.27 Kettering - Nottingham (19.48)
6	47	08.28 Nottingham - St Pancras (11.25)	THIRD CORRIDOR (42)	LMS	ST PANCRAS	KETTERING	18.27 Kettering - Nottingham (19.48)
7	47	08.28 Nottingham - St Pancras (11.25)	COMPOSITE CORRIDOR (18/24)	LMS	ST PANCRAS	KETTERING	18.27 Kettering - Nottingham (19.48)
8	47	08.28 Nottingham - St Pancras (11.25)	COMPOSITE CORRIDOR (18/24)	LMS	ST PANCRAS	KETTERING	18.27 Kettering - Nottingham (19.48)
9	47	08.28 Nottingham - St Pancras (11.25)	THIRD CORRIDOR (42)	LMS	ST PANCRAS	KETTERING	18.27 Kettering - Nottingham (19.48)
10	47	08.28 Nottingham - St Pancras (11.25)	BRAKE THIRD CORRIDOR (24)	LMS	ST PANCRAS	KETTERING	18.27 Kettering - Nottingham (19.48)

In contrast to the shunting that had to be done to the 16.15 Manchester, the 16.25 to Kettering was simplicity itself since the ten coaches arrived in London from Nottingham at 11.25 and then spent the afternoon in Cricklewood with no more attention than a clean. The principal function of the train was to give the business traffic of Luton, Bedford and Kettering - Wellingborough was served by the 16.50 St Pancras to Bradford - a fast evening service although it did, after standing in the slow line platform at Kettering for twenty-one minutes, continue forward to Nottingham as a stopping train via Melton Mowbray after connecting with the 16.50 from London.

12.40 NEWCASTLE to BRISTOL (20.27)

	C/W Previous working	Vehicle	Type	From	To	Next working
				Mondays, Wednesdays and Fridays		
1	65 10.20 Bristol - Newcastle (18.30)	BRAKE THIRD CORRIDOR (24)	BR (NER)	NEWCASTLE	BRISTOL	10.20 Bristol - Newcastle (18.30)
2	65 10.20 Bristol - Newcastle (18.30)	FIRST CORRIDOR (42)	BR (NER)	NEWCASTLE	BRISTOL	10.20 Bristol - Newcastle (18.30)
3	65 10.20 Bristol - Newcastle (18.30)	RESTAURANT FIRST (18)	LNER	NEWCASTLE	BRISTOL	10.20 Bristol - Newcastle (18.30)
4	65 10.20 Bristol - Newcastle (18.30)	THIRD OPEN (48)	LNER	NEWCASTLE	BRISTOL	10.20 Bristol - Newcastle (18.30)
5	65 10.20 Bristol - Newcastle (18.30)	THIRD CORRIDOR (48)	BR (NER)	NEWCASTLE	BRISTOL	10.20 Bristol - Newcastle (18.30)
6	65 10.20 Bristol - Newcastle (18.30)	THIRD CORRIDOR (48)	BR (NER)	NEWCASTLE	BRISTOL	10.20 Bristol - Newcastle (18.30)
7	65 10.20 Bristol - Newcastle (18.30)	THIRD CORRIDOR (48)	BR (NER)	NEWCASTLE	BRISTOL	10.20 Bristol - Newcastle (18.30)
8	65 10.20 Bristol - Newcastle (18.30)	THIRD CORRIDOR (48)	BR (NER)	NEWCASTLE	BRISTOL	10.20 Bristol - Newcastle (18.30)
9	65 10.20 Bristol - Newcastle (18.30)	THIRD CORRIDOR (48)	BR (NER)	NEWCASTLE	BRISTOL	10.20 Bristol - Newcastle (18.30)
10	65 10.20 Bristol - Newcastle (18.30)	BRAKE THIRD CORRIDOR (24)	BR (NER)	NEWCASTLE	BRISTOL	10.20 Bristol - Newcastle (18.30)
				Tuesdays and Thursdays		
1	65 10.20 Bristol - Newcastle (18.30)	BRAKE THIRD CORRIDOR (24)	BR (LM)	NEWCASTLE	BRISTOL	10.20 Bristol - Newcastle (18.30)
2	65 10.20 Bristol - Newcastle (18.30)	FIRST CORRIDOR (42)	BR (LM)	NEWCASTLE	BRISTOL	10.20 Bristol - Newcastle (18.30)
3	65 10.20 Bristol - Newcastle (18.30)	RESTAURANT COMPOSITE (12/18)	LMS	NEWCASTLE	BRISTOL	10.20 Bristol - Newcastle (18.30)
4	65 10.20 Bristol - Newcastle (18.30)	THIRD OPEN (56)	LMS	NEWCASTLE	BRISTOL	10.20 Bristol - Newcastle (18.30)
5	65 10.20 Bristol - Newcastle (18.30)	THIRD CORRIDOR (48)	BR (LM)	NEWCASTLE	BRISTOL	10.20 Bristol - Newcastle (18.30)
6	65 10.20 Bristol - Newcastle (18.30)	THIRD CORRIDOR (48)	BR (LM)	NEWCASTLE	BRISTOL	10.20 Bristol - Newcastle (18.30)
7	65 10.20 Bristol - Newcastle (18.30)	THIRD CORRIDOR (48)	BR (LM)	NEWCASTLE	BRISTOL	10.20 Bristol - Newcastle (18.30)
8	65 10.20 Bristol - Newcastle (18.30)	THIRD CORRIDOR (48)	BR (LM)	NEWCASTLE	BRISTOL	10.20 Bristol - Newcastle (18.30)
9	65 10.20 Bristol - Newcastle (18.30)	THIRD CORRIDOR (48)	BR (LM)	NEWCASTLE	BRISTOL	10.20 Bristol - Newcastle (18.30)
10	65 10.20 Bristol - Newcastle (18.30)	BRAKE THIRD CORRIDOR (24)	BR (LM)	NEWCASTLE	BRISTOL	10.20 Bristol - Newcastle (18.30)

Unlike the morning Newcastle - Bristol service which on alternate days brought to Tyneside the unaccustomed sight of Great Western vehicles, the midday express consisted very largely of BR Mark 1 stock, the only way of distinguishing between the two rakes involved in the working being the restaurant cars which alternated between LNER and LMS. An unusual feature was the way in which first class accommodation was grouped together as opposed to the usual practice of spreading it throughout the train. In this case a First Corridor vehicle was provided instead of the usual two or three Composite vehicles and placed next to the Restaurant Car which also contained first class seating.

The train was carefully timed to depart as a connection out of the 10.00 Edinburgh - Kings Cross and was sandwiched into the rather tight space between the Flying Scotsman and the 08.35 Glasgow to Kings Cross. The A1 booked to the 12.37 as far as York had to run fast to prevent delay to the latter and in fact was only six minutes slower than the Scotsman to York; five minutes being attributable to the stop at Darlington and the remainder to a minute's recovery time on the approach to York. As a result of coincidence rather than skilful planning, the train made a second connection with Scotland when it arrived in Sheffield just as the up Thames-Clyde was pulling out for London. This meant that Glasgow passengers not only sampled some of the finest scenery in the country but were spared both an early start and a change of trains in Edinburgh.

The entire 10-coach formation remained together in Bristol to form the next day's 10.20 Bristol - Newcastle express.

10.05 EDINBURGH (WAVERLEY) to ST PANCRAS (20.15)

	C/W Previous working	Vehicle	Type	From	To	Next working
1	09.00 St Pancras - Edinburgh	BRAKE THIRD CORRIDOR (24)	BR	EDINBURGH	ST PANCRAS	09.00 St Pancras - Edinburgh
2	09.00 St Pancras - Edinburgh	COMPOSITE CORRIDOR (24/18)	BR	EDINBURGH	ST PANCRAS	09.00 St Pancras - Edinburgh
3	09.00 St Pancras - Edinburgh	FIRST CORRIDOR (42)	BR	EDINBURGH	ST PANCRAS	09.00 St Pancras - Edinburgh
4	09.00 St Pancras - Edinburgh	RESTAURANT (BUFFET) THIRD (30)	LMS	EDINBURGH	ST PANCRAS	09.00 St Pancras - Edinburgh
5	09.00 St Pancras - Edinburgh	THIRD CORRIDOR (48)	BR	EDINBURGH	ST PANCRAS	09.00 St Pancras - Edinburgh
6	09.00 St Pancras - Edinburgh	THIRD CORRIDOR (48)	BR	EDINBURGH	ST PANCRAS	09.00 St Pancras - Edinburgh
7	09.00 St Pancras - Edinburgh	THIRD CORRIDOR (48)	BR	EDINBURGH	ST PANCRAS	09.00 St Pancras - Edinburgh
8	09.00 St Pancras - Edinburgh	THIRD CORRIDOR (48)	BR	EDINBURGH	ST PANCRAS	09.00 St Pancras - Edinburgh
9	09.00 St Pancras - Edinburgh	BRAKE THIRD CORRIDOR (24)	BR	EDINBURGH	ST PANCRAS	09.00 St Pancras - Edinburgh

Neither as fast nor as illustrious as its partner, the Thames-Clyde, the Waverley was nonetheless an excellent train from which to see the best of the country and savour its geographical extremes as the view changed from the lonely wilderness of the Border Counties and Yorkshire Dales to the fiery industrialisation of Rotherham and Sheffield. The first part of its journey was relatively slow since engines were changed at Carlisle, crews at Hellifield and stops made at the more important stations on the Settle and Carlisle. Progress through South Yorkshire and Derbyshire was that of a normal Midland express but at Nottingham the tempo changed quite dramatically and for just over two hours the train became one of the fastest expresses on the system by covering the 123 miles between Nottingham and London in 133 minutes plus two minutes recovery times. The 72-mile Kettering - London leg was timed at exactly 60 mph pass to stop. The nine-coach set was not broken up at Cricklewood but kept together - with the additional of a tenth vehicle for Nottingham - for the next day's down service.

16.00 MANCHESTER CENTRAL to ST PANCRAS (20.38)

	C/W Previous working	Vehicle	Type	From	To	Next working
1	28C 08.15 St Pancras - Manchester (13.02)	THIRD CORRIDOR (42)	LMS	MANCHESTER	ST PANCRAS	08.15 St Pancras - Manchester (13.02)
2	31 10.15 St Pancras - Manchester (14.32)	BRAKE THIRD CORRIDOR (24)	LMS	MANCHESTER	ST PANCRAS	10.15 St Pancras - Manchester (14.32)
3	31 10.15 St Pancras - Manchester (14.32)	COMPOSITE CORRIDOR (18/24)	LMS	MANCHESTER	ST PANCRAS	10.15 St Pancras - Manchester (14.32)
4	31 10.15 St Pancras - Manchester (14.32)	COMPOSITE CORRIDOR (18/24)	LMS	MANCHESTER	ST PANCRAS	10.15 St Pancras - Manchester (14.32)
5	31 10.15 St Pancras - Manchester (14.32)	BRAKE THIRD CORRIDOR (24)	LMS	MANCHESTER	ST PANCRAS	10.15 St Pancras - Manchester (14.32)
6	123 10.15 St Pancras - Manchester (14.32)	KITCHEN CAR	LMS	MANCHESTER	ST PANCRAS	10.15 St Pancras - Manchester (14.32)
7	123 10.15 St Pancras - Manchester (14.32)	THIRD OPEN (64)	BR	MANCHESTER	ST PANCRAS	10.15 St Pancras - Manchester (14.32)
8	29 10.15 St Pancras - Manchester (14.32)	THIRD CORRIDOR (48)	BR	MANCHESTER	ST PANCRAS	10.15 St Pancras - Manchester (14.32)
9	29 10.15 St Pancras - Manchester (14.32)	COMPOSITE CORRIDOR (24/18)	BR	MANCHESTER	ST PANCRAS	10.15 St Pancras - Manchester (14.32)
10	29 10.15 St Pancras - Manchester (14.32)	BRAKE THIRD CORRIDOR (24)	BR	MANCHESTER	ST PANCRAS	10.15 St Pancras - Manchester (14.32)

Although the LNW provided a competing service at 16.05 from London Road which got into Euston at 19.52, the Midland service was sufficiently popular to require ten coaches, a load that made it the heaviest London service out of London Road and put the train well over the limit for XL or special limit timings with a 5XP 4-6-0 on the climb to Peak Forest. By the time the service reached Derby, from which point Special Limit timings could have been observed, the train found itself so closely behind the up Waverley that no acceleration was possible and indeed the schedule of the 16.00 had to be eased by two minutes in order to allow the Edinburgh train to get clear at Kettering. Until 1955 the position of the two trains had been reversed but the running of the Manchester service had been too much of a threat to the fast Nottingham - London leg of the Waverley and the latter was given precedence. The revised position did little to favour the Manchester train's chances of a punctual arrival in St Pancras since, after calling at Kettering and Luton, it found itself following the 18.46 Bedford - London stopping train which had been turned main line to follow the Waverley from Harpenden. If all three trains happened to pass Chiltern Green on time then all was well but the chances of this happening were not such that money might be risked. The vehicles forming the 16.00 worked the 10.15 St Pancras - Manchester (the service entrusted to an LNER B1 4-6-0 during the 1948 exchange) except for one carriage which worked down in the 08.15.

16.50 ST PANCRAS to BRADFORD (22.38)

	C/W	Previous working	Vehicle	Type	From	To	Next working
1	18	09.12 Bradford - St Pancras (14.08)	BRAKE THIRD CORRIDOR (24)	BR	ST PANCRAS	BRADFORD	09.12 Bradford - St Pancras (14.08)
2	18	09.12 Bradford - St Pancras (14.08)	THIRD CORRIDOR (48)	BR	ST PANCRAS	BRADFORD	09.12 Bradford - St Pancras (14.08)
3	18	09.12 Bradford - St Pancras (14.08)	THIRD CORRIDOR (48)	BR	ST PANCRAS	BRADFORD	09.12 Bradford - St Pancras (14.08)
4	18	09.12 Bradford - St Pancras (14.08)	THIRD OPEN (64)	BR	ST PANCRAS	BRADFORD	09.12 Bradford - St Pancras (14.08)
5	18	09.12 Bradford - St Pancras (14.08)	KITCHEN CAR	LMS	ST PANCRAS	BRADFORD	09.12 Bradford - St Pancras (14.08)
6	18	09.12 Bradford - St Pancras (14.08)	FIRST OPEN (42)	LMS	ST PANCRAS	BRADFORD	09.12 Bradford - St Pancras (14.08)
7	18	09.12 Bradford - St Pancras (14.08)	FIRST CORRIDOR (36)	LMS	ST PANCRAS	BRADFORD	09.12 Bradford - St Pancras (14.08)
8	18	09.12 Bradford - St Pancras (14.08)	BRAKE FIRST CORRIDOR (30)	LMS	ST PANCRAS	BRADFORD	09.12 Bradford - St Pancras (14.08)
9	18	09.12 Bradford - St Pancras (14.08)	COMPOSITE CORRIDOR (24/18)	BR	ST PANCRAS	BRADFORD	09.12 Bradford - St Pancras (14.08)
10	18	09.12 Bradford - St Pancras (14.08)	BRAKE THIRD CORRIDOR (24)	BR	ST PANCRAS	BRADFORD	09.12 Bradford - St Pancras (14.08)
11	906		FULL BRAKE	LMS	NOTTINGHAM	LEEDS	01.15 Leeds - Carnforth (03.10)

It was not often that the postwar Great Central managed to upstage the Midland but the 1948 rearrangement of services from Marylebone - a brief flare of activity that was probably not unconnected with the arrival in Marylebone Road of the Railway Executive - saw the GC's 16.50 South Yorkshireman reaching Bradford Exchange almost half an hour before the arrival of the 16.50 ex St Pancras in Forster Square. The reason for the Great Central's performance lay in the direct routing via Sheffield, Penistone and Huddersfield; the Midland train having to languish in Leeds for eleven minutes whilst it reversed and changed engines. Had the Midland retained its interest in the 'Golden Mile' between Royston and Thornhill - the prewar 17.10 'Yorkshireman' used this route and managed for a short time to run from St Pancras to Bradford Exchange in a minute over four hours - no doubt the Great Central would have been beaten into second place but in the event the Midland decided that Leeds was too important a location to sacrifice for the interests of Bradford. In any event, talk of competitive moves between Marylebone and St Pancras was of academic interest only since the 17.30 Yorkshire Pullman from Kings Cross brought the Bradford businessman into Exchange at 21.28. The chief value of the train lay in its function as a business express to Nottingham and Sheffield.

The formation was that of the inward working, the 09.12 ex Bradford, except for the addition at Nottingham of a parcels vehicle for Carnforth.

16.45 BRISTOL to YORK (23.02)

	C/W	Previous working	Vehicle	Type	From	To	Next working
1	153A	07.42 Nottingham - Bristol (12.00)	THIRD CORRIDOR (42)	LMS	BRISTOL	DERBY	10.48 Derby - St Pancras (14.00)
2	153	10.24 Derby - Bristol (13.37)	THIRD CORRIDOR (42)	LMS	BRISTOL	DERBY	10.24 Derby - Bristol (13.37)
3	153	10.24 Derby - Bristol (13.37)	RESTAURANT COMPOSITE (12/18)	LMS	BRISTOL	DERBY	10.24 Derby - Bristol (13.37)
4	40	07.30 Bradford - Bristol (13.37)	BRAKE THIRD CORRIDOR (24)	LMS	BRISTOL	YORK	12.00 York - Bristol (18.25)
5	40	07.30 Bradford - Bristol (13.37)	THIRD CORRIDOR (42)	LMS	BRISTOL	YORK	12.00 York - Bristol (18.25)
6	40A	07.30 Bradford - Bristol (13.37)	THIRD CORRIDOR (42)	LMS	BRISTOL	YORK	
7	40A	07.30 Bradford - Bristol (13.37)	THIRD CORRIDOR (42)	LMS	BRISTOL	YORK	
8	40	07.30 Bradford - Bristol (13.37)	COMPOSITE CORRIDOR (18/24)	LMS	BRISTOL	YORK	12.00 York - Bristol (18.25)
9	40	07.30 Bradford - Bristol (13.37)	COMPOSITE CORRIDOR (18/24)	LMS	BRISTOL	YORK	12.00 York - Bristol (18.25)
10	40	07.30 Bradford - Bristol (13.37)	THIRD CORRIDOR (42)	LMS	BRISTOL	YORK	12.00 York - Bristol (18.25)
11	40	07.30 Bradford - Bristol (13.37)	BRAKE THIRD CORRIDOR (24)	LMS	BRISTOL	YORK	12.00 York - Bristol (18.25)
12	932	02.15 Derby - Bristol (07.25)	FULL BRAKE	LMS	BRISTOL	YORK	
13	946		FULL BRAKE	LMS	SHEFFIELD	YORK	00.30 York - Edinburgh (05.08)

With a maximum permitted load of thirteen vehicles (400 tons) for a 5XP 4-6-0 between Bristol and Birmingham, the 16.45 with twelve vehicles for 379 tons was the heaviest booked Midland service out of Temple Meads and, in theory, escaped having to be banked from Engine Shed Junction to Fishponds by one ton! (As an aside, it is interesting to see that in spite of Fishponds and the Lickey Incline, the loadings for engines were more generous between Bristol and Derby than they were between St Pancras and Leicester).

The reasons for the weight of the train stemmed from the fact that it not only connected with the 10.05 Penzance - Crewe - Manchester and the 10.35 'Cornishman' Penzance - Wolverhampton but departed at a time convenient for home-going business travel. The popularity of the service and the hours it spanned meant that a dining car - which actually worked as a buffet - was a mandatory inclusion although it will be noticed that the customary accompanying open coach had to be omitted for reasons of weight. It was a great pity that a class 7 Royal Scot 4-6-0 could not be spared from the West Coast since this would have permitted the train to have been expanded to fifteen vehicles. The opportunity to pick up overnight parcels from intermediate stations was too great to miss and stops were made at Mangotsfield and Tamworth in addition to the usual calls. This together with the need to detach the leading three vehicles at Derby made the service about a quarter of an hour slower to Sheffield than the best trains on the route: a circumstance that caused the connection with the northbound Aberdonian to be broken by a mere two minutes.

17.30 ST PANCRAS to NOTTINGHAM MIDLAND (20.47)

	C/W	Previous working	Vehicle	Type	From	To	Next working
1	51	09.07 Sheffield - St Pancras (13.23)	BRAKE THIRD CORRIDOR (24)	LMS	ST PANCRAS	NOTTINGHAM	07.35 Nottingham - Bristol (12.00)
2	24A	10.48 Derby - St Pancras (14.00)	THIRD CORRIDOR (42)	LMS	ST PANCRAS	NOTTINGHAM	06.40 Nottingham - St Pancras (09.55)
3	27A	00.05 Manchester - St Pancras (06.54)	COMPOSITE CORRIDOR (18/24)	LMS	ST PANCRAS	NOTTINGHAM	07.50 Nottingham - Derby (08.37)
4	51	09.07 Sheffield - St Pancras (13.23)	THIRD CORRIDOR (42)	LMS	ST PANCRAS	NOTTINGHAM	07.35 Nottingham - Bristol (12.00)
5	51	09.07 Sheffield - St Pancras (13.23)	COMPOSITE CORRIDOR (18/24)	LMS	ST PANCRAS	NOTTINGHAM	07.35 Nottingham - Bristol (12.00)
6	51	09.07 Sheffield - St Pancras (13.23)	COMPOSITE CORRIDOR (18/24)	LMS	ST PANCRAS	NOTTINGHAM	07.35 Nottingham - Bristol (12.00)
7	51	09.07 Sheffield - St Pancras (13.23)	THIRD CORRIDOR (42)	LMS	ST PANCRAS	NOTTINGHAM	07.35 Nottingham - Bristol (12.00)
8	51	09.07 Sheffield - St Pancras (13.23)	BRAKE THIRD CORRIDOR (24)	LMS	ST PANCRAS	NOTTINGHAM	07.35 Nottingham - Bristol (12.00)
9	15A	10.30 Bradford - St Pancras (15.39)	THIRD CORRIDOR (42)	LMS	ST PANCRAS	NOTTINGHAM	07.35 Nottingham - Bristol (12.00)
10	51A	15.35 Derby - St Pancras (18.14)	THIRD CORRIDOR (42)	LMS	ST PANCRAS	NOTTINGHAM	07.35 Nottingham - Bristol (12.00)

The 17.30 presented quite an interesting study in carriage workings since its inward working, the six-coach lightweight 09.09 from Sheffield, had to be split in London to allow a pair of coaches to be added between the fifth and sixth vehicles whilst two Third Corridors were attached to the trailing end. In addition to this, the following day the set, or most of it, departed from the London axis to spend several days working over the West of England main line; a series of duties that commenced with the 07.43 Nottingham to Bristol. It suggested a degree of integration between the London and West of England main lines that was perhaps missing on the Great Western where it was exceptional for a Wolverhampton-based train set to work between London and Plymouth or London and Swansea.

Although described as a Nottingham express, most of the 17.30's patronage alighted at Luton, Bedford and Wellingborough since beyond the Home Counties the train not only degenerated into a semi-fast service but completed its journey over the circuitous route via Trent in the pious hope of pleasing both Leicester and Nottingham by giving both a direct service from London at the busiest time of the evening. The result was to alienate both camps since Leicester businessmen did not care for trains that made five intermediate stops whilst to take three and a quarter hours between London and Nottingham was to make a nonsense of rail travel. Both parties were better off under the rather maligned Great Central whose 18.18 'Master Cutler' ex Marylebone reached Leicester at 20.26 and Nottingham thirty minutes later. The Cutler also had the benefit of a full-blown restaurant car.

More important in freight terms than passenger, Wellingborough was a major centre of Midland activity with extensive marshalling yards and a loco depot with an allocation of around eighty engines. On a 1959 afternoon 9F 2-10-0 92160 of Kettering passes the slow line platforms with the 12.50 Brent - Toton and is overtaken by Britannia 70004 'William Shakespeare' (Trafford Park) on the 14.25 St Pancras - Manchester Central.

With a large fleet of Black 5's playing second fiddle to the Jubilee 4-6-0's the scope for other classes on main line passenger work was limited although when large number of specials were run, some unusual sightings were possible. When they first appeared the 1947 4MT 2-6-0's were rather poor steamers; the problem being attributed t the double-chimneys with which they were first fitted. In 1950/1 43027 spent several months with a stovepipe chimney and was evaluated in several parts of the syste before the LMS standard single chimney was fitted to the class as a whole. The engine is seen at Clay Mills Junction during the summer of 1951 while working a train empty stock from Derby to Burton to form an excursion to Skegness. The best work by these engines - optimistically intended to be a replacement for the 4F 0-6-0 - w done on the Midland & Great Northern system between Peterborough and Great Yarmouth.

The rush hour gets under way on a 1955 afternoon at St Pancras as Jubilee 4-6-0 45620 'North Borneo' of Nottingham prepares to work the 16.25 express to Kettering. Judging by the smoke from the chimney, the fireman is building the fire up - 'getting the engine hot' - and in ten minutes time a solid and continuous column of steam will be shooting up to the station roof with the needle steady on the red mark. Calling only at Luton and Bedford, the 16.25 ran to Kettering in 101 minutes where it waited to connect with the 16.50 St Pancras - Bradford before continuing forward as a semi-fast to Nottingham via Melton Mowbray.

From 1951 the ranks of Black 5's were swollen by BR Standard 5MT 4-6-0's which became quite regular performers on the principal Midland routes. The first of the class, 73000, is seen ascending the Lickey Incline on Thursday 6 June 1957. It appears that most of the work is being done from the rear of the train. (W. Good)

17.16 SHEFFIELD to GLOUCESTER (21.42)

	C/W	Previous working	Vehicle	Type	From	To	Next working
1	52	16.15 York - Sheffield (18.06)	BRAKE THIRD CORRIDOR (24)	LMS	SHEFFIELD	GLOUCESTER	10.15 Gloucester - Worcester (11.20)
2	52	16.15 York - Sheffield (18.06)	THIRD CORRIDOR (42)	LMS	SHEFFIELD	GLOUCESTER	10.15 Gloucester - Worcester (11.20)
3	52	16.15 York - Sheffield (18.06)	COMPOSITE CORRIDOR (18/24)	LMS	SHEFFIELD	GLOUCESTER	10.15 Gloucester - Worcester (11.20)
4	52	16.15 York - Sheffield (18.06)	COMPOSITE CORRIDOR (18/24)	LMS	SHEFFIELD	GLOUCESTER	10.15 Gloucester - Worcester (11.20)
5	52	16.15 York - Sheffield (18.06)	THIRD CORRIDOR (42)	LMS	SHEFFIELD	GLOUCESTER	10.15 Gloucester - Worcester (11.20)
6	52	16.15 York - Sheffield (18.06)	THIRD CORRIDOR (42)	LMS	SHEFFIELD	GLOUCESTER	10.15 Gloucester - Worcester (11.20)
7	52	16.15 York - Sheffield (18.06)	THIRD CORRIDOR (42)	LMS	SHEFFIELD	GLOUCESTER	10.15 Gloucester - Worcester (11.20)
8	52	16.15 York - Sheffield (18.06)	BRAKE THIRD CORRIDOR (24)	LMS	SHEFFIELD	GLOUCESTER	10.15 Gloucester - Worcester (11.20)

The last express of the day between the North of England and the West was the 12.37 Newcastle - Bristol which left Sheffield at 15.55; a little too early for business purposes. The next was the 16.45 Bradford - Bristol (18.35 from Sheffield) which did not reach Bristol until midnight and took - thanks to lengthy stops at Derby and Birmingham - about an hour longer than the time normally granted for a fast train. Given the importance of Sheffield, there was a need for an intervening service although whether the working used to plug the gap met the bill is a matter open to question.

The departure time of the 17.16 was well suited for business needs and the train ran at a good speed to Derby, making the usual Chesterfield stop en route. Beyond Derby calls were made at Burton and Tamworth after which the picture changed considerably as the train sallied westward calling at almost every station on the line and being routed via the Worcester loop. Strangest of all, the service terminated at Gloucester - nearly forty miles short of Bristol - with no forward connection until the 16.45 from Bradford arrived eighty minutes later. To add hunger to sloth, no dining facilities of any sort were provided.

The eight coach corridor set used - an unusual formation for what was in reality a disguised stopping train - did very little work after reaching Gloucester and the sum of its activities the following day was to form a stopping train to Worcester largely to position itself for the through train to York the next morning.

15.50 BRADFORD to LEEDS (16.28)

	C/W	Previous working	Vehicle	Type	From	To	Next working
1		10.15 York - Bradford (11.44)	THIRD CORRIDOR (48)	LNER	BRADFORD	LEEDS	17.07 Leeds - Hull (18.31)
2		10.15 York - Bradford (11.44)	COMPOSITE CORRIDOR (21/32)	LNER	BRADFORD	LEEDS	17.07 Leeds - Hull (18.31)
3	128	10.15 York - Bradford (11.44)	BRAKE THIRD CORRIDOR (32)	LNER	BRADFORD	LEEDS	17.07 Leeds - Hull (18.31)
4	128	10.15 York - Bradford (11.44)	THIRD CORRIDOR (64)	LNER	BRADFORD	LEEDS	17.07 Leeds - Hull (18.31)
5	128	10.15 York - Bradford (11.44)	COMPOSITE CORRIDOR (21/32)	LNER	BRADFORD	LEEDS	17.07 Leeds - Hull (18.31)
6	128	10.15 York - Bradford (11.44)	THIRD CORRIDOR (64)	LNER	BRADFORD	LEEDS	17.07 Leeds - Hull (18.31)
7	128	10.15 York - Bradford (11.44)	BRAKE THIRD CORRIDOR (32)	LNER	BRADFORD	LEEDS	17.07 Leeds - Hull (18.31)

This was a set of LNER stock that operated a return trip from Bradford to York in the mornings, remaining at Forster Square until the evening when it returned to Leeds to re-enter its parent North Eastern workings. The service of local trains between Bradford Forster Square and Leeds was not generous - the 15.50 broke a gap of almost two hours - and the use of LNER stock in some drew attention to the far better GN service between Bradford Exchange and Leeds Central.

18.15 NOTTINGHAM to ST PANCRAS (21.56)

	C/W	Previous working	Vehicle	Type	From	To	Next working
1		14.35 Leicester - Nottingham (15..36)	BRAKE THIRD CORRIDOR (32)	LMS	NOTTINGHAM	ST PANCRAS	10.40 St Pancras - Leicester (13.32)
2		14.35 Leicester - Nottingham (15..36)	COMPOSITE CORRIDOR (18/32)	LMS	NOTTINGHAM	ST PANCRAS	10.40 St Pancras - Leicester (13.32)
3		14.35 Leicester - Nottingham (15..36)	BRAKE THIRD CORRIDOR (32)	LMS	NOTTINGHAM	ST PANCRAS	10.40 St Pancras - Leicester (13.32)
4		20.15 Kettering - Nottingham (21.11)	BRAKE THIRD CORRIDOR (32)	LMS	NOTTINGHAM	ST PANCRAS	10.40 St Pancras - Bedford (11.58)
5		20.15 Kettering - Nottingham (21.11)	COMPOSITE CORRIDOR (18/32)	LMS	NOTTINGHAM	ST PANCRAS	10.40 St Pancras - Bedford (11.58)
6		20.15 Kettering - Nottingham (21.11)	BRAKE THIRD CORRIDOR (32)	LMS	NOTTINGHAM	ST PANCRAS	10.40 St Pancras - Bedford (11.58)
7			COMPOSITE CORRIDOR (18/32)	LMS	NOTTINGHAM	ST PANCRAS	

Since the 10.05 Edinburgh - St Pancras 'Waverley' ran non-stop from Nottingham to London, passengers for intermediate stations were given the 18.15 semi-fast train which must have been a very tiresome affair for the Edinburgh - St Albans passenger who, after no less than twelve stops south of Nottingham - calls that included Old Dalby, Grimston, Corby and Flitwick, reached his destination an hour and a quarter after the Waverley had terminated in London. In common with most semi-fasts to St Pancras, this service was regarded as a local working for purposes of stock arrangements and was the return of the 10.40 St Pancras to Leicester, the gap being closed by working a stopping train from Leicester. The rear portion of the train had worked down as the Bedford section of the previous day's 10.40 making its way down to Nottingham in a succession of local workings.

15.30 LIVERPOOL CENTRAL to NOTTINGHAM (19.31)

	C/W	Previous working	Vehicle	Type	From	To	Next working
1	48	09.06 Nottingham - Liverpool (12.30)	FULL BRAKE	LMS	LIVERPOOL	NOTTINGHAM	09.06 Nottingham - Liverpool (12.30)
2	48	09.06 Nottingham - Liverpool (12.30)	BRAKE THIRD CORRIDOR (24)	BR	LIVERPOOL	NOTTINGHAM	09.06 Nottingham - Liverpool (12.30)
3	48	09.06 Nottingham - Liverpool (12.30)	THIRD CORRIDOR (48)	BR	LIVERPOOL	NOTTINGHAM	09.06 Nottingham - Liverpool (12.30)
4	48	09.06 Nottingham - Liverpool (12.30)	COMPOSITE CORRIDOR (24/18)	BR	LIVERPOOL	NOTTINGHAM	09.06 Nottingham - Liverpool (12.30)
5	48	09.06 Nottingham - Liverpool (12.30)	RESTAURANT BUFFET	LMS	LIVERPOOL	NOTTINGHAM	09.06 Nottingham - Liverpool (12.30)
6	48	09.06 Nottingham - Liverpool (12.30)	COMPOSITE CORRIDOR (24/18)	BR	LIVERPOOL	NOTTINGHAM	09.06 Nottingham - Liverpool (12.30)
7	48	09.06 Nottingham - Liverpool (12.30)	THIRD CORRIDOR (48)	BR	LIVERPOOL	NOTTINGHAM	09.06 Nottingham - Liverpool (12.30)
8	48	09.06 Nottingham - Liverpool (12.30)	BRAKE THIRD CORRIDOR (24)	LMS	LIVERPOOL	NOTTINGHAM	09.06 Nottingham - Liverpool (12.30)
9			STORES VAN	LOCO	DERBY	NOTTINGHAM	

Joint possession, with the Great Central and the Great Northern, of the Cheshire Lines Committee had given the Midland access to Liverpool and although the grouping had left Euston in command so far as Merseyside was concerned, the daily Nottingham - Liverpool working continued to operate and act as a reminder of more expansive times on the Midland. The eight coach service was based at Nottingham and worked down in the morning, returning in the afternoon and timed to leave Manchester at a time convenient to its business community.

Although the Cheshire Lines had come out of the war in very poor shape, the restoration of passenger services was given a high priority and the 45 minute timing of the hourly service was regarded as something of a showpiece in the North-West. It has to be said, however, that this timing reflected greater credit on the operating and permanent way departments rather than the motive power muscle since speed rather than tractive effort was the chief ingredient in meeting the demands of the timetable. The 33-mile route was level with very few restriction and the eight coaches of the Liverpool - Nottingham service could be timed - in theory, at any rate - with a class 3 locomotive. In fact a 5MT 4-6-0 was the diagrammed power over the CLC and even with the stops at Widnes and Warrington, this was more than sufficient. The train's limited load status was confined to the Cheshire Lines section and southwards from Manchester, in spite of being worked by a 5XP 4-6-0, the service ran to ordinary passenger timings via Stockport (Tiviot Dale), calling at eight intermediate points and taking half an hour longer to Derby than the better London trains. The relegation from limited to express at Manchester was far from being the worst indignity suffered by the train since at Derby, a loco stores van was attached to the rear and the service downgraded to local status, calling at all stations except Attenborough to Nottingham.

18.33 ST PANCRAS to SHEFFIELD MIDLAND (21.53)

C/W	Previous working	Vehicle	Type	From	To	Next working
1	907 00.05 Manchester - St Pancras (06.54)	FULL BRAKE (NON-CORRIDOR)	LMS	ST PANCRAS	DERBY	21.28 Derby - Manchester (23.05)
2	126 12.11 Sheffield - St Pancras (15.42)	THIRD OPEN (56)	LMS	ST PANCRAS	SHEFFIELD	12.11 Sheffield - St Pancras (15.42)
3	126 12.11 Sheffield - St Pancras (15.42)	RESTAURANT FIRST (24)	LMS	ST PANCRAS	SHEFFIELD	12.11 Sheffield - St Pancras (15.42)
4	15 10.30 Bradford - St Pancras (15.42)	BRAKE THIRD CORRIDOR (24)	LMS	ST PANCRAS	SHEFFIELD	07.05 Sheffield - St Pancras (10.32)
5	15 10.30 Bradford - St Pancras (15.42)	COMPOSITE CORRIDOR (24/18)	BR	ST PANCRAS	SHEFFIELD	07.05 Sheffield - St Pancras (10.32)
6	15 10.30 Bradford - St Pancras (15.42)	COMPOSITE CORRIDOR (24/18)	BR	ST PANCRAS	SHEFFIELD	07.05 Sheffield - St Pancras (10.32)
7	15 10.30 Bradford - St Pancras (15.42)	THIRD CORRIDOR (48)	BR	ST PANCRAS	SHEFFIELD	07.05 Sheffield - St Pancras (10.32)
8	15 10.30 Bradford - St Pancras (15.42)	THIRD CORRIDOR (48)	BR	ST PANCRAS	SHEFFIELD	07.05 Sheffield - St Pancras (10.32)
9	15 10.30 Bradford - St Pancras (15.42)	THIRD CORRIDOR (48)	BR	ST PANCRAS	SHEFFIELD	07.05 Sheffield - St Pancras (10.32)
10	15 10.30 Bradford - St Pancras (15.42)	BRAKE THIRD CORRIDOR (24)	BR	ST PANCRAS	SHEFFIELD	07.05 Sheffield - St Pancras (10.32)

Although the Thames-Clyde and Waverley expresses were popularly supposed to be the most important of the Midland trains, in reality the accolade went to the 18.33 St Pancras to Sheffield, partly because it ran at the busiest time of day but mainly because it ran non-stop to Derby and in doing so achieved the rare and remarkable distinction of passing through Leicester without stopping. The service was a gesture of defiance at the Great Central who, having tempted away much of the Midlands' Leicester and Nottingham business traffic with its 18.18 Master Cutler from Marylebone, could not match the postwar Midland when it came to Sheffield. London to Sheffield by the Cutler took three hours and thirty-seven minutes whilst the Midland's 18.33 managed it in seventeen minutes less. It went some way towards balancing the books although the Great Central had a better reputation for time-keeping.

Instead of the normal express running times which allowed a 5XP 4-6-0 to take a twelve-coach train, the 18.33 was given an accelerated special limit which restricted its Jubilee 4-6-0 to a maximum of eleven coaches. This gave the train an advantage of four minutes in every fifty miles, Bedford being passed in fifty-five minutes as opposed to the fifty-nine permitted most expresses. Rather curiously the full eleven coach limit was not utilised to the full since the vehicle next to the engine was a parcels brake which was transferred at Derby to the 18.40 London - Manchester.

In spite of the train's impressive running, it was not provided with its own set of coaches but was instead part of a two-day cycle which alternated with the 14.00 St Pancras to Bradford. The exception to this was the dining portion which worked in the service each day, coming up in the 10.30 Bradford - St Pancras from Sheffield.

18.40 ST PANCRAS to MANCHESTER CENTRAL (23.05)

C/W	Previous working	Vehicle	Type	From	To	Next working
1	907 18.33 St Pancras - Derby (20.53)	FULL BRAKE (NON-CORRIDOR)	LMS	DERBY	MANCHESTER	
2	30 12.05 Derby - St Pancras (15.12)	BRAKE THIRD CORRIDOR (24)	LMS	ST PANCRAS	MANCHESTER	07.24 Manchester - Derby (10.01)
3	30 12.05 Derby - St Pancras (15.12)	COMPOSITE CORRIDOR (18/24)	LMS	ST PANCRAS	MANCHESTER	07.24 Manchester - Derby (10.01)
4	30 12.05 Derby - St Pancras (15.12)	COMPOSITE CORRIDOR (18/24)	LMS	ST PANCRAS	MANCHESTER	07.24 Manchester - Derby (10.01)
5	30 12.05 Derby - St Pancras (15.12)	BRAKE THIRD CORRIDOR (24)	LMS	ST PANCRAS	MANCHESTER	07.24 Manchester - Derby (10.01)
6	119 12.05 Derby - St Pancras (15.12)	THIRD CORRIDOR (42)	LMS	ST PANCRAS	DERBY	12.05 Derby - St Pancras (15.12)
7	119 12.05 Derby - St Pancras (15.12)	THIRD CORRIDOR (42)	LMS	ST PANCRAS	DERBY	12.05 Derby - St Pancras (15.12)
8	119 12.05 Derby - St Pancras (15.12)	COMPOSITE CORRIDOR (18/24)	LMS	ST PANCRAS	DERBY	12.05 Derby - St Pancras (15.12)
9	119 12.05 Derby - St Pancras (15.12)	RESTAURANT FIRST (24)	LMS	ST PANCRAS	DERBY	12.05 Derby - St Pancras (15.12)
10	119 12.05 Derby - St Pancras (15.12)	THIRD OPEN (64)	BR	ST PANCRAS	DERBY	12.05 Derby - St Pancras (15.12)
11	119 12.05 Derby - St Pancras (15.12)	THIRD OPEN (56)	LMS	ST PANCRAS	DERBY	12.05 Derby - St Pancras (15.12)
12	119 12.05 Derby - St Pancras (15.12)	BRAKE THIRD CORRIDOR (24)	LMS	ST PANCRAS	DERBY	12.05 Derby - St Pancras (15.12)

Following in the wake of the 18.33 flier, the 18.40 to Manchester also ran to special limit timings although only as far as Leicester where it reverted to ordinary express (limited load) timings. The seven minute interval was maintained as far as Wigston but thereafter it increased in stages, thanks to stops at Kettering, Leicester and Loughborough, to twenty four minutes. Even though there were few London passengers who used the service all the way to Manchester, the 18.40 was still one of the Midland's principal trains and it may have surprised many of its patrons to learn that the stock used - or, at least, some of it - actually started the day as a rather humble local service. This extreme of fortunes concerned the Manchester coaches at the front of the train - seven of the eleven vehicles were left behind at Derby to form the next day's 12.05 to London - which commenced work as the 07.24 Manchester - Derby, a local train which in the author's opinion and experience was the most miserable in the country since it was invariably unheated and made no less than twenty-one stops before reaching Derby.

Married up to seven Derby-based vehicles, the 07.24 went forward as the 12.05 Derby to St Pancras semi-fast; a service that occasionally attracted the attention of the railway press since it was regularly used for whichever of the early BR diesels happened to be working on the Midland at the time. No alterations were made to the eleven-coach set during its three and a half hour turn-round in London although at Derby, as the Manchester coaches were being separated from the rest, a non-corridor parcels vehicle which had arrived with the 18.33 ex St Pancras was added to the front of the train.

19.10 ST PANCRAS to DERBY (22.15)

C/W	Previous working	Vehicle	Type	From	To	Next working
1	49 13.25 Nottingham - St Pancras (17.33)	BRAKE THIRD CORRIDOR (24)	LMS	ST PANCRAS	DERBY	06.18 Derby - Nottingham (07.06)
2	49 13.25 Nottingham - St Pancras (17.33)	THIRD CORRIDOR (42)	LMS	ST PANCRAS	DERBY	06.18 Derby - Nottingham (07.06)
3	49 13.25 Nottingham - St Pancras (17.33)	COMPOSITE CORRIDOR (18/24)	LMS	ST PANCRAS	DERBY	06.18 Derby - Nottingham (07.06)
4	49 13.25 Nottingham - St Pancras (17.33)	COMPOSITE CORRIDOR (18/24)	LMS	ST PANCRAS	DERBY	06.18 Derby - Nottingham (07.06)
5	49 13.25 Nottingham - St Pancras (17.33)	THIRD CORRIDOR (42)	LMS	ST PANCRAS	DERBY	06.18 Derby - Nottingham (07.06)
6	49 13.25 Nottingham - St Pancras (17.33)	BRAKE THIRD CORRIDOR (24)	LMS	ST PANCRAS	DERBY	06.18 Derby - Nottingham (07.06)
7	49A 13.25 Nottingham - St Pancras (17.33)	CAFETERIA CAR	BR	ST PANCRAS	NOTTINGHAM	13.25 Nottingham - St Pancras (17.33)
8	49A 13.25 Nottingham - St Pancras (17.33)	THIRD OPEN (56)	LMS	ST PANCRAS	NOTTINGHAM	13.25 Nottingham - St Pancras (17.33)
9	49A 13.25 Nottingham - St Pancras (17.33)	THIRD CORRIDOR (42)	LMS	ST PANCRAS	NOTTINGHAM	13.25 Nottingham - St Pancras (17.33)
10	49A 13.25 Nottingham - St Pancras (17.33)	BRAKE THIRD CORRIDOR (24)	LMS	ST PANCRAS	NOTTINGHAM	13.25 Nottingham - St Pancras (17.33)

The 19.10 was the second of the evening business expresses between London and Nottingham and the third since four o'clock to run non-stop to Kettering; then the centre of the boot and shoe trade and a far more important location that it is often given credit for being. As the 17.30 ex St Pancras illustrated the geographical flexibility of the Midland by running to Nottingham via Leicester so the 19.10 demonstrated another variation by running to Derby - with a loss of about half an hour - via Melton and Nottingham. The train was formed from two sections: one, a six car set which ran through to Derby whilst the other, which included a cafeteria car, was removed during the six-minute stop in Nottingham. The two sections were reunited at Nottingham the following morning; the Derby-based coaches being used to form the 06.18 Derby - Nottingham local service.

16.15 YORK to SHEFFIELD (18.06)

	C/W	Previous working	Vehicle	Type	From	To	Next working
1	54	07.54 Worcester - York (12.50)	BRAKE THIRD CORRIDOR (24)	LMS	YORK	SHEFFIELD	17.16 Sheffield - Gloucester (21.49)
2	54	07.54 Worcester - York (12.50)	THIRD CORRIDOR (42)	LMS	YORK	SHEFFIELD	17.16 Sheffield - Gloucester (21.49)
3	54	07.54 Worcester - York (12.50)	COMPOSITE CORRIDOR (18/24)	LMS	YORK	SHEFFIELD	17.16 Sheffield - Gloucester (21.49)
4	54	07.54 Worcester - York (12.50)	COMPOSITE CORRIDOR (18/24)	LMS	YORK	SHEFFIELD	17.16 Sheffield - Gloucester (21.49)
5	54	07.54 Worcester - York (12.50)	THIRD CORRIDOR (42)	LMS	YORK	SHEFFIELD	17.16 Sheffield - Gloucester (21.49)
6	54	07.54 Worcester - York (12.50)	THIRD CORRIDOR (42)	LMS	YORK	SHEFFIELD	17.16 Sheffield - Gloucester (21.49)
7	54	07.54 Worcester - York (12.50)	THIRD CORRIDOR (42)	LMS	YORK	SHEFFIELD	17.16 Sheffield - Gloucester (21.49)
8	54	07.54 Worcester - York (12.50)	BRAKE THIRD CORRIDOR (24)	LMS	YORK	SHEFFIELD	17.16 Sheffield - Gloucester (21.49)

Now and again one found oneself waiting for a local train at a wayside station such as Sherburn-in-Elmet or Burton Salmon when instead of the expected 2-6-4T and three or four non-corridors, a Black Five 4-6-0 would grind to a hand with no less than eight corridor coaches in tow; the last thing one expected. The 16.15 York to Sheffield Midland was one such service.

Ending the day after arriving in York with the morning through train from Worcester, had it not been for the need to return the stock to Sheffield for the next day's working, it is hardly likely that the 16.15 Swinton & Knottingley service would have comprised as many as eight main line corridor vehicles; the more so since it did not connect with anything of note at York whilst the connection at Sheffield - the 16.45 Bradford to Bristol - gave no advantage to the West of England passenger over the 15.57 Newcastle to Birmingham.

York to Sheffield was not always the easiest of journeys and although an express could cover the forty-six miles in about seventy-five minutes, they were few and far between especially in the late afternoon when there was a long gap between the 15.22 ex York (12.57 Newcastle - Bristol) and the 17.40 (15.57 Newcastle - Birmingham). For those leaving York between the two expresses there was only the 16.15 which, apart from its length of corridor stock, was notable only for calling at every one of the eighteen intermediate stations.

16.45 BRADFORD to BRISTOL (23.56)

	C/W	Previous working	Vehicle	Type	From	To	Next working
1	969		FULL BRAKE	LMS	DERBY	BRISTOL	
2	43A	11.10 Derby - Bradford (14.03)	RESTAURANT BUFFET (24)	LMS	BRADFORD	DERBY	11.10 Derby - Bradford (14.03)
3	43	07.35 Bristol - Bradford (14.03)	BRAKE THIRD CORRIDOR (24)	LMS	BRADFORD	BRISTOL	07.35 Bristol - Bradford (14.03)
4	43	07.35 Bristol - Bradford (14.03)	THIRD CORRIDOR (42)	LMS	BRADFORD	BRISTOL	07.35 Bristol - Bradford (14.03)
5	43	07.35 Bristol - Bradford (14.03)	COMPOSITE CORRIDOR (18/24)	LMS	BRADFORD	BRISTOL	07.35 Bristol - Bradford (14.03)
6	43	07.35 Bristol - Bradford (14.03)	COMPOSITE CORRIDOR (18/24)	LMS	BRADFORD	BRISTOL	07.35 Bristol - Bradford (14.03)
7	43	07.35 Bristol - Bradford (14.03)	THIRD CORRIDOR (42)	LMS	BRADFORD	BRISTOL	07.35 Bristol - Bradford (14.03)
8	43	07.35 Bristol - Bradford (14.03)	FULL BRAKE	LMS	BRADFORD	BRISTOL	07.35 Bristol - Bradford (14.03)
9	967		FULL BRAKE	LMS	BRADFORD	BRISTOL	
10	968		FULL BRAKE	LMS	BRADFORD	BRISTOL	
11	43B	01.10 Bristol - Derby (05.45)	TPO	LMS	DERBY	BRISTOL	01.10 Bristol - Derby (05.36)

The return working of part of the 07.35 ex Bristol - a train notable for being brought in by an LNER D49 4-4-0 - the night West of England Mail had to maintain a critical path since it had to connect at Sheffield with an afternoon service from York before exchanging a considerable amount of traffic at Derby with the 17.55 Manchester to St Pancras. Whilst engaged with the latter, the 5MT 4-6-0 of the 16.45 shunted the buffet car into a bay platform and exchanged it for a loaded Full Brake whilst at the rear of the train the station pilot attached a Travelling Post Office sorting coach for Bristol. In the midst of this activity the platform rang with the noisy clatter of confused passengers threading their way through scurrying mail and parcels trolleys as they tried to establish which train was which. There was an added urgency to the mele since the two services provided the last service of the day between Sheffield and London. A punctual departure from Derby by the Mail was essential since it was closely followed by the 15.57 Newcastle - Birmingham express, the latter running to a margin which narrowed to only six minutes by New Street. The Newcastle invariably conveyed numerous passengers for Bristol together with a considerable weight of parcels and mail for Devon and Cornwall and to ensure that the 16.45 left Birmingham on time, twenty-one minutes were allowed in New Street.

Between Birmingham and Cheltenham the Mail became something of a semi-fast, calling at Barnt Green, Wadborough (unadvertised and for five minutes!) and Ashchurch; express running not being resumed until after leaving Gloucester from whence it ran non-stop to reach Bristol a few minutes before midnight.

17.55 MANCHESTER CENTRAL to ST PANCRAS (22.52)

	C/W	Previous working	Vehicle	Type	From	To	Next working
1	25	08.15 St Pancras - Manchester (13.02)	BRAKE THIRD CORRIDOR (24)	LMS	MANCHESTER	ST PANCRAS	08.15 St Pancras - Manchester (13.02)
2	25	08.15 St Pancras - Manchester (13.02)	COMPOSITE CORRIDOR (18/24)	LMS	MANCHESTER	ST PANCRAS	08.15 St Pancras - Manchester (13.02)
3	25	08.15 St Pancras - Manchester (13.02)	FIRST CORRIDOR (36)	LMS	MANCHESTER	ST PANCRAS	08.15 St Pancras - Manchester (13.02)
4	25	08.15 St Pancras - Manchester (13.02)	THIRD OPEN (56)	LMS	MANCHESTER	ST PANCRAS	08.15 St Pancras - Manchester (13.02)
5	25	08.15 St Pancras - Manchester (13.02)	THIRD CORRIDOR (42)	LMS	MANCHESTER	ST PANCRAS	08.15 St Pancras - Manchester (13.02)
6	25	08.15 St Pancras - Manchester (13.02)	THIRD CORRIDOR (42)	LMS	MANCHESTER	ST PANCRAS	08.15 St Pancras - Manchester (13.02)
7	25	08.15 St Pancras - Manchester (13.02)	BRAKE THIRD CORRIDOR (24)	LMS	MANCHESTER	ST PANCRAS	08.15 St Pancras - Manchester (13.02)
8	25	08.15 St Pancras - Manchester (13.02)	FULL BRAKE	LMS	MANCHESTER	ST PANCRAS	08.15 St Pancras - Manchester (13.02)
9	901	04.18 St Pancras - Manchester (09.49)	FULL BRAKE	LMS	MANCHESTER	ST PANCRAS	04.18 St Pancras - Manchester (09.49)
10	902	17.55 Newark - Leicester (19.56)	FULL BRAKE	LMS	LEICESTER	ST PANCRAS	04.18 St Pancras - Wellingborough (06.03)
11	903	07.02 Wellingborough - Leicester (08.09)	FULL BRAKE	LMS	LEICESTER	ST PANCRAS	04.18 St Pancras - Wellingborough (06.03)

With the Comet leaving London Road at 17.50 on a three and a half hour timing to Euston, the operators were of the opinion that the 16.00 Manchester Central to St Pancras was sufficient for Midland business purposes and the 17.55 from Central, in spite of being, like most Midland expresses, very popular, was rather a poor affair. Calling only at Chinley, Millers Dale and Matlock, the first half of the journey was covered in the normal time for a London express; timekeeping being more than usually important since a connection was made at Derby with the 16.45 Bradford - Bristol: a meeting that involved a heavy exchange of mail and parcels and for which two Full Brakes were marshalled at the rear of the train.

Up to Leicester the main complaint about the train concerned the lack of dining facilities and it was quite extraordinary that a London express running at a time that encompassed the dinner hours should lack a restaurant car. The running to Leicester had been that of an express but from arriving in London Road matters degenerated as, first of all, the train stood for eight minutes whilst another pair of Full Brakes - including one from Newark - was attached after which calls were made at Kettering, Wellingborough, Bedford and Luton until, five hours after leaving Manchester Central, the 5XP and its coaches pulled into St Pancras just in time for its passengers to witness the closing of the Underground for the night.

Most of the stock was that which had worked north in the 08.15 St Pancras - Manchester whilst three of the four BG's came from the 04.18 Newspaper train.

In 1954 one of the authors was a Motive Power Inspector supervising the tests of Britannia Pacifics on fitted trains between Toton and Cricklewood. Knowing that the test engines were not required on Saturdays and knowing - as an enthusiast - that the sight of a Pacific in St Pancras would give lineside observers something to talk about for years to come, a couple of telephone calls were all that was necessary to have 70043 booked to the 12.05 Derby - St Pancras and the 20.10 St Pancras - Derby. Having made the arrangements, the next job was to scale a suitable signal ladder - the Spondon down starter - and take a photograph of 70043 as it passed Way & Works Sidings, near Spondon, a few minutes out of Derby. Through the murk blowing over from Derby loco on the right, Leicester Compound 41089 can be seen undergoing preparation for its next job.

	C/W Previous working	Vehicle	Type	From	To	Next working
		19.55 ST PANCRAS to NOTTINGHAM (23.17)				
1		FULL BRAKE	LMS	ST PANCRAS	NOTTINGHAM	
2	11.47 Bedford - St Pancras (13.04)	**THIRD CORRIDOR (42)**	LMS	ST PANCRAS	NOTTINGHAM	07.16 Nottingham - Leicester (08.25)
3	11.47 Bedford - St Pancras (13.04)	**THIRD CORRIDOR (42)**	LMS	ST PANCRAS	NOTTINGHAM	07.16 Nottingham - Leicester (08.25)
4	11.47 Bedford - St Pancras (13.04)	**BRAKE THIRD CORRIDOR (32)**	LMS	ST PANCRAS	NOTTINGHAM	07.16 Nottingham - Leicester (08.25)
5	11.47 Bedford - St Pancras (13.04)	**COMPOSITE CORRIDOR (18/32)**	LMS	ST PANCRAS	NOTTINGHAM	07.16 Nottingham - Leicester (08.25)
6	11.47 Bedford - St Pancras (13.04)	**BRAKE THIRD CORRIDOR (32)**	LMS	ST PANCRAS	NOTTINGHAM	07.16 Nottingham - Leicester (08.25)
7		FULL BRAKE	LMS	ST PANCRAS	NOTTINGHAM	

Technically a local train since the operators drew a sharp distinction between the stock that worked the expresses and vehicles that went no further from London than either Leicester or Nottingham, the 19.55 ran as a semi-fast to Nottingham via Leicester for the purpose of providing a connection at Nottingham into the 21.05 St Pancras to Edinburgh. One mystery surrounding the train concerned Wellingborough, a town whose claim for an Edinburgh connection was as sound as any. For some reason the timing office decided not to include Wellingborough in the list of stops and although the service was shown in the timetable as calling only at Kettering between Bedford and Leicester, the diagramming office decided that the train's locomen had to be relieved in Wellingborough and duly inserted an unadvertised stop...... Left hands and right hands!

The stock remained in the working on a daily basis and started its day with the 07.16 Leicester to Nottingham via Trent, going on to work the 09.48 Leicester to Bedford and the 11.47 Bedford to St Pancras.

	C/W Previous working	Vehicle	Type	From	To	Next working
		20.10 ST PANCRAS to DERBY (23.40)				
1	27B 06.40 Nottingham - St Pancras (09.55)	**THIRD CORRIDOR (42)**	LMS	ST PANCRAS	DERBY	
2	32 07.55 Derby - St Pancras (10.42)	**THIRD CORRIDOR (42)**	LMS	ST PANCRAS	DERBY	07.55 Derby - St Pancras (10.42)
3	32 07.55 Derby - St Pancras (10.42)	**THIRD CORRIDOR (42)**	LMS	ST PANCRAS	DERBY	07.55 Derby - St Pancras (10.42)
4	32 07.55 Derby - St Pancras (10.42)	**BRAKE THIRD CORRIDOR (24)**	BR	ST PANCRAS	DERBY	07.55 Derby - St Pancras (10.42)
5	32 07.55 Derby - St Pancras (10.42)	**THIRD CORRIDOR (48)**	BR	ST PANCRAS	DERBY	07.55 Derby - St Pancras (10.42)
6	32 07.55 Derby - St Pancras (10.42)	**FIRST CORRIDOR (42)**	BR	ST PANCRAS	DERBY	07.55 Derby - St Pancras (10.42)
7	32 07.55 Derby - St Pancras (10.42)	**COMPOSITE CORRIDOR (24/18)**	BR	ST PANCRAS	DERBY	07.55 Derby - St Pancras (10.42)
8	32 07.55 Derby - St Pancras (10.42)	**THIRD CORRIDOR (48)**	BR	ST PANCRAS	DERBY	07.55 Derby - St Pancras (10.42)
9	32 07.55 Derby - St Pancras (10.42)	**BRAKE THIRD CORRIDOR (24)**	BR	ST PANCRAS	DERBY	07.55 Derby - St Pancras (10.42)
10	908	FULL BRAKE	LMS	ST PANCRAS	DERBY	**01.25 Derby - York (04.25)**
11	909	FULL BRAKE	LMS	ST PANCRAS	DERBY	**01.25 Derby - York (04.25)**

A popular train, not only for returning visitors from London but for overnight passengers from stations such as Luton and Bedford for Newcastle and Scotland; the service connecting with the overnight London - Edinburgh express at Kettering and at Derby with the 19.20 Bristol - Newcastle. In having to change trains at Derby, passengers for the North East were less fortunate than the several tons of parcels picked up en route which were provided with through carriage to York and Newcastle respectively. The two full brakes used for this purpose were transferred at Derby to the 23.05 Birmingham - York parcels train.

The 08.45 Paignton - Bradford 'Devonian' runs into Gloucester Eastgate on Saturday 30th May 1959 behind BR 5MT 4-6-0 73050 and 5XP 45662 'Kempenfelt' of Bath and Bristol respectively. The service was unique in that instead of running over the Midland route from Bristol to Yate via Mangotsfield, it was booked to run via Stapleton Road to Filton Junction where it ran for a short distance along the GWR South Wales - London main line before taking the Westerleigh - Yate spur to rejoin the Midland. Seven services followed this routing on summer Saturdays but the Devonian was the only example to do so on weekdays; the reason being to ensure that a link of Midland crews were able to retain route knowledge without the need for refreshing. The maximum load permitted to a Jubilee 4-6-0 was slightly less than allowed via Mangotsfield and on Summer Saturdays a pilot - in this instance 73050 - was generally taken as far as Gloucester.

		15.57 NEWCASTLE to BIRMINGHAM (21.05)					
	C/W	Previous working	Vehicle	Type	From	To	Next working
1	39	08.02 Birmingham - Newcastle (13.03)	**BRAKE THIRD CORRIDOR (24)**	**LMS**	**NEWCASTLE**	**BIRMINGHAM**	06.40 Birmingham - Bradford (11.04)
2	39	08.02 Birmingham - Newcastle (13.03)	**THIRD CORRIDOR (42)**	**LMS**	**NEWCASTLE**	**BIRMINGHAM**	06.40 Birmingham - Bradford (11.04)
3	39	08.02 Birmingham - Newcastle (13.03)	**COMPOSITE CORRIDOR (18/24)**	**LMS**	**NEWCASTLE**	**BIRMINGHAM**	06.40 Birmingham - Bradford (11.04)
4	39	08.02 Birmingham - Newcastle (13.03)	**COMPOSITE CORRIDOR (18/24)**	**LMS**	**NEWCASTLE**	**BIRMINGHAM**	06.40 Birmingham - Bradford (11.04)
5	39	08.02 Birmingham - Newcastle (13.03)	**THIRD CORRIDOR (42)**	**LMS**	**NEWCASTLE**	**BIRMINGHAM**	06.40 Birmingham - Bradford (11.04)
6	39	08.02 Birmingham - Newcastle (13.03)	**BRAKE THIRD CORRIDOR (24)**	**LMS**	**NEWCASTLE**	**BIRMINGHAM**	06.40 Birmingham - Bradford (11.04)

Alone of the Tyneside 'Midland' trains, the stock of the 15.57 ex Newcastle made a return trip each day, arriving with the 08.02 from Birmingham and leaving after less than three hours in the area. This short turn-round called for some hard work by the carriage servicing staff since the stock arrived in Heaton sidings at 13.28, exchanged its A2 for an A3 Pacific and left again less than two hours later. The activity in the carriage sidings when the down train arrived late had to be seen to be believed. The operation could not be conducted in Newcastle Central because there were only three through platforms. The formation shown above was the basic and varied considerably from day to day. On Mondays a pair of additions TK's were conveyed behind the first vehicle whilst on Tuesdays and Wednesdays a three-coach set (BTK,CK,BTK) was added to the front of the train at Sheffield. In addition a three-coach dining set was attached for the North Eastern leg of the journey as far as York. The 'core' six coaches did not spent more than a day on the Newcastle working but followed a lengthy and complex cyclic working which saw them at Bradford the following day and at St Pancras the day after that. Although terminating at Birmingham the service ran into New Street alongside the 16.45 Bradford - Bristol which provided a useful connection to the West Country, reaching Temple Meads at midnight.

		17.25 BRADFORD to SHEFFIELD (19.23)					
	C/W	Previous working	Vehicle	Type	From	To	Next working
1	38A	06.40 Birmingham - Bradford (11.04)	**BRAKE THIRD CORRIDOR (24)**	**LMS**	**BRADFORD**	**SHEFFIELD**	09.09 Sheffield - St Pancras (13.21)
2	38A	06.40 Birmingham - Bradford (11.04)	**THIRD CORRIDOR (42)**	**LMS**	**BRADFORD**	**SHEFFIELD**	09.09 Sheffield - St Pancras (13.21)
3	38A	06.40 Birmingham - Bradford (11.04)	**COMPOSITE CORRIDOR (18/24)**	**LMS**	**BRADFORD**	**SHEFFIELD**	09.09 Sheffield - St Pancras (13.21)
4	38A	06.40 Birmingham - Bradford (11.04)	**COMPOSITE CORRIDOR (18/24)**	**LMS**	**BRADFORD**	**SHEFFIELD**	09.09 Sheffield - St Pancras (13.21)
5	38A	06.40 Birmingham - Bradford (11.04)	**THIRD CORRIDOR (42)**	**LMS**	**BRADFORD**	**SHEFFIELD**	09.09 Sheffield - St Pancras (13.21)
6	38A	06.40 Birmingham - Bradford (11.04)	**BRAKE THIRD CORRIDOR (24)**	**LMS**	**BRADFORD**	**SHEFFIELD**	09.09 Sheffield - St Pancras (13.21)

Stopping trains were generally formed of local sets that did not stray from their allotted beaten tracks but there were exceptions where unbalanced main line stock was used and the 17.25 Bradford - Sheffield was one such. The train was the return of the unbalanced 06.40 Birmingham to Bradford, the six coaches being pressed into stopping service principally to get them to Sheffield in order to work a morning express to London the following morning. This was the last leg of a ten-day cycle that had taken the carriage set on every section of the Midland system except Shipley to Carlisle whilst it had also travelled down the North Eastern main line as far as Newcastle.

	C/W	Previous working	Vehicle	Type	From	To	Next working
		19.20 BRISTOL to NEWCASTLE (04.21)					
1	66	19.05 Newcastle - Bristol (05.21)	FULL BRAKE	LMS	BRISTOL	NEWCASTLE	19.05 Newcastle - Bristol (05.21)
2	66	19.05 Newcastle - Bristol (05.21)	**BRAKE THIRD CORRIDOR (24)**	BR	BRISTOL	NEWCASTLE	19.05 Newcastle - Bristol (05.21)
3	66	19.05 Newcastle - Bristol (05.21)	**THIRD CORRIDOR (48)**	BR	BRISTOL	NEWCASTLE	19.05 Newcastle - Bristol (05.21)
4	66	19.05 Newcastle - Bristol (05.21)	**THIRD CORRIDOR (48)**	BR	BRISTOL	NEWCASTLE	19.05 Newcastle - Bristol (05.21)
5	66	19.05 Newcastle - Bristol (05.21)	**COMPOSITE CORRIDOR (24/18)**	BR	BRISTOL	NEWCASTLE	19.05 Newcastle - Bristol (05.21)
6	66	19.05 Newcastle - Bristol (05.21)	FULL BRAKE	LMS	BRISTOL	NEWCASTLE	19.05 Newcastle - Bristol (05.21)
7	66	19.05 Newcastle - Bristol (05.21)	TPO	LMS	BRISTOL	NEWCASTLE	19.05 Newcastle - Bristol (05.21)
8	66	19.05 Newcastle - Bristol (05.21)	TPO	LMS	BRISTOL	NEWCASTLE	19.05 Newcastle - Bristol (05.21)
9	66	19.05 Newcastle - Bristol (05.21)	TPO	LMS	BRISTOL	NEWCASTLE	19.05 Newcastle - Bristol (05.21)
10	948	23.30 Sheffield - Bristol (05.20)	FULL BRAKE	LMS	BRISTOL	SHEFFIELD	02.10 Sheffield - Bradford (04.41)
11	951	**16.18 Bailey Gate - Mangotsfield**	FULL BRAKE	LMS	MANGOTSFIELD	SHEFFIELD	02.10 Sheffield - Bradford (04.41)

Based on the rather precarious presumption that passengers joining at Birmingham would be balanced by those alighting from Bristol, accommodation on the Newcastle mail was limited in all but name and the experience of using the service - as the author can testify - put the lie to many of the claims made by the press and others who should know better about the romance and charms of night travel. On Friday nights the operators relented to the extent of attaching a pair of additional third corridors at New Street but so far as Bristol was concerned, they preferred to stay well inside the loading limit for a Black 5 4-6-0. A sleeping car might well have been a popular adjunct and although the mid-1950's saw the facility introduced in the 16.45 Penzance - Manchester over the Bristol - Crewe route, no such parallel proposal was made in respect of the Midland. Passengers for Scotland, however, were able to book berths from Derby in the 21.15 ex St Pancras.

The real importance of the service lay in mail traffic and no less than three Royal Mail sorting coaches were included in the formation together with four full brakes containing bagged mails and parcels post. Of the latter, two went through to Newcastle with the rest of the train whilst two (including one that was attached at Mangotsfield and came from the Somerset & Dorset) were detached at Sheffield and transferred to the 02.10 express to Bradford Forster Square.

In addition to overcrowding, another frustration endured by through passengers was the fifty minutes that the train spent in New Street loading transfer mails from other parts of the system.

	C/W	Previous working	Vehicle	Type	From	To	Next working
		21.05 ST PANCRAS to EDINBURGH WAVERLEY (07.54)					
1	913	18.20 Hull - Leeds (20.17)	VANFIT (Fish)	LMS	LEEDS	CARLISLE	06.20 Carlisle - Whitehaven (08.05)
2	9	21.53 Edinburgh - St Pancras (09.12)	FULL BRAKE	LMS	ST PANCRAS	EDINBURGH	21.53 Edinburgh - St Pancras (09.12)
3	9	21.53 Edinburgh - St Pancras (09.12)	**SLEEPING CAR COMPOSITE**	LMS/LNER*	ST PANCRAS	EDINBURGH	21.53 Edinburgh - St Pancras (09.12)
4	9	21.53 Edinburgh - St Pancras (09.12)	**SLEEPING CAR COMPOSITE**	LMS/LNER*	ST PANCRAS	EDINBURGH	21.53 Edinburgh - St Pancras (09.12)
5	9	21.53 Edinburgh - St Pancras (09.12)	**SLEEPING CAR THIRD**	LMS/LNER*	ST PANCRAS	EDINBURGH	21.53 Edinburgh - St Pancras (09.12)
6	9	21.53 Edinburgh - St Pancras (09.12)	**SLEEPING CAR FIRST**	LMS/LNER*	ST PANCRAS	EDINBURGH	21.53 Edinburgh - St Pancras (09.12)
7	9	21.53 Edinburgh - St Pancras (09.12)	**COMPOSITE CORRIDOR (18/24)**	LMS	ST PANCRAS	EDINBURGH	21.53 Edinburgh - St Pancras (09.12)
8	9	21.53 Edinburgh - St Pancras (09.12)	**COMPOSITE CORRIDOR (18/24)**	LMS	ST PANCRAS	EDINBURGH	21.53 Edinburgh - St Pancras (09.12)
9	9	21.53 Edinburgh - St Pancras (09.12)	**THIRD CORRIDOR (42)**	LMS	ST PANCRAS	EDINBURGH	21.53 Edinburgh - St Pancras (09.12)
10	9	21.53 Edinburgh - St Pancras (09.12)	**THIRD CORRIDOR (42)**	LMS	ST PANCRAS	EDINBURGH	21.53 Edinburgh - St Pancras (09.12)
11	9	21.53 Edinburgh - St Pancras (09.12)	**THIRD CORRIDOR (42)**	LMS	ST PANCRAS	EDINBURGH	21.53 Edinburgh - St Pancras (09.12)
12	9	21.53 Edinburgh - St Pancras (09.12)	FULL BRAKE	LMS	ST PANCRAS	EDINBURGH	21.53 Edinburgh - St Pancras (09.12)
13	910	18.45 St Pancras - Nottingham (23.10)	FULL BRAKE	LMS	NOTTINGHAM	PERTH	
14	911	19.40 Luton - Nottingham (23.10)	FULL BRAKE	LMS	NOTTINGHAM	GLASGOW	09.20 Glasgow - St Pancras (19.19)

* Alternating daily.   The service reversed at Leeds and the order of leaving St Pancras in shown

For a service that was supposed to be secondary to those of the East Coast, the overnight Midland express to Edinburgh was no mean train and one of several notable features was the high proportion of first class accommodation with five of the nine passenger vehicles containing first class seats or berths. The presence of LNER sleeping cars on alternate evening gave one a sense of reassurance that the world was not changing as quickly as some would have believe. Not, on the other nights of the week, that there was anything wrong with the LMS cars, the solidity of whose bulbous sides and 12-wheel bogies virtually guaranteed a good nights sleep although during the summer, a sleeping berth was a waste of several hours of unrivalled scenic pageantry and all that was required was a good book that would last as far as sunrise at Settle and a window seat thereafter. A considerable amount of non-passenger tonnage was also conveyed in the four full brakes included in the formation: two for Edinburgh and one each for Perth and Glasgow. The last two were attached to the rear of the train at Nottingham but actually came through from London, working down in the 18.45 St Pancras - Leicester slow and the 22.08 Leicester - Nottingham stopping train. A rather unlikely addition to the formation came at Leeds where a wagon of fish en route from Hull to Whitehaven was attached to the train.

	C/W	Previous working	Vehicle	Type	From	To	Next working
		21.15 ST PANCRAS to GLASGOW ST ENOCH (08.30)					
1	912		FULL BRAKE	LMS	ST PANCRAS	KILMARNOCK	
2	7	21.10 Glasgow - St Pancras (08.05)	FULL BRAKE	LMS	ST PANCRAS	GLASGOW	21.10 Glasgow - St Pancras (08.05)
3	7	21.10 Glasgow - St Pancras (08.05)	**BRAKE THIRD CORRIDOR (24)**	LMS	ST PANCRAS	GLASGOW	21.10 Glasgow - St Pancras (08.05)
4	7	21.10 Glasgow - St Pancras (08.05)	**THIRD CORRIDOR (42)**	LMS	ST PANCRAS	GLASGOW	21.10 Glasgow - St Pancras (08.05)
5	7	21.10 Glasgow - St Pancras (08.05)	**THIRD CORRIDOR (42)**	LMS	ST PANCRAS	GLASGOW	21.10 Glasgow - St Pancras (08.05)
6	7	21.10 Glasgow - St Pancras (08.05)	**THIRD CORRIDOR (42)**	LMS	ST PANCRAS	GLASGOW	21.10 Glasgow - St Pancras (08.05)
7	7	21.10 Glasgow - St Pancras (08.05)	**SLEEPING CAR THIRD**	LMS	ST PANCRAS	GLASGOW	21.10 Glasgow - St Pancras (08.05)
8	7	21.10 Glasgow - St Pancras (08.05)	**SLEEPING CAR FIRST**	LMS	ST PANCRAS	GLASGOW	21.10 Glasgow - St Pancras (08.05)
9	7	21.10 Glasgow - St Pancras (08.05)	**SLEEPING CAR FIRST**	LMS	ST PANCRAS	GLASGOW	21.10 Glasgow - St Pancras (08.05)
10	7	21.10 Glasgow - St Pancras (08.05)	**COMPOSITE CORRIDOR (18/24)**	LMS	ST PANCRAS	GLASGOW	21.10 Glasgow - St Pancras (08.05)
11	7	21.10 Glasgow - St Pancras (08.05)	FULL BRAKE	LMS	ST PANCRAS	GLASGOW	21.10 Glasgow - St Pancras (08.05)
12	914		FULL BRAKE	LMS	LEEDS	GLASGOW	

The service reversed at Leeds and the order of leaving St Pancras in shown

Whilst intended primarily to give a direct service between the East Midlands and Scotland, no objections (at least in the author's hearing) were ever raised to the train being used throughout and although the West Coast had its points of interest, there was at least one small group of regular travellers who used the Midland route partly because of the Settle & Carlisle but also because there was a feeling of supporting the underdog. (In this connection there was a considerable sense of pride generated by the sight of two Anglo-Scottish trains following each other from St Pancras - it meant that the Midland was still in the big league!). Sometimes the underdog took on the appearance of a mastiff since on Summer Fridays, the usual diet of two Scottish trains expanded to eight: six from St Pancras and one each from Nottingham and Manchester.

The accommodation provided was interesting in that a high proportion of the sleeping berths were for first class traffic whilst all but half a coach of the seating section was for third class ticket holders thus making something of a contrast with the preceding Edinburgh train. It is interesting to note that neither of the night trains - which were invariably well used to the point of overcrowding - used the new BR standard coaching stock which the Midland seemed to embrace more readily than other constituents of British Railways. It is a fact that the new vehicles were poor riders and had aroused a number of complaints on this score. The Midland, it seems, was disinclined to extend the experiment through the long night hours.

20.00 LINCOLN to TAMWORTH (22.24)

	C/W	Previous working	Vehicle	Type	From	To	Next working
1	986		FULL BRAKE	LMS	NOTTINGHAM	TAMWORTH	00.26 Tamworth - Crewe
2	125	02.25 Tamworth - Lincoln (04.45)	BRAKE THIRD CORRIDOR (32)	LMS	LINCOLN	TAMWORTH	02.25 Tamworth - Lincoln (04.45)
3	125	02.25 Tamworth - Lincoln (04.45)	COMPOSITE CORRIDOR (18/32)	LMS	LINCOLN	TAMWORTH	02.25 Tamworth - Lincoln (04.45)
4	125	02.25 Tamworth - Lincoln (04.45)	BRAKE THIRD CORRIDOR (32)	LMS	LINCOLN	TAMWORTH	02.25 Tamworth - Lincoln (04.45)
5	125	02.25 Tamworth - Lincoln (04.45)	TPO	LMS	LINCOLN	TAMWORTH	02.25 Tamworth - Lincoln (04.45)
6	125	02.25 Tamworth - Lincoln (04.45)	FULL BRAKE	LMS	LINCOLN	TAMWORTH	02.25 Tamworth - Lincoln (04.45)
7		16.48 Grimsby - Nottingham	VANFIT	Fish	NOTTINGHAM	BURTON	
8		16.48 Grimsby - Nottingham	VANFIT	Fish	NOTTINGHAM	DERBY	

The 'Tamworth Mail' was something of an institution amongst railwaymen (and not a few enthusiasts) in the Nottingham area whose pride in the fact that two of the minor provinces should have a train service devoted to them was palpable. In fact the train had very little to do with either Lincoln or Tamworth but collected mail from East Lincolnshire, Nottingham and Derby and delivered it to Tamworth solely because it was a convenient point to hand over the traffic to the West Coast Postal which called at the low level platforms at 22.39. What made the train particularly notable was the inclusion of a TPO which allowed mail to be sorted en route. The service also conveyed a small amount of fish traffic from Nottingham - two vanfits brought in by the 16.48 ex Grimsby - which was detached at Derby and Burton-on-Trent. Passenger accommodation was provided throughout although it was of limited use to Anglo-Scottish passengers since they had over an hour and a half to wait for a northbound service from Tamworth. For more local needs the train was quite a good service since it ignored most of the stops on the Lincoln - Nottingham branch, pausing only at Collingham, Newark and Rolleston Junction only - after which the train called at Trent, Derby, Repton and Burton. Access to Derby was via the Chaddesden curve to avoid reversing in the station.

On arrival at Tamworth the Scotch mails were unloaded and taken down to the LNW platforms to await the 20.30 Euston - Aberdeen and Glasgow TPO. Mails that had been sorted and bagged for other destinations in the North West were transferred to the leading Full Brake which was shunted down the single-line connection to the LNW by the 2-6-4T that had brought the train in from Lincoln. The remainder of the stock returned to Lincoln at 02.25 after connecting with the 15.35 Glasgow - Euston Postal.

16.00 GLASGOW (ST ENOCH) to LEEDS (21.41)

	C/W	Previous working	Vehicle	Type	From	To	Next working
1	12	10.35 Leeds - Glasgow (15.53)	FULL BRAKE	LMS	GLASGOW	LEEDS	10.35 Leeds - Glasgow (15.53)
2	12	10.35 Leeds - Glasgow (15.53)	BRAKE THIRD CORRIDOR (24)	LMS	GLASGOW	LEEDS	10.35 Leeds - Glasgow (15.53)
3	12	10.35 Leeds - Glasgow (15.53)	THIRD CORRIDOR (42)	LMS	GLASGOW	LEEDS	10.35 Leeds - Glasgow (15.53)
4	12	10.35 Leeds - Glasgow (15.53)	THIRD CORRIDOR (42)	LMS	GLASGOW	LEEDS	10.35 Leeds - Glasgow (15.53)
5	12	10.35 Leeds - Glasgow (15.53)	COMPOSITE CORRIDOR (24/18)	BR	GLASGOW	LEEDS	10.35 Leeds - Glasgow (15.53)
6	12	10.35 Leeds - Glasgow (15.53)	COMPOSITE CORRIDOR (24/18)	BR	GLASGOW	LEEDS	10.35 Leeds - Glasgow (15.53)
7	12	10.35 Leeds - Glasgow (15.53)	THIRD CORRIDOR (42)	LMS	GLASGOW	LEEDS	10.35 Leeds - Glasgow (15.53)
8	12	10.35 Leeds - Glasgow (15.53)	THIRD CORRIDOR (42)	LMS	GLASGOW	LEEDS	10.35 Leeds - Glasgow (15.53)
9	12	10.35 Leeds - Glasgow (15.53)	BRAKE THIRD CORRIDOR (42)	LMS	GLASGOW	LEEDS	10.35 Leeds - Glasgow (15.53)
10	11A	10.35 Leeds - Kilmarnock (15.13)	COMPOSITE OPEN (18/18)	LMS	KILMARNOCK	LEEDS	10.35 Leeds - Kilmarnock (15.13)
11	11A	10.35 Leeds - Kilmarnock (15.13)	RESTAURANT CAR (12/18)	LMS	KILMARNOCK	LEEDS	10.35 Leeds - Kilmarnock (15.13)

By and large Midland carriage utilisation was quite good: most main line sets achieved about 400 miles per day - many of the Manchester and West Riding trains managed a daily return trip - and where this was not possible it was usually because time rather than the will intervened. One or two of the Bradford sets only ran single trips because a return working would have meant running a train very early in the morning or in the dead of night but these were the exception to the rule. More inexplicable was the daily Leeds to Glasgow working which did not more than a single trip - 229 miles - each day. Before the war and for as long as anyone could remember there had been a daily round trip leaving Leeds at 10.00 and returning from Glasgow after a turn-round of 130 minutes at 17.30. Somehow this very neat and convenient arrangement failed to survive the war and for more than fifteen years afterwards the gap between the arrival of the down train in Glasgow and the departure of the corresponding southbound service was no more than seven minutes. This ruled out any question of the same set of coaches being used and the only section of the train that came close to managing the journey in both directions in the same day was the two-coach restaurant portion which came off the down train at Kilmarnock and was attached to the rear of the up train an hour and a half later. Quite why the prewar arrangement could not have been reverted to - there was still a 17.30 St Enoch to Carlisle which could have been extended to Leeds - is one of those mysteries which may never be addressed. The one departure from the arrangement was that the 10.35 from Leeds on Fridays worked the relief Thames-Clyde express to St Pancras on Summer Saturdays, picking up its normal Glasgow duty by forming the 14.45 (Sunday) St Pancras to Leeds.

19.05 NEWCASTLE to BRISTOL (05.21)

	C/W	Previous working	Vehicle	Type	From	To	Next working
1	947		FULL BRAKE	LMS	SHEFFIELD	BRISTOL	
2	67	19.20 Bristol - Newcastle (04.21)	FULL BRAKE	BR (LM)	NEWCASTLE	BRISTOL	19.20 Bristol - Newcastle (04.21)
3	67	19.20 Bristol - Newcastle (04.21)	BRAKE THIRD CORRIDOR (24)	BR (LM)	NEWCASTLE	BRISTOL	19.20 Bristol - Newcastle (04.21)
4	67	19.20 Bristol - Newcastle (04.21)	THIRD CORRIDOR (48)	BR (LM)	NEWCASTLE	BRISTOL	19.20 Bristol - Newcastle (04.21)
5	67	19.20 Bristol - Newcastle (04.21)	THIRD CORRIDOR (48)	BR (LM)	NEWCASTLE	BRISTOL	19.20 Bristol - Newcastle (04.21)
6	67	19.20 Bristol - Newcastle (04.21)	COMPOSITE CORRIDOR (24/18)	BR (LM)	NEWCASTLE	BRISTOL	19.20 Bristol - Newcastle (04.21)
7	67	19.20 Bristol - Newcastle (04.21)	FULL BRAKE	BR (LM)	NEWCASTLE	BRISTOL	19.20 Bristol - Newcastle (04.21)
8	67	19.20 Bristol - Newcastle (04.21)	TPO	LMS	NEWCASTLE	BRISTOL	19.20 Bristol - Newcastle (04.21)
9	67	19.20 Bristol - Newcastle (04.21)	TPO	LMS	NEWCASTLE	BRISTOL	19.20 Bristol - Newcastle (04.21)
10	67	19.20 Bristol - Newcastle (04.21)	TPO	LMS	NEWCASTLE	BRISTOL	19.20 Bristol - Newcastle (04.21)
11	949	22.00 Leeds - Derby (23.07)	FULL BRAKE	LMS	DERBY	WORCESTER	

Although it included in its formation four passenger coaches the 19.05 ex Newcastle was primarily a mail train and because of this, had to be timed to reach Bristol as early as possible in order that its mail could be made ready for the first delivery. Thus, passengers found themselves ejected from the relative warmth of a railway compartment at rather an unpleasant time in the morning - when travelling overnight, it was generally best to give mail trains a wide berth if one wanted to alight at a reasonable time of day. It is interesting to note that the passenger accomodation of the train consisted of BR Mark 1 stock and one wonders if the concealing of brand new coaches in a service that spent most of the daylight hours in carriage sidings was a reflection of the public reception that had been accorded these rather unpleasant vehicles.

The most active section of the train was the Travelling Post Office and the inclusion of three such vehicles in one train testifies to the amount of work that had to be done. A Full Brake was conveyed for the sorted and bagged mail with others being added at Sheffield and Derby; the latter travelling only as far as Worcester. Every effort was made to have the North Eastern mail sorted and bagged by the time the train reached Midland metals since at Sheffield the service took on a fresh load of unsorted mail from the 20.55 Bradford - Bristol which did not carry a TPO. If they wished, passengers could transfer from the Newcastle to the Bradford train which reached Bristol three-quarters of an hour earlier, at 04.33.

BR Standard 5MT 4-6-0 73054 (Holbeck) passes Burton on Trent with the 10.53 Birmingham - Newcastle during the summer of 1955. This was a summer Saturday working designed to relieve the 08.30 Cardiff - Newcastle.

	C/W	Previous working	Vehicle	Type	From	To	Next working
		02.10 SHEFFIELD to LEEDS (03.41)					
1	954	00.09 Sheffield - Normanton (01.02)	FULL BRAKE	LMS	**NORMANTON**	**LEEDS**	07.20 Leeds - Bradford (08.03)
2	442	16.10 Leeds - Sheffield (17.52)	**BRAKE THIRD CORRIDOR (32)**	LMS	**SHEFFIELD**	**LEEDS**	06.30 Leeds - Sheffield (17.52)
3	442	16.10 Leeds - Sheffield (17.52)	**COMPOSITE CORRIDOR (18/32)**	LMS	**SHEFFIELD**	**LEEDS**	06.30 Leeds - Sheffield (17.52)
4	442	16.10 Leeds - Sheffield (17.52)	**BRAKE THIRD CORRIDOR (32)**	LMS	**SHEFFIELD**	**LEEDS**	06.30 Leeds - Sheffield (17.52)
5	948	19.20 Bristol - Sheffield (00.48)	FULL BRAKE	LMS	**SHEFFIELD**	**LEEDS**	07.20 Leeds - Bradford (08.03)
6	951	16.18 Bailey Gate - Sheffield (00.48)	FULL BRAKE	LMS	**SHEFFIELD**	**LEEDS**	07.20 Leeds - Bradford (08.03)
7	950		FULL BRAKE	LMS	**SHEFFIELD**	**LEEDS**	07.20 Leeds - Bradford (08.03)
8	952	22.10 Derby - Sheffield (23.28)	FULL BRAKE (Loco Stores)	LMS	**SHEFFIELD**	**LEEDS**	
9	953	22.10 Derby - Sheffield (23.28)	FULL BRAKE	LMS	**SHEFFIELD**	**LEEDS**	07.20 Leeds - Bradford (08.03)

More of a parcels than a passenger train, the service picked up a collection of parcels vehicles that had come in from Derby and worked them (together with any extras needed for balancing reasons) to Leeds, running in the wake of the 21.15 St Pancras to Glasgow. The train also conveyed mail traffic together with a three coach passenger formation which was a useful passenger facility since a connection was made at Normanton with the 03.15 Lancashire and Yorkshire service to Manchester Victoria via Wakefield and Todmorden.

The routing of the train made an interesting alternative to the usual Rotherham route; the service leaving the main line at Wincobank Junction , three miles north of Sheffield, and travelling via Chapeltown, the main line being rejoined at Cudworth. Although well used by parcels, goods and mineral trains as well local trains between Sheffield, Cudworth and Barnsley, it was an unusual route for a through service; the only other express routinely being sent via Chapeltown being the 14.00 St Pancras to Bradford Forster Square.

	C/W	Previous working	Vehicle	Type	From	To	Next working
		23.50 ST PANCRAS to LEEDS (06.24)					
1	915	22.10 Hendon - St Pancras	FULL BRAKE	LMS	**ST PANCRAS**	**LEEDS**	06.55 Leeds - Bradford
2	916	Kensington - St Pancras	FULL BRAKE	LMS	**ST PANCRAS**	**LEEDS**	06.55 Leeds - Bradford
3	8	21.28 Bradford - St Pancras (05.16)	**THIRD CORRIDOR (42)**	LMS	**ST PANCRAS**	**LEEDS**	06.55 Leeds - Bradford
4	0	21.20 Bradford - St Pancras (05.16)	**THIRD CORRIDOR (42)**	LMS	**ST PANCRAS**	**LEEDS**	06.55 Leeds - Bradford
5	8	21.28 Bradford - St Pancras (05.16)	**COMPOSITE CORRIDOR (18/24)**	LMS	**ST PANCRAS**	**LEEDS**	06.55 Leeds - Bradford
6	8	21.28 Bradford - St Pancras (05.16)	**BRAKE THIRD CORRIDOR (24)**	LMS	**ST PANCRAS**	**LEEDS**	06.55 Leeds - Bradford
7	22A	02.45 Leeds - St Pancras (08.05)	**SLEEPING CAR FIRST**	LMS	**ST PANCRAS**	**LEEDS**	02.45 Leeds - St Pancras (08.05)
8	22A	02.45 Leeds - St Pancras (08.05)	**SLEEPING CAR THIRD**	LMS	**ST PANCRAS**	**LEEDS**	02.45 Leeds - St Pancras (08.05)
9	917	21.20 Bradford - St Pancras (05.16)	FULL BRAKE	LMS	**ST PANCRAS**	**LEEDS**	06.55 Leeds - Bradford
10	918	22.12 Leeds - St Pancras (05.16)	FULL BRAKE	LMS	**ST PANCRAS**	**LEEDS**	22.12 Leeds - St Pancras (05.16)
11	919		FULL BRAKE	LMS	**ST PANCRAS**	**DERBY**	
12	920		FULL BRAKE	LMS	**ST PANCRAS**	**DERBY**	03.57 Derby - Nottingham
13	921	16.25 Leicester - St Pancras (19.00)	FULL BRAKE	LMS	**ST PANCRAS**	**LEICESTER**	16.25 Leicester - St Pancras (19.00)
14	922		FULL BRAKE	LMS	**ST PANCRAS**	**KETTERING**	

While the Midland generally had to take second place to the Great Northern so far as travel to the West Riding was concerned, it held a trump card in that its night parcels train left St Pancras in the late evening and took nearly seven hours to reach Leeds. As such it was the ideal vehicle for an overnight passenger service and accordingly in conveyed a first and third class sleeping car together with a quartet of day coaches; the latter actually going through, albeit unadvertised, to Bradford. This for many was a much more civilised arrangement than that of the Great Northern whose train - day accommodation only - left Kings Cross at 22.45 and ejected its passengers onto the streets of Leeds about four and a half hours later. On the Midland you stood a chance of a decent night's sleep.

Strangely, the combined sleeper and day coach service operated in one direction only and the various components made their way back to London separately. This was because the through service reached London at 05.16 which meant that the sleeping cars would have to be held in St Pancras throughout the greater part of the rush-hour which was not a practicable proposition at a station with a busy service and only seven platforms. The solution to the problem was to attach the sleeping cars to the up overnight Glasgow service which reached London at a far more convenient time.

The use of Burton Black 5 4-6-0 45262 on the down Devonian (09.25 Bradford - Paignton) as it pulls away from Derby during the summer of 1955 suggests a shortage of motive power somewhere along the line. Although highly capable engines, the Black Five was not the equal of a Jubilee and a few minutes dropped every fifty miles can be expected on this particular journey.

20.55 BRADFORD to BRISTOL (04.33)

	C/W Previous working	Vehicle	Type	From	To	Next working
1	960	FULL BRAKE	LMS	LEEDS	BIRMINGHAM	02.15 Birmingham - Bath (06.09)
2	961	FULL BRAKE	LMS	LEEDS	BIRMINGHAM	
3	962	FULL BRAKE	LMS	LEEDS	BRISTOL	
4	963	FULL BRAKE	LMS	BRADFORD	BIRMINGHAM	
5	85 07.35 Bristol - Bradford (14.03)	THIRD CORRIDOR (42)	LMS	BRADFORD	BRISTOL	07.35 Bristol - Bradford (14.03)
6	85 07.35 Bristol - Bradford (14.03)	COMPOSITE CORRIDOR (18/24)	LMS	BRADFORD	BRISTOL	07.35 Bristol - Bradford (14.03)
7	85 07.35 Bristol - Bradford (14.03)	BRAKE THIRD CORRIDOR (24)	LMS	BRADFORD	BRISTOL	07.35 Bristol - Bradford (14.03)
8	964	FULL BRAKE	LMS	BRADFORD	BRISTOL	
9	964	FULL BRAKE	LMS	BRADFORD	BRISTOL	
10	966	FULL BRAKE	LMS	BRADFORD	BRISTOL	
11	949	FULL BRAKE	LMS	BRADFORD	DERBY	00.38 Derby - Worcester (03.12)

Shown in order leaving Leeds

The Midland ran extremes of night trains: it had both the best and the worst.   The overnight service from St Pancras could be a heavenly experience - the Bradford to Bristol was hellish.   Intended primarily for parcels traffic, three passenger coaches were added almost as an after thought with no consideration for the hordes who invariably boarded the train at Leeds and Sheffield and jammed solid the seats, luggage racks, corridors and brake compartment.   Many passengers would have travelled more comfortably on the floor of one of the full brakes and probably would have had there been a chance of getting in.

Of the four parcels vans conveyed from Bradford, three were for Bristol with transfer traffic for the Great Western whilst the fourth was a vehicle for Worcester which was taken to Derby where it was transferred to the 19.05 Newcastle to Bristol which unlike the Bradford train ran via Worcester.   Three further vans were added during the reversal at Leeds, two for Birmingham and one for Bristol.   One of the Birmingham vehicles was loaded with traffic for Dorset and the Wessex area and was transferred at New Street to the 00.40 Leicester - Bath parcels.   Later in the morning it was taken forward to Bournemouth West in the 09.05 Bristol - Bournemouth.   By attaching them to the front of the train at Leeds as opposed to the rear, the Midland was twisting the blade of passenger discomfort a little further.   Because they had to be uncoupled at Birmingham, the fireman would have to ensure that the heating was turned off somewhere in the Burton area to ensure that the pipes were not too hot to handle.   Thus the existing discomfiture of the long suffering passenger complement would be made complete through a lack of heat.

21.20 BRADFORD to ST PANCRAS (05.16)

	C/W Previous working	Vehicle	Type	From	To	Next working
1	925	FULL BRAKE	LMS	SHEFFIELD	ST PANCRAS	07.08 St Pancras - Hendon (07.30)
2	924	FULL BRAKE	LMS	LEEDS	ST PANCRAS	23.50 St Pancras - Leeds (06.24)
3	915A	FULL BRAKE	LMS	BRADFORD	ST PANCRAS	
4	916A	FULL BRAKE	LMS	BRADFORD	ST PANCRAS	
5	21 06.55 Leeds - Bradford (07.40)	BRAKE THIRD CORRIDOR (24)	LMS	BRADFORD	ST PANCRAS	23.50 St Pancras - Leeds (06.24)
6	21 06.55 Leeds - Bradford (07.40)	COMPOSITE CORRIDOR (18/24)	LMS	BRADFORD	ST PANCRAS	23.50 St Pancras - Leeds (06.24)
7	21 06.55 Leeds - Bradford (07.40)	THIRD CORRIDOR (42)	LMS	BRADFORD	ST PANCRAS	23.50 St Pancras - Leeds (06.24)
8	21 06.55 Leeds - Bradford (07.40)	THIRD CORRIDOR (42)	LMS	BRADFORD	ST PANCRAS	23.50 St Pancras - Leeds (06.24)
9	970	FULL BRAKE	LMS	BRADFORD	LEICESTER	02.20 Leicester - Marylebone (06.05)
10	971 19.18 Sheffield - Derby (20.36)	FULL BRAKE	LMS	DERBY	LEICESTER	02.20 Leicester - Marylebone (06.05)
11	972 18.05 Bradford - Derby (22.38)	FULL BRAKE	LMS	DERBY	LEICESTER	02.20 Leicester - Marylebone (06.05)
12	973 23.55 Nottingham - Derby (00.28)	FULL BRAKE	LMS	DERBY	LEICESTER	02.20 Leicester - Marylebone (06.05)

Shown in order leaving Leeds

The criticisms made of the night express from Bradford to Bristol applied almost equally to the overnight train to London which had only four passenger coaches even though half of Yorkshire seemed to want to join at Leeds and Sheffield.   Travelling overnight from Bradford to London sometimes called for a judgement of Paris.   On the one hand the Kings Cross train contained almost twice as many coaches but one was ejected from the train at three in the morning whilst on the Midland you had more than two hours extra sleep - provided the overcrowding allowed you to doze off.   Those with funds could, of course, travel in the sleeping car which was picked up at Leeds by the Glasgow - St Pancras express.

The passenger accommodation - the return of the 23.50 ex St Pancras - occupied the centre of the train whilst the front was reserved for parcels traffic for London, vans being picked up at Leeds and Sheffield.   The rear of the train, also vans of parcels traffic, was interesting since all four were destined for Marylebone and all four originated from locations that had a direct Great Central service.   The quartet came off at Leicester and formed the 02.20 to Marylebone via Market Harborough, Northampton, Blisworth, Bletchley and Claydon LNE Junction.   They reached their destination only three quarters of an hour after the Bradford train arrived in St Pancras.

An atmospheric scene is an atmospheric environment. 5XP 4-6-0 45731 'Perseverance' of Carlisle waits in Leeds City to take over the northbound 09.00 St Pancras - Edinburgh when it arrives from London. Unlike the Thames-Clyde Express which was worked by a rebuilt Royal Scot between Leeds and Glasgow, the Waverley remained as a Jubilee 4-6-0 working; the engine going only as far as Carlisle where it was replaced by an ex-LNER A3 Pacific for the final leg to Edinburgh.

Nearly three hours out of London and the 09.00 St Pancras - Edinburgh 'Waverley' rejoins the main line at Trowell after deviating via Melton and Nottingham in early 1957. The service will now travel through one of the most densely trafficked sections of the Midland as it passes through the Nottingham/Derby coalfield which extends for twenty miles as far as Chesterfield. The train is worked by the booked 5XP 4-6-0 and has 4P Compound 4-4-0 41095 of Leicester as pilot.

MAIN LINE CARRIAGE WORKINGS : 1955

10: BTK, 3TK, TO, RK, FO, 2CK, BTK (BR SET)
1 | St Pancras | 10.00
19.41 | Glasgow | (09.20)

10: BTK, 2CK, FO, RK, TO, 3TK, BTK (BR SET)
2 | Glasgow | 09.20
19.28 | St Pancras | (10.00)

9: BTK, CK, FK, RT, 4TK, BTK (BR SET)
4 | Edinburgh | 10.05
20.45 | St Pancras | (09.00)

9: BTK, 4TK, RT, FK, CK, BTK (BR SET)
5 | St Pancras | 09.00
19.15 | Edinburgh | (10.05)

1: CK
5A | St Pancras | 09.00
11.25 | `Nottingham | 17.50
20.00 | Sheffield | (12.11)

10: BG, BTK, 3TK, SLT, 2SLF, CK, BG
7 | St Pancras | 21.15
08.30) | Glasgow | (21.10)

10: BG, CK, 2SLF, SLT, 3TK, BTK, BG
8 | Glasgow | 21.10
02.33 | Leeds | 02.45
08.05 | St Pancras | (21.15)

11: BG, 2SLC, SLT, SLF, 2CK, 3TK, BG
9 | St Pancras | 21.05
07.54 | Edinburgh | (21.53)

11: BG, 3TK, 2CK, SLF, SLT, 2SLC, BG
10 | Edinburgh | 21.53
09.12 | St Pancras | (21.05)

9: BTK, 2TK, 2CK, 2TK, BTK, BG
11 | Leeds | 10.35
15.53 | Glasgow | (16.00)

2: CO RC
11A | Leeds | 10.35
15.13 | Kilmarnock | 16.40
21.41 | Leeds | (10.35)

9: BTK, 2TK, 2CK, 2TK, BTK, BG
12 | Glasgow | 16.00
21.41 | Leeds | (10.35)

7: BTK, 3TK, 2CK, BTK (BR SET)
14 | Sheffield | 07.05
10.31 | St Pancras | 14.00
19.26 | Bradford | (10.30)

7: BTK, 2CK, 3TK, BTK (BR SET)
15 | Bradford | 10.30
15.30 | St Pancras | 18.33
21.53 | Sheffield | (07.05)

1: TK
15A | Bradford | 10.30
15.30 | St Pancras | 17.32
20.47 | Nottingham | (07.42)

11: BTK, CK, FK, FO, RK, TO, 3TK, BTK, TK (BR SET)
16 | Bradford | 11.50
17.52 | St Pancras | (11.45)

11: TK, BTK, 3TK, TO, RK, FO, FK, CK, BTK (BR SET)
17 | St Pancras | 11.45
17.15 | Bradford | (11.58)

10: BTK, 2TK, TO, RK, FO, FK, BFK, CK, BTK (BR SET)
18 | Bradford | 09.12
14.08 | St Pancras | 16.50
22.38 | Bradford | (09.12)

7: BTK, 2CK, 3TK, BTK (BR SET)
19 | Bradford | 07.15
12.18 | St Pancras | 15.15
20.50 | Bradford | (07.15)

4: 2TK, CK, BTK
21 | Bradford | 21.20
05.16 | St Pancras | (23.50)

2: SLF, SLT
21B | Leeds | 02.45
08.05 | St Pancras | (23.50)

4: 2TK, CK, BTK
22 | St Pancras | 23.50
06.20 | Leeds | 06.55
07.40 | Bradford | (21.20)

2: SLF, SLT
22A | St Pancras | 23.50
06.20 | Leeds | (02.45)

8: BTK, CK, FK, RF, TO, 2TK, BTK
23 | Manchester | 07.20
11.31 | St Pancras | 14.15
18.35 | Manchester | (09.00)

8: BTK, CK, FK, RF, TO, 2TK, BTK
24 | Manchester | 09.00
14.01 | St Pancras | 16.15
 | Manchester | (07.20)

1: TK
24A | Derby | 10.48
14.01 | St Pancras | 17.30
20.47 | Nottingham | (06.40)

1: FK
24B | Derby | 09.00
11.31 | St Pancras | 16.15
19.01 | Derby | (09.00)

1: CK
24C | Manchester | 09.00
14.01 | St Pancras | 16.15
20.47 | Manchester | (09.00)

8: BG, BTK, 2TK, TO, FK, CK, BTK,
25 | St Pancras | 08.15
13.02 | Manchester | 17.55
22.55 | St Pancras | (08.15)

6: BTK, FK, CK, TK, TK, BTK (BR SET)
26 | St Pancras | 04.18
09.46 | Manchester | 13.55
18.14 | St Pancras | (04.18)

2: 2TK
26A | Leicester | 07.13
09.46 | Manchester |

10 : BTK, SFO, RT, TO, 2CK, BTK, 2TK
27 | Nottingham | 06.40
09.55 | St Pancras | 12.50
15.25 | Leicester | 15.35
16.22 | Nottingham | (06.40)

1: CK
27A | Manchester | 00.05
06.54 | St Pancras | 17.30
20.37 | Nottingham | (07.50)

1: TK
27B | Nottingham | 06.40
09.55 | St Pancras | 20.10
23.40 | Derby | (15.35)

1: TK
27C | St Pancras | 16.15
20.50 | Manchester | 00.05
06.54 | St Pancras | (16.15)

2: RC. TO
28A | St Pancras | 08.15
11.19 | Derby | 15.35
18.14 | St Pancras | (08.15)

1: TK
28B | Derby | 15.35
18.14 | St Pancras |

1: TK
28C | St Pancras | 08.15
13.02 | Manchester | 16.00
20.38 | St Pancras | (08.15)

3: BTK, CK, TK (BR SET)
29 | St Pancras | 10.15
14.32 | Manchester | 16.00
20.34 | St Pancras | (10.15)

1: CK
29A | St Pancras | 10.15
12.50 | Derby | 15.35
18.14 | St Pancras | (10.15)

4: BTK, 2CK, BTK
30 | Manchester | 07.24
10.01 | Derby | 12.05
15.12 | St Pancras | 18.40
23.05 | Manchester | (07.24)

4: BTK, 2CK, BTK
31 | St Pancras | 10.15
14.32 | Manchester | 16.00
20.34 | St Pancras | (10.15)

8: BTK, TK, CK, FK, TK, BTK, 2TK
32 | Derby | 08.05
10.45 | St Pancras | 20.10
23.40 | Derby | (08.05)

1: BTK
32A | Derby | 08.05
10.45 | St Pancras | 14.15
16.52 | Derby | (08.05)

5: BTK, CK, 2TK, BTK (BR SET)
33 | Bradford | 09.25
19.25 | Paignton | (09.15)

5: BTK, CK, 2TK, BTK (BR SET)
34 | Paignton | 09.15
19.09 | Bradford | (09.25)

6: BTK, TK, CK, RC, TO, BTK (BR SET)
35 | Bradford | 09.25
18.52 | Newton Abbot | 19.30
20.45 | Plymouth | (08.15)

6: BTK, TK, CK, RC, TO, BTK (BR SET)
36 | Plymouth | 08.45
09.45 | Newton Abbot | 09.50
19.09 | Bradford |

6: BTK, TK, 2CK, TK, BTK
38 | Birmingham | 06.40
11.04 | Bradford | 17.25
19.23 | Sheffield | (09.09)

1: TK
38A | Sheffield | 09.07
11.04 | Bradford |

6: BTK, TK, 2CK, TK, BTK
39 | Kings Norton | 07.40
07.52 | Birmingham | 08.05
13.03 | Newcastle | 15.57
21.05 | Birmingham | 21.25
21.45 | Kings Norton | (07.40)

6: BTK, TK, 2CK, TK, BTK
40 | Bradford | 07.30
13.42 | Bristol | 16.45
23.02 | York | (12.00)

2: 2TK
40A | Bradford | 07.30
13.42 | Bristol | 16.45
23.02 | York |

10: BTK, TK, 2CK, TK, 4TK, BTK
41 | Bradford | 08.46
11.14 | Scarborough | 16.22
19.00 | Bradford | (08.46)

6: BTK, TK, 2CK, TK, BTK
42 | Bristol | 01.10
06.59 | Sheffield | 07.50
09.55 | Bradford | (07.30)

1: TK
42A | Nottingham | 07.43
12.00 | Bristol | 01.10
06.59 | Sheffield | 07.50
09.55 | Bradford | (10.30)

6: BG, TK, 2CK, TK, BTK
43 | Bristol | 07.35
13.58 | Bradford | 16.45
23.56 | Bristol | (07.35)

	1: RB	
43A	Derby	11.10
13.58	Bradford	16.45
19.29	Derby	(11.10)

	1: TPO	
43B	Derby	19.52
23.56	Bristol	01.10
05.36	Derby	(19.52)

	6: BTK, TK, 2CK, TK, BTK	
44	Bristol	14.15
20.00	York	(09.43)

	6: BTK, TK, 2CK, TK, BTK	
46	Nottingham	07.35
12.00	Bristol	(01.10)

	10: BTK, 5TK, 2CK, TK, BTK	
47	Nottingham	08.28
11.25	St Pancras	16.25
18.06	Kettering	18.27
19.48	Nottingham	(08.28)

	8: BTK, TK, CK, RB, CK, TK, BTK, BG	
48	Nottingham	09.06
11.29	Manchester	11.40
12.25	Liverpool	15.30
16.15	Manchester	16.32
19.31	Nottingham	(09.06)

	6: BTK, TK, 2CK, TK, BTK	
49	Derby	06.18
07.06	Nottingham	13.25
17.05	St Pancras	19.10
22.15	Derby	(06.18)

	4: BTK, TK, TO, CAFÉ	
49A	Nottingham	13.25
17.05	St Pancras	19.10
21.40	Nottingham	(13.25)

	6: BTK, TK, 2CK, TK, BTK	
50	Sheffield	10.10
12.09	Birmingham	12.30
12.45	Kings Norton CS	(07.40)

	6: BTK, TK, 2CK, TK, BTK	
51	Sheffield	09.09
13.21	St Pancras	17.30
20.47	Nottingham	(07.43)

	1: TK	
51A	St Pancras	17.30
20.47	Nottingham	

	8: BTK, TK, 2CK, 3TK, BTK	
52	Sheffield	17.15
21.49	Gloucester	(10.15)

	8: BTK, TK, 2CK, 3TK, BTK	
52A	Gloucester	10.15
11.20	Worcester	(07.45)

	6: BTK, TK, 2CK, TK, BTK	
53	York	09.42
10.56	Sheffield	(10.10)

	8: BTK, TK, 2CK, 3TK, BTK	
54	Worcester	07.54
12.50	York	16.15
18.06	Sheffield	(17.15)

	6: BTK, TK, 2CK, TK, BTK	
55	York	12.20
18.25	Bristol	(14.15)

	5: BTK, RT, CK, TK, BTK	
57	Bristol (MWFO)	08.45
09.48	Gloucester	10.04
16.57	Newcastle	(08.15)

	5: BTK, RT, CK, TK, BTK	
57A	Newcastle (TThO)	08.15
14.49	Gloucester	14.55
15.52	Bristol	(08.45)

	5: BTK, RU, CK, TK, BTK (BR/NER SET)	
58	Bristol (TThO)	08.45
09.48	Gloucester	10.04
16.57	Newcastle	(08.15)

	5: BTK, RU, CK, TK, BTK (BR/NER SET)	
58A	Newcastle (MWFO)	08.15
14.49	Gloucester	14.55
15.52	Bristol	(08.45)

	7: BTK, TK, CK, 3TK, BTK (GWR SET)	
59	Cardiff (MWFO)	08.30
09.48	Gloucester	10.04
16.57	Newcastle	(08.15)

	7: BTK, TK, CK, 3TK, BTK (GWR SET)	
59A	Newcastle (TThO)	08.15
14.49	Gloucester	14.57
16.36	Cardiff	(08.30)

	7: BTK, TK, CK, 3TK, BTK (BR/NER SET)	
60	Cardiff (TThO)	08.30
09.48	Gloucester	10.04
16.57	Newcastle	(08.15)

	7: BTK, TK, CK, 3TK, BTK (BR/NER SET)	
60A	Newcastle (MWFO)	08.15
14.49	Gloucester	14.57
16.36	Cardiff	(08.30)

	10: BTK, 5TK, TO, RC, FK, BTK (BR SET)	
64	Bristol (MWFO)	10.20
18.30	Newcastle	(12.37)

	10: BTK, 5TK, TO, RC, FK, BTK (BR SET)	
64A	Newcastle (TThO)	12.37
20.23	Bristol	(10.20)

	10: BTK, 5TK, TO, RF, FK, BTK (BR/NER SET)	
65	Bristol (TThO)	10.20
18.30	Newcastle	(12.37)

	10: BTK, 5TK, TO, RF, FK, BTK (BR/NER SET)	
65A	Newcastle (MWFO)	12.37
20.23	Bristol	(10.20)

	9: BG, BTK, 2TK, CK, BG, 3TPO (BR SET)	
66	Bristol	19.20
04.21	Newcastle	(19.05)

	9: BG, BTK, 2TK, CK, BG, 3TPO (BR SET)	
67	Newcastle	19.05
05.20	Bristol	(19.20)

	2: BTK, CK	
68	Sheffield	10.10
12.09	Birmingham	12.42
17.32	Bournemouth West	(09.45)

	2: BTK, CK	
69	Bournemouth West	09.45
14.23	Birmingham	14.38
16.33	Sheffield	(10.10)

	1: TK	
69A	Kings Norton	14.03
14.15	Birmingham	14.38
16.33	Sheffield	19.05
21.05	Birmingham	21.25
21.45	Kings Norton	(14.03)

	2: BTK, CK	
72	Liverpool LS	10.15
11..01	Crewe	11.20
12.29	Birmingham	12.42
17.32	Bournemouth West	(09.45)

	7: BCK, CK, TK, TO, RT, CO, BTK	
73	Bournemouth West	09.45
14.23	Birmingham	14.33
16.35	Manchester (Mayfield)	(10.25)

	2: BTK, CK	
73A	Bournemouth Wes	
14.23	Birmingham	
15.41	Crewe	
16.50	Liverpool LS	

	7: BCK, CK, TK, TO, RT, CO, BTK	
74	Manchester LR	
11.13	Crewe	
12.29	Birmingham	
17.32	Bournemouth Wes	

	3: BTK, CK, TK	
85	Bristol	
13.58	Bradford	
04.33	Bristol	

	1: CK	
86	Nottingham	
08.37	Derby	
19.08	Manchester	

	5: BTK, TK, CK, TK, BTK	
87	Cleethorpes	
11.13	Birmingham	
14.21	Gloucester	

	5: BTK, TK, CK, TK, BTK	
88	Gloucester	
15.59	Birmingham	
21.28	Cleethorpes	

	4: CK, BTK, CK, BTK	
88A	Bristol	
12.05	Gloucester	
19.23	Bournemouth	

	4: CK, BTK, CK, BTK	
88B	Bournemouth	
13.53	Bath	
14.50	Gloucester	
17.24	Bristol	

	2: TK, BCK	
89	Kings Norton	
12.55	Birmingham	
18.12	Melton Constable	
19.12	Cromer	

	3: 2TK, BCK	
90	Kings Norton	
12.55	Birmingham	
19.34	Yarmouth	

	2: TK: BCK	
91	Kings Norton	
12.55	Birmingham	
18.12	Melton Constable	
19.00	Norwich (City)	

	2: TK, BCK	
92	Cromer	
10.18	Melton Constable	
15.38	Birmingham	
16.00	Kings Norton	

	3: 2TK, BCK	
93	Yarmouth	
15.38	Birmingham	
16.00	Kings Norton	

	2: TK: BCK	
94	Norwich (City)	
10.14	Melton Constable	
15.38	Birmingham	
16.00	Kings Norton	

	1: TK	
95	Carlisle	
08.05	St Pancras	

MAIN LINE CARRIAGE WORKINGS : 1955

96 — 3: BTK, CK, BTK

	Leeds	02.55
07.56	Birmingham	08.05
08.23	Kings Norton	16.40
16.55	Birmingham	17.15
18.40	Derby	19.42
21.18	Sheffield	22.05
23.38	Leeds	(02.55)

100 — 1: BCK

	Buxton	09.39
14.01	St Pancras	(14.15)

101 — 1: BCK

	St Pancras	14.15
17.43	Millers Dale	17.56
18.06	Buxton	(09.39)

117 — 3: FK, FO, RT

	Nottingham	08.15
10.31	St Pancras	14.00
16.17	Nottingham	(08.15)

119 — 7: 2TK, CK, RF, 2 TO, BTK

	Derby	12.05
15.12	St Pancras	18.40
21.17	Derby	(12.05)

123 — 2: TO, KB

	St Pancras	10.15
14.30	Manchester	16.00
20.38	St Pancras	(10.15)

124 — 3: RF, TO, TK

	Sheffield	08.58
12.18	St Pancras	15.15
18.56	Sheffield	(08.58)

125 — 5: BTK, CK, BTK, TPO, BG

	Lincoln	20.00
22.24	Tamworth	02.25
	Lincoln	(20.00)

126 — 2: RF, TO

	Sheffield	12.11
15.39	St Pancras	18.33
21.53	Sheffield	(12.11)

126A — 1: CK

	Sheffield	12.11
15.39	St Pancras	

128 — 5: BTK, TK, CK, TK, BTK (LNER SET)

	Bradford	06.42
08.19	York	10.15
11.44	Bradford	15.50
16.28	Leeds	(16.24)

128A — 5: BTK, TK, CK, TK, BTK (LNER SET)

	York	15.10
15.50	Leeds	16.24
17.04	Bradford	(06.42)

129 — 6: BTK, CK, 2TK, BTK, T (LNER SET)

	Hull	09.15
11.03	Sheffield	15.10
17.10	Hull	(09.15)

130 — 7: BTK, 2TK, FK, CK, TK, BTK (BR/NER SET)

	Hull	10.42
12.57	Bradford	15.00
17.17	Hull	(10.42)

132 — 3: BTK, CK, BTK

	Sheffield	08.06
11.29	Worcester	11.35
12.34	Gloucester	13.51
15.59	Birmingham	17.15
18.40	Derby	19.42
21.18	Sheffield	(08.06)

133 — 3: BTK, CK, BTK

	Sheffield	08.06
11.29	Worcester	16.25
19.18	Derby	22.10
23.28	Sheffield	(08.06)

150 — 2: 2TK

	Bristol	14.15
20.00	York	(12.00)

151 — 2: 2TK

	York	12.00
18.26	Bristol	(14.15)

152 — 3: 3 TK

	Bristol	14.15
18.42	Sheffield	

153 — 2: TK, RC

	Derby	10.24
13.42	Bristol	16.45
20.22	Derby	(10.24)

153A — 1: TK

	Nottingham	07.43
12.00	Bristol	16.45
20.22	Derby	(10.48)

441 — 6: BTK, TK, 2CK, TK, BTK

	Derby	07.20
11.40	Llandudno	18.15
22.02	Derby	(07.20)

442 — 3: BTK, CK, BTK

	Sheffield	02.40
03.41	Leeds	06.30
08.25	Sheffield	11.33
13.08	Leeds	16.10
17.52	Sheffield	(02.40)

901 — 1: BG

	St Pancras	04.18
09.46	Manchester	17.55
22.55	St Pancras	(04.18)

902 — 1: BG (non-corr)

	St Pancras	04.18
06.03	Wellingborough	07.02
08.09	Leicester	08.37
09.32	Nottingham	12.50
13.30	Newark	17.55
19.59	Leicester	20.36
22.55	St Pancras	(04.18)

903 — 1: BG (non-corr)

	St Pancras	04.18
06.03	Wellingborough	07.02
08.09	Leicester	20.36
22.55	St Pancras	(04.18)

904 — 2: 2 BG (non-corr)

	St Pancras	04.18
05.36	Bedford	

905 — 1: BG (non-corr)

	St Pancras	04.18
05.07	Luton	

906 — 1: BG

	Nottingham	19.23
21.50	Leeds	01.15
03.10	Carnforth	

907 — 1: BZ

	St Pancras	18.33
20.53	Derby	21.27
23.05	Manchester	

908 — 1: BG

	St Pancras	20.10
23.40	Derby	01.25
04.25	York	05.06
07.56	Newcastle	

909 — 1: BG

	St Pancras	20.10
23.40	Derby	01.25
04.25	York	

910 — 1: BG

	St Pancras	18.45
23.10	Nottingham	23.52
07.54	Edinburgh	08.45
10.34	Perth	

911 — 1: BG

	Luton	19.40
23.10	Nottingham	23.52
07.54	Carlisle	07.45
11.03	Glasgow (St E)	

912 — 1: BG

	St Pancras	21.15
07.35	Kilmarnock	

913 — 1: VANFIT (FISH)

	Hull	18.20
20.17	Leeds	02.50
05.17	Carlisle	06.20
08.05	Whitehaven	

914 — 1: BG

	Leeds	02.50
08.30	Glasgow (St E)	

915 — 1: BG

	Hendon	22.10
22.38	St Pancras	23.50
06.24	Leeds	06.55
07.40	Bradford	

915A — 1: BG

	Bradford	21.20
05.16	St Pancras	

916 — 1: BG

	Kensington	19.55
20.37	St Pancras	23.50
06.24	Leeds	06.55
07.40	Bradford	

916A — 1: BG

	Bradford	21.20
05.16	St Pancras	

917 — 1: BG

	St Pancras	23.50
06.24	Leeds	06.55
07.40	Bradford	(21.28)

918 — 1: BG

	St Pancras	23.50
06.24	Leeds	

919 — 1: BG

	St Pancras	23.50
03.20	Derby	06.22
07.35	Sheffield	(23.50)

920 — 1: BG

	St Pancras	23.50
03.20	Derby	03.57
04.37	Nottingham	

921 — 1: BG

	St Pancras	23.50
02.34	Leicester	16.25
19.00	St Pancras	

922 — 1: BG (non-corr)

	St Pancras	23.50
01.48	Kettering	

923 — 1: BG

	Bradford	21.28
05.16	St Pancras	20.05
20.30	Willesden	03.15
03.25	Kensington	(22.10)

924 — 1: BG

	Leeds	22.12
05.16	St Pancras	(23.50)

MAIN LINE CARRIAGE WORKINGS : 1955

925 — I: BG

	Sheffield	23.50
05.16	St Pancras	07.08
07.30	Hendon	(22.10)

926 — I: BG

	Bradford	21.28
05.16	St Pancras	(23.50)

930 — I: BG

	Plymouth	17.05
	Bristol	01.10
06.59	Sheffield	07.50
09.55	Bradford	

931 — I: BG

	Bristol	01.10
06.59	Sheffield	07.50
08.48	Leeds	

931A — I: BG

	Leeds	02.55
06.00	Derbu	

932 — I: BG

	Manchester	00.05
02.00	Derby	02.15
07.25	Bristol	16.45
23.02	York	

933 — I: BG

	Manchester	00.05
02.51	Leicester	

934 — I: BG

	Liverpool	22.10
23.36	Manchester	00.05
06.54	St Pancras	

935 — I: BG

	Manchester	00.05
06.54	St Pancras	

936 — I: BG

	Manchester	00.05
06.54	St Pancras	

937 — I: BG

	Manchester	00.05
02.00	Derby	03.57
04.37	Nottingham	

938 — I: BG

	Liverpool	22.10
23.36	Manchester	00.05
02.00	Derby	03.57
04.37	Nottingham	

939 — I: BG

	Birmingham	23.35
01.42	Leicester	03.35
06.54	St Pancras	

940 — I: BG

	Birmingham	23.35
01.42	Leicester	03.35
06.54	St Pancras	

941 — I: BG

	Bolton	20.37
02.53	Leicester	03.35
06.54	St Pancras	

942 — I: BG

	Bolton	20.37
02.53	Leicester	03.35
06.54	St Pancras	

943 — I: BG

	Leeds	02.55
06.00	Derby	

944 — I: BG

	Leeds	02.55
07.56	Birmingham	

945 — I: BG

	Glasgow	09.20
19.19	St Pancras	

946 — I: BG

	Sheffield	21.37
23.02	York	00.30
05.08	Edinburgh	

947 — I: BG

	Sheffield	23.30
05.20	Bristol	(19.20)

948 — I: BG

	Bristol	19.20
00.48	Sheffield	(23.30)

949 — I: BG

	Bradford	20.55
23.07	Derby	00.38
03.12	Worcester	

950 — I: BG

	Sheffield	02.10
03.41	Leeds	(21.55)

951 — I: BG

	Bailey Gate	16.18
18.56	Bath	19.03
19.20	Mangotsfield	19.42
00.48	Sheffield	02.10
03.41	Leeds	07.20
08.03	Bradford	

952 — I: BG

	Derby	22.10
23.38	Sheffield	02.10
03.41	Leeds	

953 — I: BG

	Derby	22.10
23.38	Sheffield	02.10
03.41	Leeds	07.20
08.03	Bradford	

954 — I: BG

	Sheffield	00.09
01.02	Normanton	03.16
03.37	Leeds	07.20
08.03	Bradford	

960 — I: BG

	Leeds	21.55
01.35	Birmingham	02.15
06.09	Bath	06.55
09.57	Bailey Gate	(16.18)

961 — I: BG

	Leeds	21.55
01.35	Birmingham	

962 — I: BG

	Leeds	21.55
04.33	Bristol	

963 — I: BG

	Bradford	20.55
01.35	Birmingham	

964 — I: BG

	Bradford	20.55
04.33	Bristol	

965 — I: BG

	Bradford	20.55
04.33	Bristol	

966 — I: BG

	Bradford	20.55
04.33	Bristol	

967 — I: BG

	Bradford	16.45
23.56	Bristol	

968 — I: BG

	Bradford	16.45
23.56	Bristol	

969 — I: BG

	Derby	19.52
23.56	Bristol	

970 — I: BG

	Bradford	21.20
01.44	Leicester	02.20
06.05	Marylebone	

971 — I: BG

	Sheffield	19.18
20.36	Derby	01.00
01.44	Leicester	02.20
06.05	Marylebone	

972 — I: BG

	Bradford	18.05
22.38	Derby	01.00
01.44	Leicester	02.20
06.05	Marylebone	

973 — I: BG

	Nottingham	23.55
00.28	Derby	01.00
01.44	Leicester	02.20
06.05	Marylebone	

974 — I: BG

	Bristol	01.10
02.00	Gloucester	02.35
07.35	Sheffield	

975 — I: BG

	Leeds	02.55
04.05	Cudworth	04.25
04.36	Barnsley	07.00
08.15	Leeds	(02.55)

980 — I: BG

	Newcastle	20.10
23.38	York	02.08
02.40	Normanton	03.45
06.00	Derby	08.15
09.15	Birmingham	16.10
21.00	Bristol	

981 — I: BG

	Durham	21.00
23.38	York	02.08
02.40	Normanton	03.45
06.00	Derby	08.15
09.15	Birmingham	16.10
21.00	Bristol	

982 — I: BG

	York	02.08
02.40	Normanton	03.45
06.00	Derby	08.15
09.15	Birmingham	16.10
21.00	Bristol	

983 — I: BG

	West Hartlepool	20.33
22.25	York	02.08
02.40	Normanton	03.45
06.00	Derby	08.15
09.15	Birmingham	16.10
21.00	Bristol	

984 — I: BG

	Blackpool N	21.20
01.11	Leeds	02.55
04.48	Sheffield	

985 — I: BG

	Blackpool N	21.20
01.11	Leeds	02.55
06.00	Derby	

In Spring 1957 a Compound 4-4-0 and a 5XP 4-6-0 accelerate the down Waverley, 09.00 St Pancras to Edinburgh towards Chesterfield and Sheffield and away from the 20 mph speed restriction affecting trains coming through Trowell Junction from the Nottingham direction. Traffic was so dense on this section of line - the Erewash Valley - that five running lines were provided for the six miles between Toton and Ilkeston South Junction: up and down goods, up and down main and an additional goods line, the last mentioned allowing trains to run from Toton to Ilkeston without conflicting with services on the up and down main lines. 8F 2-8-0 48082 of Hasland works a train of mineral empties down this addition line which was known as the second down goods.

MAIN LINE ARRIVALS & DEPARTURES : ST PANCRAS (1955)

Train From	Arr	C/W	Formation	Dep	Destination
13.50 Manchester	18.14	26	6: BTK, FK, CK, TK, TK, BTK (BR SET)	04.18	Manchester
17.55 Manchester	22.55	901	1: BG	04.18	Manchester
20.36 Leicester	22.55	902	1: BG (non corridor)	04.18	Wellingborough
		903	1: BG (non corridor)	04.18	Wellingborough
		904	2: BG (non corridor)	04.18	Bedford
		905	1: BG (non corridor)	04.18	Luton
17.55 Manchester	22.55	25	8: BG, BTK, 2TK, TO, FK, CK, BTK.	08.15	Manchester
16.00 Manchester	20.38	28C	1: TK	08.15	Manchester
13.50 Manchester	18.14	28A	2: RC. TO	08.15	Derby
10.05 Edinburgh	20.15	5	9: BTK, 4TK, RT, FK, CK, BTK (BR SET)	09.00	Edinburgh
12.11 Sheffield	15.39	5A	1: CK	09.00	Nottingham
		Local 3: 3 TK		09.05	Leicester
16.25 Leicester	19.00	Local 5: 2 TK, BTK, CK, BTK		09.05	Leicester
		Local 2: 2 CK		09.05	Bedford
09.20 Glasgow	19.19	1	10: BTK, 3TK, TO, RK, FO, 2CK, BTK (BR SET)	10.00	Glasgow
16.00 Manchester	20.38	29	3: BTK, CK, TK	10.15	Manchester
16.00 Manchester	20.38	123	2: TO, KB	10.15	Manchester
16.00 Manchester	20.38	31	4: BTK, 2CK, BTK	10.15	Manchester
15.35 Derby	18.14	29A	1: CK	10.15	Derby
		Local 1: TK		10.40	Nottingham
18.15 Nottingham	21.56	Local 3: BTK, CK, BTK		10.40	Nottingham
18.15 Nottingham	21.56	Local 3: BTK, CK, BTK		10.40	Bedford
11.58 Bradford	17.52	17	11: TK, BTK, 3TK, TO, RK, FO, FK, CK, BTK (BR SET)	11.45	Bradford
06.40 Nottingham	09.55	27	10: BTK, SFO, RT, TO, 2CK, BTK, 2TK	12.50	Leicester
07.00 Sheffield	10.31	14	7: BTK, 3TK, 2CK, BTK (BR SET)	14.00	Bradford
08.16 Nottingham	10.31	117	3: FK, FO, RT	14.00	Nottingham
07.20 Manchester	11.31	23	8: BTK, CK, FK, RF, TO, 2TK, BTK	14.15	Manchester
10.05 Millers Dale	14.01	101	1: BCK	14.15	Millers Dale
08.05 Derby	10.45	32A	1: BTK	14.15	Derby
07.15 Bradford	12.18	124	7: BTK, 2CK, 3TK, BTK (BR SET)	15.15	Bradford
08.58 Sheffield	12.18	19	3: RF, TO, TK	15.15	Sheffield
09.00 Manchester	14.01	24	8: BTK, CK, FK, RF, TO, 2TK, BTK	16.15	Manchester
09.00 Manchester	14.01	24C	1: CK	16.15	Manchester
00.05 Manchester	06.54	27C	1: TK	16.15	Manchester
09.00 Derby	11.31	24B	1: FK	16.15	Derby
08.28 Nottingham	11.25	47	10: BTK, 5TK, 2CK, TK, BTK	16.25	Nottingham
09.12 Bradford	14.08	18	10: BTK, 2TK, TO, RK, FO, FK, BFK, CK, BTK (BR SET)	16.50	Bradford
09.09 Sheffield	13.21	51	6: BTK, TK, 2CK, TK, BTK	17.30	Nottingham
10.48 Derby	14.01	24A	1: TK	17.30	Nottingham
10.30 Bradford	15.39	15A	1: TK	17.30	Nottingham
00.05 Manchester	06.54	27A	1: CK	17.30	Nottingham
15.35 Derby	18.14	28B	1: TK	17.30	Nottingham
10.20 Bradford	15.39	15	7: BTK, 2CK, 3TK, BTK (BR SET)	18.33	Sheffield
12.11 Sheffield	15.39	126	2: RF, TO	18.33	Sheffield
00.05 Manchester	06.54	907	1: BZ	18.33	Derby
12.05 Derby	15.12	30	4: BTK, 2CK, BTK (BR SET)	18.40	Manchester
12.05 Derby	15.12	119	7: 2TK, CK, RF, 2 TO, BTK	18.40	Manchester
13.35 Nottingham	17.05	49	6: BTK, TK, 2CK, TK, BTK	19.10	Derby
13.35 Nottingham	17.05	49A	4: BTK, TK, TO, CAFÉ	19.10	Nottingham
		Local 1: BG		19.55	Nottingham
11.47 Bedford	13.01	Local 5: 2 TK, BTK, CK, BTK		19.55	Nottingham
		Local 1: BG		19.55	Nottingham
08.05 Derby	10.45	32	8: BTK, TK, CK, FK, BTK, 2TK	20.10	Derby
06.40 Nottingham	09.55	27B	1: TK	20.10	Derby
		908	1: BG	20.10	Derby
		909	1: BG	20.10	Derby
21.53 Edinburgh	09.12	9	11: BG, 2SLC, SLT, SLF, 2CK, 3TK, BG	21.05	Edinburgh
21.05 Glasgow	08.05	7	9: BG, BTK, 3TK, SLT, 2SLF, CK, BG	21.15	Glasgow
		912	1: BG	21.15	Kilmarnock
22.10 Hendon	22.38	915	1: BG	23.50	Leeds
22.10 Hendon	22.38	916	1: BG	23.50	Leeds
21.20 Bradford	05.16	22	4: 2TK, CK, BTK	23.50	Leeds
21.05 Glasgow	08.05	22A	2: SLF, SLT	23.50	Leeds
21.20 Bradford	05.16	917	1: BG	23.50	Leeds
21.20 Leeds	05.16	918	1: BG	23.50	Leeds
		919	1: BG	23.50	Derby
		920	1: BG	23.50	Derby
		921	1: BG	23.50	Leicester
		922	1: BG (non corridor)	23.50	Kettering
21.20 Sheffield	05.16	925	1: BG		
09.20 Glasgow	19.19	945	1: BG		
21.20 Bradford	05.16	9	1: BG		
22.10 Liverpool	06.54	934	1: BG		
03.35 Leicester	06.54	939	1: BG		
00.05 Manchester	06.54	940	1: BG		
00.05 Manchester	06.54	941	1: BG		
00.05 Manchester	06.54	942	1: BG		